Management for Professionals

The Springer series "Management for Professionals" comprises high-level business and management books for executives, MBA students, and practice-oriented business researchers. The topics cover all themes relevant to businesses and the business ecosystem. The authors are experienced business professionals and renowned professors who combine scientific backgrounds, best practices, and entrepreneurial vision to provide powerful insights into achieving business excellence.

The Series is SCOPUS-indexed.

Pierre Ollivier • Graham Bell •
Victor De Leon • Sylvain Roy
Editors

Business Secrets Management

Strategies to Protect, Extract and Maximize Value

Springer

Editors
Pierre Ollivier
Winnotek
Paris, France

Graham Bell
Cubicibuc
Cambridge, UK

Victor De Leon
Accralaw
Manila, Philippines

Sylvain Roy
SRA
Montréal, QC, Canada

ISSN 2192-8096 ISSN 2192-810X (electronic)
Management for Professionals
ISBN 978-3-031-82511-8 ISBN 978-3-031-82512-5 (eBook)
https://doi.org/10.1007/978-3-031-82512-5

This Springer imprint is published by the registered company Springer Nature Switzerland AG
The registered company address is: Gewerbestrasse 11, 6330 Cham, Switzerland

Preface

Secrets are often the silent engines of business success. From Coca Cola's recipe and KFC's iconic 11 herbs and spices to Amazon's recommendation engine or Apple's face ID technology, businesses have developed winning products and services by carefully managing their companies' business secrets, e.g. trade secrets, sensitive information, etc. Exclusive access to these valuable assets has enabled corporations to innovate, fund, and deliver transformative solutions — sometimes benefiting society with substantial productivity gains and advancements.

Secrets in the form of formulas, algorithms, composition, and processes have shaped industries, driven innovation, and touched nearly every aspect of daily life. Looking ahead, new technologies protected as trade secrets —including generative AI algorithms, autonomous driving, biologics manufacturing processes, and space innovations like SpaceX's rocket landing systems—promise to drive economic growth, influence national and international politics, and reshape the relationship between citizens, states, and businesses.

Unlike patents which are formalized by disclosure and registration, business secrets remain, by definition, "secret." Their protection relies on meticulous management of employment policies, IT infrastructure, and commercial agreements. A single misstep—a careless disclosure or a lapse in internal controls—can result in the irreversible loss of what may be company's most valuable asset. While resources abound on intellectual property strategies—patents, copyrights, trademarks, and design—there is a notable scarcity of practical guides focused on business secret management. The need for a dedicated management handbook on this subject was clear.

This book on *Strategies to Protect, Extract and Maximize Value* is designed as an accessible yet comprehensive guide for business managers seeking to better understand and use business secrets. It provides actionable insights and strategies for protecting, monetizing, and leveraging confidential information in an increasingly competitive and interconnected world, all by balancing legal and operation considerations.

Authored by a dozen legal and consulting advisors, all members of the Licensing Executives Society (LES), this book draws on the expertise of practitioners at the forefront of innovation and commerce. The idea for this volume originated with our esteemed colleague and co-author, Véronique Chapuis. It is our sincere hope that this book will illuminate the nuances of business secret strategy and equip readers with the tools to protect and harness these relating invaluable assets effectively.

All the best,

Pierre, Graham, Vic, Sylvain

Paris, France Pierre Ollivier
Cambridge, UK Graham Bell
Manila, Philippines Victor De Leon
Montréal, Canada Sylvain Roy

Contents

Book Reference Terms, Definitions, and Cases

Graham Bell, Ferzana Haq, Victor De Leon, Pierre Ollivier, Sylvain Roy, and Philippe Simon

Abstract

This book is addressed to business and academic executives and senior managers in small and medium-sized businesses or scale-ups that need to understand how to effectively manage the business secrets within their organisation, particularly during new product launches, finance raising, and mergers and acquisitions (M&A). The book keeps away from technical legal details that are important for legal experts but are not absolutely necessary for managers and executives in their daily lives. It may happen, nevertheless, that some of these terms appear while reading the chapters below, because the authors believed they were necessary to reach some level of understanding the strategic issues concerning business secrets.

The authors also believe that non-legal business executives can grasp the essentiality of these terms and then use them to design and implement

G. Bell
Cambridge, UK
e-mail: graham@cubicibuc.com

F. Haq
Singapore, Singapore
e-mail: ferzanahaq@hslegal.com.sg

V. De Leon (✉)
Manila, Philippines
e-mail: vnlllb@gmail.com

P. Ollivier · P. Simon
Paris, France
e-mail: pierre.ollivier@winnotek.com; philippe.simon@winnotek.com

S. Roy
Montreal, Canada
e-mail: sylvain@sroy.ca

P. Ollivier et al. (eds.), *Business Secrets Management*, Management for Professionals, https://doi.org/10.1007/978-3-031-82512-5_1

comprehensive business secrets strategies for all employees. Moreover, having a foundational understanding of the legal concepts at play will also increase their ability to communicate with companies' legal teams and external advisers.

A number of recent confidential information and secret-related legal cases are believed to be representative of the issues that require attention from managers and executives. These are also summarised in this section. These cases come from small to big size companies and involving multiple industries such as chemicals, drugs, biotechnology, information technology, car fleets, car manufacturing, food technology, pharmacy, admin services, and metal industry.

This section summarises the elements that are useful to refer to when reading its chapters.

1 Glossary of Terms

This section is a summary of the technical terms, concepts, and expressions that are used throughout the book.

"Absence of IP assets from corporate accounting statements": Because intellectual property (IP) assets are intangible, they are usually not grasped by corporate accounting which lacks adequate knowledge and tools to assess a confidence interval for their monetary value. At best, an efficient cost accounting system may allow identification of the historical R&D, engineering, and legal costs incurred while creating the invention and use these as a proxy for the value of the corresponding IP asset; however, a historic sum of costs is seldom a reflection of current realistic monetary value which may be significantly more or less than the sum of costs. Although national reporting standards like the International Financial Reporting Standards (IFRS) now require the reporting of intangible assets, experience shows that in liquidation contexts for example, liquidators value a failing company's IP assets at best at the legal costs incurred for filing and prosecution of patents, trademarks, etc., and at worst value them at zero.

"Breach of confidence": Action by the recipient of confidential information which violates a confidentiality clause applying to said information, whereby said clause restricts the freedom of said recipient to disseminate, share, use, etc., the information. Such clauses typically appear in employment contracts, non-disclosure agreements (NDAs), collaborative projects, and suppliers or subcontractors' agreements.

"Breach of duty of confidentiality": An action whereby the recipient of confidential information violates one or several confidentiality clauses applying to said information spelled out in a contractual agreement the recipient has signed and to which the recipient is legally bound. Whether the violation is unintentional (e.g. negligence) or intentional (e.g. counterfeiting or malevolence) is irrelevant to the materiality of the breach once it is established.

"Burden of proof": In the framework of litigation, it is a responsibility assigned to one party by law or by the court to find and exhibit material proofs, either that their own claim is legitimate or that the other party's claim is invalid or untrue.

"Business secret or Trade secret value estimates": These estimates are heuristical methods used either internally (by the owner of a business secret) or by courts (in litigation contexts) to assign a financial value to the business secret, even though it is not a registered IP asset that is liable to "classical" value estimate methods. Most often, the assigned value is an estimate of the financial damage incurred by the legitimate owner if the business secret is leaked, pilfered, pirated, unlawfully used, etc. The nature of the damage may cover loss of revenues/margins, loss of future sales opportunities, equity losses due to harmed image/reputation, etc. As for all heuristical methods, the assigned value is assessed as a confidence interval, not a single amount.

"Confidentiality clauses": Contractual clauses of an employment contract, NDA, collaborative project agreement, supplier contract, or subcontractor contract, restricting the freedom of recipients of a defined set of data to disclose, share, or use the same, in order to preserve the interests of the legitimate data owner. Recipients may be employees, partners, subcontractors, suppliers, etc. The sets of data covered by the clauses must be spelled out in the contract but may encompass up to 100% of all information labelled as "confidential" by the owner.

"Discovery" and "e-discovery": "*Discovery*" is a legal procedure whereby a court authority orders the seizure of part or all of a company's documents, files, e-mails, etc., relative to an ongoing litigation, so that the court and the opposing party may, through a detailed review and analysis of contents, find and exhibit evidence supporting or invalidating the plaintiff's claims or the defendant's defence. "*E-discovery*" is the method of executing the discovery with the help of IT / AI tools to handle massive, digitalised data and speed up the sorting out of relevant versus irrelevant data, via machine learning (ML) algorithms.

"Document Classification": The process of assigning one or more class or categories to documents created within an organisation. Distinct from indexing which may seek to identify the contents of a document for search purposes, classification typically allocates a label to a document that signifies how the document is to be controlled based on sensitivity and business context. Labelling may use levels of confidentiality such as: Public, Internal, Restricted, and Confidential.

"Dual-use technology": Technology that can be used for both civilian and military purposes in the broader sense.

"FMEA", or "Failure Mode Economic Analysis": A formal method of quality assurance and risk reduction leveraged during design of a product or process. The method identifies how the system, product, or process may fail, and what the most likely consequences would be in terms of performance, user safety, durability, and repair/restoration costs (including catastrophic failure). It assigns probabilities to each failure mode and leads to design or manufacturing process changes in order to minimise these probabilities.

"Gardening leave": A human relations (HR) management practice whereby an employee who resigns or is dismissed remains on the payroll during his advance notice period but is forbidden from visiting the company's premises or from starting a new job until the advance notice period is exhausted. This method is very rigorously applied in particular by British courts especially when the employee initially refuses to abide by his advance notice period and wishes to leave immediately.

"Good conscience": A state of mind of a stakeholder having access to confidential information, whereby the stakeholder sincerely believes that the way they use said information is lawful, legitimate, and does not harm the interests of the original owner of the confidential information. This commonly signifies that the stakeholder has no conscious intention of causing damage to the original owner, even though they may actually do so (e.g. by negligence).

"Informal or non-registered IP assets": Confidential information that holds value for its owner but does not qualify for registration or for labelling as legally recognised intellectual property (patents, trademarks, designs & models, databases, copyrighted documents, algorithms, and formalised know-how). Business secrets are initially considered "informal IP assets" before they may mature or graduate into formal IP assets.

"Innovation cycle": An outline of the step-by-step process undertaken by organisations to bring new innovations or inventions to life, from idea generation and conceptualisation (in-process assets) to development and execution, and ultimately, protection (formal and identified assets).

"Intangible asset": A non-physical asset such as—but not limited to—a patent, brand, trademark, copyright, trade name, software code, etc.

"Interests served by business secrets": A typology of stakeholders each possessing a vested interest in secrecy protection, or conversely, in the disclosure of a business secret. This typology is usually established in litigation contexts where a plaintiff claims a defendant has unlawfully accessed and/or used a business secret. At a minimum, the typology includes: (a) Interests of the legitimate owner and its shareholders, (b) Interests of competitors, (c) Interest of the end users or the public at large (in the case of a business secret generated within a Public Research Organisation), and (d) "National strategic interest" (secrets relating to defence, diplomacy, strategic resources, etc.).

"Key questions for employees receiving information": A set of questions any employee receiving information labelled as "confidential" should promptly seek answers to. They concern the legitimacy of the person transmitting the information to do so, the legitimacy of the recipient to receive it, the recipient's degrees of freedom (to solely detain the information; to share it with peers; to disclose it to third parties; to use it internally or with outsiders, etc.), the positioning of the information on a secrets classification scale ("fit for disclosure"; "restricted"; "sensitive"; "critical", etc.), and the identity of the other employees competent to give directions to the recipient on how to behave. Ideally, all these questions may be addressed in the company's business secrets policy as taught to all employees once formalised.

"Knowledge management system": A system utilised by an organisation or entity to keep track of, manage, and protect, among other things, their internal business and trade secrets and confidential and sensitive information. When properly utilised, it protects the confidentiality of the information it contains.

"Need to know basis": A rule governing the dissemination of confidential information within an organisation or towards its business partners. It generally states that any employee, regardless of hierarchical level, seniority, or function, is only allowed to access, hold, and use specific confidential information if that information is required for him to efficiently perform his daily duties or other duties specific to a given project he is assigned to. (E.g., a sales manager may be prevented from accessing the detailed cost structure of a product whereas the lower ranking design technician in charge of "target costing" may be allowed access to such information in order to perform his job.)

"Open data environment": A movement originating in the United States of America (USA) and the United Kingdom (UK) which aims to promote and generalise online disclosure by public sector stakeholders (government agencies, state and local administrations, PROs, universities, etc.) of part of their own databases for the benefit of the public at large.

"Open science": The movement that aims to make scientific research, data, code, and publications freely accessible to everyone without barriers.

"Open source": Originally coined for software, Open source promotes universal access via open-source licenses. Software source code, which is typically released under the terms of an open source software license, may generally be downloaded and modified, and then published back to the community (sometimes mandatorily with the same licensing terms).

"Open standards": A standard that is openly accessible and usable (be implemented) by anyone. Open standards may have open source obligations, but not all do.

"Public disclosure": These are certain business secrets that may already be publicly available or have been previously disclosed.

"Reverse engineering (RE)": A method whereby a research and development (R&D) department or a laboratory breaks down a product or system into its primary components to identify its bill of materials and to understand its design and the technical explanation of its features and performances. The same method applies to analysing a machine or manufacturing system to understand and reconstitute each step of a manufacturing process in order to identify the technical innovations leading to its level of performance as expressed by a set of key progress indicators (KPIs).

"Sensitive information": Intermediate grade on a classification scale for business secrets, above "restricted" and below "critical". Its leakage or capture may cause serious damage to the company but may not harm it to the point of liquidation, unlike "critical" business secrets. Symmetrically, leakage of "restricted" business secrets may cause damages which are non-trivial but are usually controllable and are not lethal.

"Strategic information": Confidential information with commercial value that competitors do not have access to. Such information must also be kept confidential with some legal, contractual, digital, and safety protection measures.

"Unauthorised use": An action by the recipient of information labelled as "confidential" (or explicitly labelled as a business secret) that infringes the explicit restrictions binding the recipient, either through contractual confidentiality clauses or as spelled out in the company's business secrets protection policy. This may include the recipient sharing the information whereas they are only authorised to hold it, using it without explicit clearance from their hierarchy, disclosing it to outsiders, using it for other purposes than their professional duties warrant it, or using it malevolently to serve personal interests and/or harm the firm (such as leaking it to a competitor, e.g.)

"Undisclosed information": This means information that fulfils three conditions stated in the Agreement on Trade-Related Aspects of Intellectual Property Rights (TRIPS): "(1) it is secret in the sense that it is not, as a body or in the precise configuration and assembly of its components, generally known among or readily accessible to persons within the circles that normally deal with the kind of information in question; (2) it has commercial value because it is secret; and (3) has been subject to reasonable steps under the circumstances, by the person lawfully in control of the information, to keep it secret".

"Wrongful gain/loss": "*Wrongful gain*" is a quantifiable and/or qualitative gain achieved by the recipient of confidential information (by leveraging this information in various ways), where said information was obtained by unlawful means and leveraged without explicit authorisation from the original owner of the information. "*Wrongful loss*" is symmetrically the quantifiable and/or qualitative damage incurred by the original legitimate owner of the information due to the fact that a third party detains and uses said information without his authorisation and against his will.

2 A Few Definitions to Keep in Mind

"Business secret" is here defined as any information that (1) is not, in itself or in the exact configuration and assembly of its elements, generally known or easily accessible to persons familiar with this type of information because of their sector of activity; (2) has commercial value, actual or potential, by virtue of its secrecy; (3) is the subject of reasonable protective measures by its legitimate holder, given the circumstances, to maintain its secrecy.

In other words, a business secret: (1) must be known within the organisation, (2) must not be known to anyone outside the organisation, and (3) results in loss of value to the organisation and / or gain in value to the external entity *if leaked.*

If a piece of information meets all three of these criteria, it should be considered a business secret.

Of course, the second test can be modified to "it must not be known to anyone outside the organisation in the absence of suitable legal obligations such as NDAs"—but this is a topic that will be covered extensively in this book.

"Trade secret" would usually be more rigorously defined as a piece of information that passes the three following tests:

1. It is not known to the professional sector or field of activity concerned. (i.e., *it is not naturally or effortlessly accessible to stakeholders of the trade who would, in the course of their professional duty, want or need to access it*)
2. It is valuable in view of the fact that the information is secret (i.e., *it can be assigned a commercial value, explicit or latent)*
3. The company endeavours to keep it secret by taking reasonable protective measures (i.e., *its legitimate owner has already enforced specific protection measures to preserve secrecy*)

"Sensitive information" has different meanings in various contexts. It may mean both:

- A catch-all word that designates in practice any confidential information or data that is important to a company because it is relevant for its business and
- Depending on jurisdiction, a precise word with significant meaning. For example, in France, it is used in the Protection of the Scientific and Technical Heritage of the Nation (PSTH, PPST in French) and the Blocking Act of 1968,[1] revised by the Decree of 22 February 2022(**).

The interest in qualifying the information a company possesses is to know one's rights and obligations but also the value one can generate from such information, according to the operational context. For example, if confidential information is considered "sovereign sensitive" in the sense of the Blocking Act,[2] it cannot be communicated to foreign authorities.

Therefore, in this book, Trade secrets or a sensitive information are business secrets, but the reverse may not be true, specifically due to differences in national laws around the world.

3 Examples Showing Key Situations and Issues Behind Business Secrets

This section outlines cases that show how decisions related to confidential information have developed in today's worldwide economic environment. They represent examples demonstrating key scenarios and issues introducing the importance of business secrets management.

[1] Law 68–678 of July 26, 1968 relating to the communication of documents and information of an economic, commercial, industrial, financial, or technical nature to foreign natural or legal persons.

[2] Decree n° 2022-207 of February 18, 2022 relating to the communication of documents and information of an economic, commercial, industrial, financial, or technical nature to foreign natural or legal persons. The SISSE (Service de l'information stratégique et de la sécurité économiques du Ministère de l'Économie et des Finances) provides explanations (https://sisse.entreprises.gouv.fr/fr/actualites/accueil/loi-de-blocage-revision-des-modalites-et-publication-d-guide-d-aide).

3.1 Case 1: Kolon

Full name: **E.I. Dupont De Nemours & Company v. Kolon Industries Incorporated** (United States).

Facts	Subsequent decision	Main takeaways for management
Facts: Dupont produces Kevlar fibre. Kolon was in the same business when it sought five (5) former Dupont employees to work as consultants to improve its product. Through the new employees, Kolon obtained information regarding the manufacturing process of Kevlar. Dupont sued Kolon. Kolon wanted to introduce evidence to show that some of Dupont's trade secrets were publicly available information as they appeared in the records of an earlier intellectual property case between Dupont and another competitor. Dupont objected to Kolon presenting evidence or arguments concerning another case.	The court ruled that a new trial is warranted in order to give Kolon an opportunity to prove its theory that the alleged trade secrets are in fact publicly available information.	1. Implement protective actions to prevent leakage such as (a) listing the key information to be protected, in a document signed by the employee by the time he/she leaves, and (b) identify potential claims by the company against a former employee as well as the duration of the validity of these potential claims. 2. Trade secrets presented as evidence in a prior litigation may later be classified as publicly available information. 3. Information released to government authorities (i.e. courts during litigation) should be treated and reviewed carefully in light of a clear trade secret IP strategy.

3.2 Case 2: Hytera

Full name: **Motorola Solutions, Inc, et. Al. v. Hytera Communications Corp. Ltd.** (United States).

Facts	Subsequent decision	Main takeaways for management
Facts: Hytera hired Motorola engineers who gave the former more than 10,000 technical documents downloaded from Motorola's database which were used by Hytera on a product similar to that of Motorola. Motorola sued Hytera et al. for trade secrets misappropriation and copyright infringement.	The jury decided in favour of Motorola, and Hytera's subsequent motions for judgment as a matter of law and for a new trial were denied. The court disagreed with Hytera's assertion that Motorola *"failed to satisfy the elements of a trade secret claim"* and *"failed to use*	1. Put in place minimum reasonable protection measures such as (a) having employees sign confidentiality agreements and (b) classifying and storing trade secrets in a database with limited and controlled access from employees. 2. Including non-compete clauses in employee contracts

(continued)

Facts	Subsequent decision	Main takeaways for management
	reasonable security measures to protect its secrets".	may also be a good protection measure. 3. Employees should be made aware of the consequences of stealing trade secrets.

3.3 Case 3: Waymo

Full name: **Waymo LLC v. Uber Technologies** (United States).

Facts	Subsequent decision	Main takeaways for management
Facts: Mr. Levandowski resigned from Waymo and started his own self-driving vehicle company called Otto. Mr. Levandowski then was suspected of having taken with him, together with other Waymo employees who joined him at Otto, confidential information about Waymo's LiDAR technology. Otto was bought by Uber who investigated former Waymo employees (which led to a report called "the Stroz report"). Waymo sued Levandowski and Uber for patent infringement and trade secret violation.	A settlement agreement was reached.	1. Be aware of unusual pre-separation activities, which give rise to an inference of misappropriation of business secrets. 2. Consider imposing activity restrictions on employees intending to move to competitors. 3. Consider requiring new employees to confirm in writing that they have completed a thorough analysis of their possessions and returned any confidential information to their former employer. 4. When illicit information is suspected within the company, do not dispose of it but call legal experts to address the problem. 5. Consider having a plan of action where something is suspected, including doing potential early forensic investigations.

3.4 Case 4: Dohme

Full name: **Merck Sharp & Dohme Corp. v. Pfizer Inc. et al.** (United States).

Facts	Subsequent decision	Main takeaways for management
Facts: Dr. Wendy Watson, an employee of Merck, had access to confidential	The court partly granted and denied the motions of both parties.	1. Be conscious of unusual use of business secrets access through discreet

(continued)

Facts	Subsequent decision	Main takeaways for management
information on Merck's vaccine programme. Dr. Watson left Merck and worked at Pfizer in a similar position. Merck filed a case for trade secrets misappropriation against Pfizer and Dr. Watson, claiming that after an investigation was conducted, it was found that before Dr. Watson left, she downloaded thousands of documents prior to her departure, copied them, and transferred them to her devices and Pfizer's computers. Both parties aimed to compel the other to disclose specific information on their own cases to each other.	On the issue of trade secrets, the court stated that a business pursing a trade secret suit must "identify its trade secrets *with a reasonable degree of precision and specificity that is particular enough as to separate the trade secret from matters of general knowledge in the trade or of special knowledge of persons skilled in the trade*". In other words, trade secrets must be "identified with sufficient particularity so that the reader understands how each such claim differs from public domain information-including public patent filings".	investigations, specially for departing employees who had access to such. 2. This practice may be standardised and carried out on a regular basis across all employees who have access to a company's business secrets. 3. Formulate a precise description of your trade secrets such that they are distinguishable and distinct from public information.

3.5 **Case 5:** Wyeth

Full name: **Wyeth v. Natural Biologics Inc.** (United States).

Facts	Subsequent decision	Main takeaways for management
Facts: Wyeth developed the "Brandon Process" for making conjugated oestrogens used in Premarin. Natural Biologics sold conjugated oestrogens. It used an extraction process that yielded material which was the same as Premarin. Natural Biologics claims to have independently developed its process through a review of Wyeth's expired patents, scientific literature, and Wyeth's Brandon Facility waste manifests, which reveal the names and volumes of chemicals used at the	The court ruled that Wyeth had implemented reasonable efforts to maintain the secrecy of the Brandon Process, given the following: *The lack of repeated losses of confidential information regarding the Brandon Process, the use of physical security, limited access to confidential information, employee training, document control, and oral and written understandings of confidentiality.* Additionally, the court ruled that that since no one had previously duplicated the	1. Put clear indications that certain information is (a company's) secret. 2. Make it a practice to manage and protect business secrets relating to manufacturing processes for as long as possible as this may give rise to future business secrets. 3. Be aware of the synergy between patents and business secrets.

(continued)

Facts	Subsequent decision	Main takeaways for management
Brandon Facility. It was contended that Wyeth did not adequately protect its trade secret.	Brandon Process, it is unlikely that Natural Biologics had succeeded in doing so legally.	

3.6 **Case 6:** Coco

Full name: **Coco v A.N. Clark (Engineers) Ltd [1969] RPC 41** (United Kingdom).

Facts	Subsequent decision	Main take aways for management
The plaintiff (Coco) shared confidential information with the defendant (A.N. Clark Engineers Ltd.) in the course of negotiations for a potential business collaboration to manufacture a new motor scooter engine. The negotiations fell through, but the defendant later produced a similar product. Plaintiff claimed that the defendant had used his confidential information in the production process. Plaintiff sought an injunction to prevent the defendant from using the confidential information, alleging a breach of confidence.	The court established a three-part test to determine the existence of a breach of confidence: (1) The information must be confidential in nature and possess the necessary quality of confidentiality (i.e. it must not be public knowledge). (2) The information must have been communicated in circumstances importing an obligation of confidence. (3) There must be an unauthorised use of the information to the detriment of the party who communicated it. The High Court ruled that the defendants were not in breach of confidence, as there was no unauthorised use of the plaintiff's confidential information. Although the information was shared in circumstances that imposed an obligation of confidence, the court found insufficient evidence of misuse in the production of the defendant's product. The case did not progress to the court of appeal, further to the plaintiff arguing that the High Court took a too narrow view of unauthorised use.	1. Ensure that the information you seek to protect qualifies as confidential. Clearly identify this information as confidential through documentation and reference disclosure of such information in your confidentiality agreements. 2. Be explicit about the confidential nature of disclosed information and ensure that all parties involved understand their non-disclosure and non-use obligations. 3. Document any case of unauthorised use and collect evidence that the information was used without permission or that unauthorised use caused harm or a competitive disadvantage. 4. Improve your confidentiality agreements. Explicitly outline the recipient duties and ensure these agreements are legally enforceable in the event of a breach. 5. Develop strategies to monitor and enforce the proper use of confidential information. This includes tracking the flow of sensitive information within and

(continued)

Facts	Subsequent decision	Main take aways for management
	This judgment remains influential in trade secret law, particularly in cases where confidential information is shared during business negotiations, but no clear evidence of misuse or damage can be proven. It highlights the importance of demonstrating actual harm from unauthorised use when pursuing a claim for breach of confidence.	outside the company, especially during negotiations, collaborations, or employee departures.

3.7 **Case 7:** Clearlab

Full name: **Clearlab SG Pte Ltd v Ting Chong Chai and others [2015] SLR 163** (Singapore).

Facts	Subsequent decision	Main takeaways for management
The plaintiff Clearlab, a Singaporean company, had employees who signed an express confidentiality clause. The employees resigned and subsequently went into a business with another party to set up a competing business in the field of production of contact lenses.	The court applied the three-part test used in the *Coco* case and held that all three elements were present: (1) The primary defendants were former Clearlab employees and were therefore under an implied obligation of confidentiality and good faith during their employment. However, they were also obliged to keep Clearlab's information confidential post-employment because of an express confidentiality clause in their employment agreements. (2) The third-party recipient of the information (who was not a former employee) was also bound by an equitable obligation of confidence, because the documents containing the information were marked as confidential, and that he had objective	1. There should be express confidentiality clauses in employment agreements that cover both the period of employment and post-employment. 2. Information should be marked as confidential to ensure that any third-party recipients have objective notice of confidentiality and are therefore bound by an equitable duty of confidence. 3. Wide confidentiality clauses are enforceable and can protect any information of the company which is not public information. However, the express confidentiality clause cannot be relied upon to restrict a former employee from using his skill and knowledge. There may be practical issues in assessing and distinguishing information that is skill and

(continued)

Facts	Subsequent decision	Main takeaways for management
	notice of its confidentiality. (3) The law does not distinguish between degrees of confidentiality, *provided the information is not publicly available.* Therefore, an express confidentiality clause that is drafted widely and including all information belonging to Clearlab was enforceable against the primary defendants subject to the principle that any information which is part of the former employee's skill and knowledge is not the employer's confidential information.	knowledge from the plaintiff's confidential information. To this end, in any lawsuit, the types of confidential information alleged to have been breached must be specified with sufficient clarity.

3.8 **Case 8:** i-Admin

Full name: **i-Admin v Hong Ying Ting [2020] SGCA 32** (Singapore).

Facts	Subsequent decision	Main takeaways for management
The appellant, I-Admin (Singapore) Pte Ltd. is in the business of payroll administrative data processing services and human resource information systems. The first and second respondents of the case were the former employees of the appellant and its subsidiary, respectively. The first and second respondents left I-Admin and set up their own company together with the third respondent, which was in the competing business of providing payroll outsourcing services and HR management functions. The appellant came across the third respondent's website	The High Court ruled out the appellant action, holding that the respondents were not in breach of their obligations of confidence because there was no unauthorised use of its confidential information in the relevant sense. The appellant appealed against the High Court on the grounds, inter alia, that the High Court took an unduly narrow approach to the requirement of unauthorised use of confidential information. The court of appeal ruled that protecting the wrongful loss interest of businesses is more important in the modern-day, hence there must be stronger measures to protect owners	1. It is possible that a former employee could breach a duty of confidentiality and find themselves liable for damages simply by taking confidential information, without using or disclosing the confidential information. 2. The good conscience aspect is coming up in more and more cases around the world. Breach of confidentiality by employees is now easier to prove with the upcoming "good conscience aspect" in cases. This aspect is advantageous as it dispenses with the need to prove any use of the concerned confidential information by an employee without permission.

(continued)

Facts	Subsequent decision	Main takeaways for management
and decided to conduct forensic investigations into the respondents. Shortly after, it successfully applied for an Anton Pillar Order (APO). The APO was executed at the third respondent's premises. A number of the appellant's materials were recovered from the first respondent's laptop and third respondent's server. It also came to light that the first and second respondents had circulated some of these materials via email.	from loss. As a result, the court stated that the respondents had not displaced the presumption that their conscience was negatively affected, and that they had accordingly acted in breach of confidence.	3. In any exchange of information, watch particularly what information is taken from and given to third parties, whose culture may be different. It becomes important to protect the company against "unjustified enriching" since simple acquisition can already become misappropriation, then used, then disclosed. 4. Notwithstanding, employers should still introduce or maintain measures to preserve the confidentiality of their business secrets.

3.9 **Case 9:** Manufacturing SME IP Leakage by Visitors

Facts	Subsequent decision	Main takeaways for management
Engineers at a UK SME manufacturing company were proud that they had been able to improve the performance of a key piece of production equipment—a CNC metal lathe. When the supplier of the lathe visited them, the engineers mentioned the improvements to the lathe configuration. The supplier did not believe that they could have improved the product and asked to see it for themselves. Being proud of their development, the engineers took the supplier to see the lathe in action. Two months later, at a tradeshow, the same improvement appeared as an upgrade to the lathe for an additional cost.	Following this incident, stricter NDA requirements were put in place for visitors. (Note: This was a company decision, not from the court)	1. It is not just competitors that could benefit from accessing business secrets, other external stakeholders including suppliers and customers should be considered when looking at the risks of business secret leakage. 2. Misappropriation is not always an intentional or malicious act, and IP value can leak through unintentional actions. 3. Business secrets exist in all functions and departments of organisations. It is vital that all employees are made aware of the importance of treating company materials in an appropriate manner.

3.10 **Case 10:** Manufacturing SME—Well-Meaning IP Leakage

Facts	Subsequent decision	Main takeaways for management
A UK SME manufacturing company lost a customer that moved to a competing provider of their products. After a long investigation, it was established that the customer had been trying to integrate the latest product from the company. The customer had experienced issues with the product and had contacted the technical support team within the manufacturing business. The tech support team offered several solutions but were unable to identify the specific problem experienced by the customer. Ultimately, the tech support team offered to provide "all the known problems with the product" and supplied copies of all problem reports and known bugs. The customer took the product and set of problem reports to the competitor and said "here's the current product, and here's what's wrong with it. Please make us a better one…"	Following the identification of this incident, the business determined to establish more rigorous processes internally, and to put in place a companywide awareness training on the issues of IP value, and the need for securing core IP of the business. (Note: This was a company internal decision).	1. Value in businesses is not always in the hard IP such as patents: IP management and "knowledge management" are on the same spectrum. 2. The impact of IP value leakage is not always "seen" as an IP issue. 3. Misappropriation is not always an intentional or malicious act, and IP value can leak through unintentional, well-meaning actions. 4. Business secrets exist in all functions and departments of organisations. It is vital that all employees are made aware of the importance of treating company materials in an appropriate manner. 5. Whenever information is passed through an external interface such as between the company and a customer or supplier, consider the benefits of having NDAs or other legal protections in place.

3.11 **Case 11:** Writers Studio

Full name: **Writers Studio v Chin Kwok Yung** (Singapore).

Facts	Subsequent decision	Main takeaways for management
Defendant was an independent contractor of the plaintiff and signed an NDA. Their relationship soured and defendant left. Defendant allegedly took or copied	The court dismissed the claim for breach of NDA/confidentiality. (i) Plaintiffs pleaded that the defendant had wrongfully gained from the plaintiff's	1. Claims must be carefully pleaded. If a wrongful gain is pleaded, it is not subsequently open to the court to consider if there was a wrongful loss and vice versa.

(continued)

Facts	Subsequent decision	Main takeaways for management
information and worksheets from the plaintiff (a Singaporean company) for his own use. Defendant sued the plaintiff for, among other things, breach of his NDA and/or duty of confidentiality.	confidential information (and this was not proven). The plaintiff later claimed that it had suffered a wrongful loss. However, as the plaintiff had not specifically pleaded a wrongful loss, it was not open to the court to consider whether the plaintiff had indeed suffered a wrongful loss. (ii) The defendant had not taken or copied the confidential information, but it was made available to the defendant with the plaintiff's knowledge and consent. The plaintiff was unable to prove that there was unauthorised use of the information and that the defendant had wrongfully gained from such use.	2. There must be an unauthorised taking or copying of the information, and the defendant's conscience is not affected by simply having the information.

Why Business Secrets Are or Should Be a Concern for Companies?

Graham Bell, Véronique Chapuis-Thuault, André Gorius, Victor De Leon, and Pierre Ollivier

Abstract

This chapter reviews the macro-level drivers for the need to develop better practices for business secrets, which include but are not limited to trade secrets and sensitive information, and are the basic elements necessary to build Intangible Assets.

Many companies focus on specific types of Intangible Assets particularly patents, which may bring high value due to their monopoly power. But patents may no longer ensure good future revenues in an IT and data driven economy; in many sectors, technologies' lifetime is shorter, and it becomes easier for competitors to bypass patented technology.

Business secrets have become more important, as secrecy is sometimes the only way to protect their competitive advantage (whether strategic, business, technical, financial, etc.) in a context of strong competition worldwide (and even more so where international trade restrictions are imposed). But an increasing digital world creates new risks of information leakage.

G. Bell
Cambridge, UK
e-mail: graham@cubicibuc.com

V. Chapuis-Thuault · P. Ollivier (✉)
Paris, France
e-mail: chapuisthuaultveronique@gmail.com; pierre.ollivier@winnotek.com

A. Gorius
Lyon, France
e-mail: andre.gorius@winnotek.com

V. De Leon
Manila, Philippines
e-mail: vnlllb@gmail.com

P. Ollivier et al. (eds.), *Business Secrets Management*, Management for Professionals, https://doi.org/10.1007/978-3-031-82512-5_2

We set out the global trends and some of the obstacles that companies face when trying to control business secrets; we look at how financial reporting standards play a role in establishing support for proactive management of business secrets as well as how HR, IT, and Legal functions support an overall governance—to address the question: "*How can* ***Confidential Information*** *become a* ***business secret****, benefiting from legal protection and, as a consequence, how can its value and even therefore its recognition as an* ***Intangible Asset*** *be established to the benefit of the company and its users?*"

1 Strategic Situations and Stakes

1.1 Confidential Information Issues in a Global Digital World: What Is the Answer?

For companies and organisations, confidential Information has become more and more important, as secrecy is sometimes the only way to protect their competitive advantage (whether strategic, business, technical, financial, etc.) in a context of strong competition worldwide (and even more so where international trade restrictions are imposed). Confidential information that has potential strategic value to the company is sometimes also named "sensitive information" (see the Chapter 1 "Book reference terms, definitions and cases" for more details on these terms).

Increasingly, companies are turning to secrecy for reasons that are mainly due to open platforms, IT, and global business changes:

- They are turning their backs from one of the most popular ways to secure technical inventions, patent protection: this costs more and more due to the need to protect it in multiple countries, in a global business environment
- The ability to control counterfeits and infringements has become more difficult, particularly due to knowledge management and because of this globalisation
- The development of IT and AI relies mainly on confidential algorithms and methodologies; areas in which patents are not always relevant, at least in some countries
- The Internet offers various possibilities to catch strategic information. The business of information search named "business intelligence" has expanded, whether done legally (information made publicly available) or illegally (cyber-attack or human error).

In addition, this present digital era actually creates **high risks of information leakage**, as compared to the economy of past decades. Moreover, while companies generalise the implementation and the **use of knowledge management systems**, such systems create new management issues, since they may become a major source of information leakage if not correctly managed and if not aware of how, with which IT solution, and where to identify Confidential Information. There are many **obstacles to controlling information leakage**:

- Patents are seen as a guarantee of protection to the detriment of sensitive data, but they are neither always an option nor desirable
- Without a method, it is difficult to isolate valuable information in the mass of information that the company processes
- One can think, obviously wrongly, that the protection of information would slow down desired communication with partners
- Organisations do not see the benefits or do not know how to protect data on digital collaborative platforms
- The proliferation of threat warnings and the incentive to ultra-protection tend to discourage efforts: why bother?

Indeed, information leakage remains a major concern for companies, with an increased risk due to dematerialisation. According to IBM in 2022,[1] the average global cost of a data leak is $3.86 M, a figure that is constantly growing. At a national level, misappropriation or theft of trade secrets is said to cost 1–3% of GDP (gross domestic product) in a number of countries.[2] According to Verizon:[3] 58% of information compromises come from insider or partner errors and misbehaviour! (18% by insiders +39% by partners) and the median size (measured in number of compromised records) of an insider breach exceeds that of a third-party breach by more than ten to one. And also, errors in delivery and configuration by employees are the top two causes of threat. Information leakage takes various forms, among which the most commonly cited are the **departure of an employee** for the competition, **electronic exchanges,** and **information exchanges with partners**.

It is estimated that the **most exposed companies are innovative companies (70% of UK firms who develop product and process innovations use trade secrets to protect these innovations.**[4]) For instance, a December 2020 note from the French Ministry of the Interior on economic interference alerts companies, especially the most innovative ones, on the risks of undue appropriation of know-how or essential technological bricks by foreign actors in the context of partnerships. This risk has also increased following the COVID health crisis. Before COVID, according to a European Commission study in 2013,[5] 56% of the companies surveyed said they had suffered lost sales. 44% have incurred internal investigation costs to identify the cause of information loss. In response, 35% of them had increased their protection expenses.

But the main concern today is that **many companies believe they do not hold strategic information** (57% do so, according to a survey by the CCI Paris Ile de

[1] (IBM) Cost of a data breach 2022: A million-dollar race to detect and respond.

[2] Passman, 2014.

[3] (Verizon) 2022 Data Breach Investigations Report—DBIR.

[4] Hall, Helmers, Sena & Rogers, 2012.

[5] Study on Trade Secrets and Confidential Business Information for the European Commission (2013).

France in 2018).[6] Practically, many companies consider that IT security plus having NDAs (non-disclosure agreements) in place are sufficient measures to ensure their protection. They do not wish to spend more time and effort. Why is that? Is it the result of the lack of law protecting confidential information—in the European Union[7]—until 2016? Do they realise that violation of confidentiality is frequent and difficult to detect? Are they just not equipped to grasp and understand the high potential value of the information they hold? Or simply do they not find the time and energy to tackle this mountain of issues, as the mass of data has increased? This book aims to unravelling this knot and help managers demystify the problem. First, we take a step by, out of the pure legal sphere, and take a managerial approach.

1.2 Consider Strategic Information as Business Secret

Strategic information must be confidential so that competitors do not have access to it. It certainly also has a "commercial value", even though this value is yet to evaluate and confirm. And it must also be kept confidential with some legal, digital, and safety protection measures. This type of information may be a Trade Secret as per the applicable law and therefore benefit from a legal protection in addition to organisational, material, and contractual protection; but maybe not fully so, depending on the specific legal terms.

For this reason, the authors of the present book invite the reader, as a business-related approach, to use the concept of "business secret" to cover a wide range of internal secrets, which legal status is defined in national laws as "Trade Secret".[8] "Business secret" is then defined, at a general and strategic business view, as *confidential information that has a commercial value and is subject to reasonable protection measures depending on circumstances.*

The authors wanted to illustrate as much as possible the interest of having executive management of companies and organisations take care of these business secrets. The reader can view the various use cases supporting the insights of this book, which are gathered in the Chapter 1 "Book reference terms, definitions and cases".

[6] Guide: "Secret des affaires, Comment bénéficier de la protection prévue par la loi du 30 juillet 2018?" https://www.cci-paris-idf.fr/sites/default/files/2020-12/guide-secret_des_affaires.pdf.

[7] cf. 2016/943 Directive European Law 2016 "on the protection of undisclosed know-how and business information (trade secrets) against their unlawful acquisition, use and disclosure".

[8] "Business secrets, high potential assets under development", by Pierre Ollivier, André Gorius, Philippe Simon, and Véronique Chapuis (https://papers.ssrn.com/sol3/papers.cfm?abstract_id=3897814).

1.3 From Business Secrets to Intangible Assets: A Virtuous Circle

A key objective for managers and business owners, in the current IT driven economy, is to find ways to create sustainable revenue, i.e. in practice to use assets that are mainly intangible and at the origin of, on average, 90% of a company value.[9] So, intangible assets are the most desirable objects to own for a manager. It should be noted that there can be no Intangible Asset without having initially collected, and then constantly protected, some key confidential information. This confidential information would then regularly grow in time, by adding new confidential information to it; this growing set of confidential information would naturally become a more valuable package of information, which may then be categorised as "business secret" at some point, and eventually transform into Intangible Asset. By definition, this resulting Intangible Asset would then generate revenue to its owner on a regular basis. According to the International Accounting Standard IAS 38, "*an Intangible Asset is recognised when it meets the following criteria: identifiability, probability of future economic benefits, control over the future economic benefits, reliable measurement of cost*".

Many companies already focus on other types of Intangible Assets particularly patents, which potentially bring high value due to the monopoly they can bring and to the formal registration given by government authorities (the various national patent offices). But patents may no longer ensure good future revenues in an IT and data driven economy; in many sectors, technologies' lifetime is getting shorter, and it becomes easier and easier for a competitor to bypass a technology or to find a better one, thanks to artificial intelligence and related IT tools. It has to be noted, also, that any patent creation has also started with an invention that was kept secret for a sufficiently long time to publish a valid patent application.

More and more SMEs in various sectors see little value in patents as they are mostly developing software, and either patenting software is a challenge to them, e.g. for pure software algorithms, or where patents may be potentially available but they claim that the technology moves too quickly to benefit from patents. Many companies generate value from non-patentable assets. For example, IoT (Internet of Things) or AI/ML (Artificial Intelligence/ Machine Learning) mostly derive value from data that may have limited longevity. Thus, they must consider other types of Intangible Assets, hence focusing on business secrets first rather than trying to file patents.

In other words, a **virtual value creation circle** would well be, consciously and constantly, to create and properly manage **Confidential Information**, the status of which would then move thanks to a given strategy towards **business secret**, and then again **towards Intangible Asset** recognised as having the most sustainable value for a company, be they patents, trademarks, know-how, designs and models, methods, algorithms, codes, databases, etc.

---

[9] Ocean Tomo, LLC Intangible Asset Market Value Study 2020.

1.4 Business Secrets and Financial Reporting

Do Financial Reporting Standards Play a Role for Business Secrets?

Financial reporting standards play a crucial role in ensuring transparency and accountability in corporate disclosures. In addition to the necessity for transparency, businesses also face the challenge of protecting their trade secrets, proprietary information, and confidential data. This delicate balance between disclosure and confidentiality is addressed through various reporting standards such as the International Financial Reporting Standards (IFRS), International Valuation Standards Council (IVSC), and local Generally Accepted Accounting Principles (GAAPs). Additionally, the recent proposal of the Corporate Sustainability Reporting Directive (CSRD) by the European Commission adds another layer of consideration in managing trade secrets within financial reporting frameworks. This section explores how these standards accommodate the need to safeguard and manage trade secrets while ensuring transparency and reliability in financial reporting.

Trade secrets encompass valuable proprietary information, including formulas, processes, customer lists, and other confidential data that provide businesses with a competitive advantage. Protecting these secrets is crucial for sustaining innovation, competitiveness, and market positioning. However, as businesses expand globally and face regulatory requirements for financial disclosures, maintaining confidentiality becomes increasingly challenging. Financial reporting standards must strike a balance between fulfilling disclosure obligations and safeguarding sensitive information.

Let us quickly illustrate these facts on a few examples.

International Financial Reporting Standards (IFRS)

IFRS, developed by the International Accounting Standards Board (IASB), sets principles-based accounting standards followed by entities globally. While IFRS primarily focuses on transparency and comparability, it recognises the importance of protecting commercially sensitive information. The standards require entities to disclose information necessary for understanding their financial position and performance without compromising confidentiality. For instance, IFRS 13 Fair Value Measurement outlines guidance on disclosing fair value measurements while protecting proprietary valuation techniques and assumptions.

International Valuation Standards Council (IVSC)

The IVSC develops global valuation standards to ensure consistency, transparency, and reliability in asset valuation. Valuation disclosures are integral to financial reporting, particularly in fair value measurements and business combinations. IVSC standards emphasise the disclosure of valuation methodologies and inputs while respecting the confidentiality of proprietary data. By providing guidance on transparent disclosure practices, IVSC standards facilitate the protection of trade secrets while enhancing the credibility of financial reports.

Local Generally Accepted Accounting Principles (GAAPs)

Many jurisdictions maintain their own GAAPs, which may differ from IFRS or other international standards. While promoting harmonisation, local GAAPs also address unique regulatory requirements and business practices. Local GAAPs recognise the importance of protecting trade secrets within financial reporting frameworks. For example, US GAAP includes provisions for disclosing material information while preserving confidentiality through exemptions for sensitive data, such as trade secrets or proprietary technology.

Corporate Sustainability Reporting Directive (CSRD)

The proposed CSRD by the European Commission aims to enhance sustainability disclosures and integrate non-financial information into corporate reporting. While sustainability reporting focuses on environmental, social, and governance (ESG) factors, it also raises concerns about the disclosure of sensitive business information. The CSRD emphasises the need for proportionate reporting, allowing companies to withhold confidential information that could harm their competitive position. This directive underscores the evolving landscape of financial reporting, incorporating considerations for trade secret protection within sustainability disclosures.

Importance of Safeguarding Proprietary Data

As a conclusion, financial reporting standards play a pivotal role in balancing transparency with the protection of trade secrets and confidential information. Standards such as IFRS, IVSC, and local GAAPs recognise the importance of safeguarding proprietary data while ensuring disclosure requirements are met. The proposed CSRD further highlights the need to manage trade secrets within evolving reporting frameworks, particularly in the context of sustainability disclosures. As businesses navigate complex regulatory environments, adherence to these standards fosters trust, integrity, and competitiveness in financial reporting practices. Moving forward, continued collaboration between standard-setting bodies, regulators, and businesses is essential to adapt reporting frameworks that effectively manage trade secrets while promoting transparency and accountability.

2 Complication: Should We Build an Open or a Closed World?

So business secrets are valuable and the regulatory environment is changing. But **how practical** is it nowadays to **identify** and manage business secrets in order to maximise the benefit from their protection? In fact, almost every company faces the problem of massive data generation, collection, share and storage. In such an environment, it may feel quite discouraging to develop a strategy around business secrets, which means spending dedicated time and costs, and consider a small return on investment due to many uncontrolled factors resulting in information leakage. For this reason, many companies hesitate to start such a strategy, and they do not see how to do it either.

Indeed, a business secret strategy would at least deal with identifying and protecting Confidential Information. In that respect, companies tend to systematically mark all information as confidential, classify it in a single platform; unfortunately, this does not create a good protection since it loses the key information within a mass of unsortable data. At the same time, no one single person could alone, continuously, **sort out** what is important, what is confidential, **decide** how it should be shared or not, and **find out** which is a candidate to become a business secret and potentially gain a status as valuable Intangible Asset. In addition, the company should **ensure** that everybody is up to date all the time and that they correctly behave while doing their job!

Developing a business secret strategy goes hand-in-hand with having the organisational capacity to defend its rights when leakage happens. How to prepare one's own company to have the capacity to detect violation and react, including with legal battles? Many companies, faced with proven information leaks, refrain from taking legal action because of difficulties in **gathering evidence**, fear of the **impact on their reputation**, or to **avoid legal costs**.

This fear of the cost of justice illustrates the **lack of understanding of the financial impact of protection**. The perception of the loss as a low probability obviates the loss of future income, hence the **loss of value** to the company.

Last but not least is the recurring theme of this book, developing a business secret strategy means having a clear idea of its **strategic and financial value**, and how it relates to creating and valuing Intangible Assets.

3 Options But Not Recommendations

In this book, we present options for managers for the various topics relating to business secrets. The discussion of options includes observations of best practice. We do not however provide recommendations on the selection of such options within each topic as this is a highly contextual matter, which depends on the organisation in question and its overall business strategy.

For example, an organisation operating in a highly competitive environment, e.g. a manufacturer of consumer electronics, may adopt an organisational strategy (corporate strategy in this instance) that seeks to minimise the ability of competitors to offer similar products. Such a strategy is likely to imply behaviours that create barriers to entry for competitors. This may therefore imply behaviours that seek strong IP protections such as patents, for the purposes of enforcement. It is not uncommon for such companies to also use trade secrets to hide particular technologies—reducing the market signals / business intelligence.

Alternatively, an organisation operating in a collaborative environment, or seeking to build consensus around the adoption of new technologies or solutions may adopt a more open approach. Such a business may file patents, but utilise them very differently—pledging them (e.g. Tesla) to be freely available to companies that want to utilise the technology, the strategic goal being to build a viable new ecosystem before letting members compete to capture the created value.

4 Middle Ground and Medium Levels

How shall we describe the possible different levels and types of business secrets, as simple as possible? It may be necessary to define more than the two levels of business secrets and non-business secrets. In large organisations, for example, business secrets may be compartmentalised in some way—not everyone that has access to some business secrets needs to see all business secrets. Business secrets may be restricted on per-function basis, by project, or by customer.

Likewise, there may be sets of information that while not business secrets, may be more sensitive than non-business secrets. Exact product specifications or performance ahead of product launch for example—the automotive sector typically releases images of new vehicles prior to launch to build user appetite, but may not provide exact engine size or performance figures ahead of time. The organisation has every intention to make this information public, but in time for market launch—such slow release, or drip feeding of information is typically used by marketing campaigns to build excitement and hype around a product. Companies such as Samsung and Apple hold conferences and launch events attended by hundreds of users and press that have been tempted in by rumour and "controlled leaks" about next-gen products.

Ahead of product launches information may be restricted; it may be shared with key customers or suppliers, and even selected press or reviewers, but may be embargoed until launch date. Such practices are common in the media sector, where movies may be screened to the press ahead of formal premieres, but any reviews embargoed until that date. Such controlled management of release of information means organisations must have a sophisticated understanding of different levels (classifications) of business secrets.

How many levels of classification an organisation needs, and whether compartmentalisation between projects or function is necessary is a decision for that organisation alone. What is important is that those levels are defined, suitable labelling identified, deployed, and used; alongside this, organisation policies may be necessary for access control and audit purposes.

When business secrets are lost, the loss is often unintentional and may occur in any department or function in the organisation. While the role of the IP Manager is important to establishing the business secrets policies and processes, on the day-to-day basis the organisation needs to maintain the position that, indeed, business secrets subject falls on the shoulders of all employees.

Case studies provided in this book provide examples of unintentional business secrets leakage due to marketing departments, engineering departments, and customer support teams. It is one of the intentions of this book to raise awareness of business secrets to non-IP managers, but in doing so, the authors hope that the need for raising a general awareness throughout the organisation is made clear.

5 Business Secrets Are Alive and Not Cast in Stone

5.1 Timely and Actively Changing

Business secret information may be perceived as valuable within a certain time window and then change due to business environment modifications. Therefore, it is not static—that is, **it is a constantly changing set of information.** Any audit of business secrets done at a certain time will, at best, provide a snapshot of the current situation, but surely new information will become business secret, and existing business secret may later stop being business secret. For example, registering AI training data may not be considered as relevant as registering the actual characteristics of that data.

This changing situation of business secret information will challenge companies with respect to the question of having one single centralised register or multiple dispatched registers, in relation to the IT complexity and cost, and to the alignment policy with their organisational structure.

For example, on one particular day, the top secret within an organisation may be the name of a target for M&A activity. Such information will be a closely guarded secret known by a small set of senior decision-makers. The leaking of such an identity may have major impacts on market valuations for both businesses involved. However, as soon as the M&A deal has completed it is likely made public, with little or no further strategic value.

5.2 HR Contracts Relevance Is Regularly Challenged

While employment contracts can contain suitable terms to deal with business secrets, it should be noted that, like other aspects of managing business secrets, changes in business secrets handling procedures within the organisation, and changes in information management technology (the use of social media, the use of cloud storage systems such as OneDrive, Google Drive, or Dropbox) mean that these terms are likely becoming irrelevant over time.

Organisations may wish to consider notice periods and "gardening leave". While it may be tempting to extend notice periods for senior staff (it is common for example to change notice periods from 1 month to 3 months for staff when they reach particular seniority) such long notice periods extend the time where employees on notice may have access to business secrets. As an alternative approach some organisations immediately revoke all access to all company information upon notice of intention to leave and put employees on extended gardening leave—obviously the balance here is whether notice periods are required for employees to "tidy up" projects and ongoing work before leaving vs. the risk of business secret "leakage".

5.3 Role of IT in Enabling Business Secrets Appropriation

The Cloud and the general use of IT through connected mobile devices (phones, cars, mobile equipment, etc.) create massive digital data that in return have high value to their recipient. For example, a car company knows where a driver goes minute by minute, when one fills the tank, controls the tyres pressure, etc. By optimising the collection and use of this information, new business opportunities arise (ex: travel-time optimising applications). Car companies also send emails to the drivers when they expect possible change of ownership from their behaviour deducted from data analysis, for example to propose to change the car for a new one. In general, such confidential information coming from collecting private user data has a high value, particularly to the advertisement business.

IT has also obviously the property to increase information leakage via hackers and other negligent behaviours from IT users. In order to protect in extreme cases where there is no need for IT systems to be connected online, IT could decide to use air gaps to isolate machines with highly sensitive systems. There is indeed little opportunity to be hacked if the IT system is isolated with an air gap between it and any network.

While inconvenient for employees it is possible to lock down USB ports restricting the use of USB drives. Likewise, IT could decide to limit access to cloud storage—perhaps to corporate provided and managed solutions. Considerations should be made about the nature of the needs of employees to engage with external parties.

6 Business Secrets Governance and Management Issues: What? Why? How?

The obstacles to **controlling information leakage**, as identified in Sect. 1.1 above, can be overcome if we look at the major interests of companies for protecting information:

- Allows companies to value the Intangible Assets, which in turn may attract investors and partners, but also allows to motivate the internal teams
- Allows companies to manage communication with their ecosystem and to strengthen their own influence
- Protection is obviously a deterrent to looting, but also to the appropriation or unauthorised use of information by employees and partners
- Finally, protection allows one to react quickly in court at a lower cost, thanks to its ability to present a solid case

In summary, **awareness** of the existence of important information to be protected, its identification and management, **in itself creates value** for the company. In other words, as one digs into company's value creation, a multi-facet approach shows up.

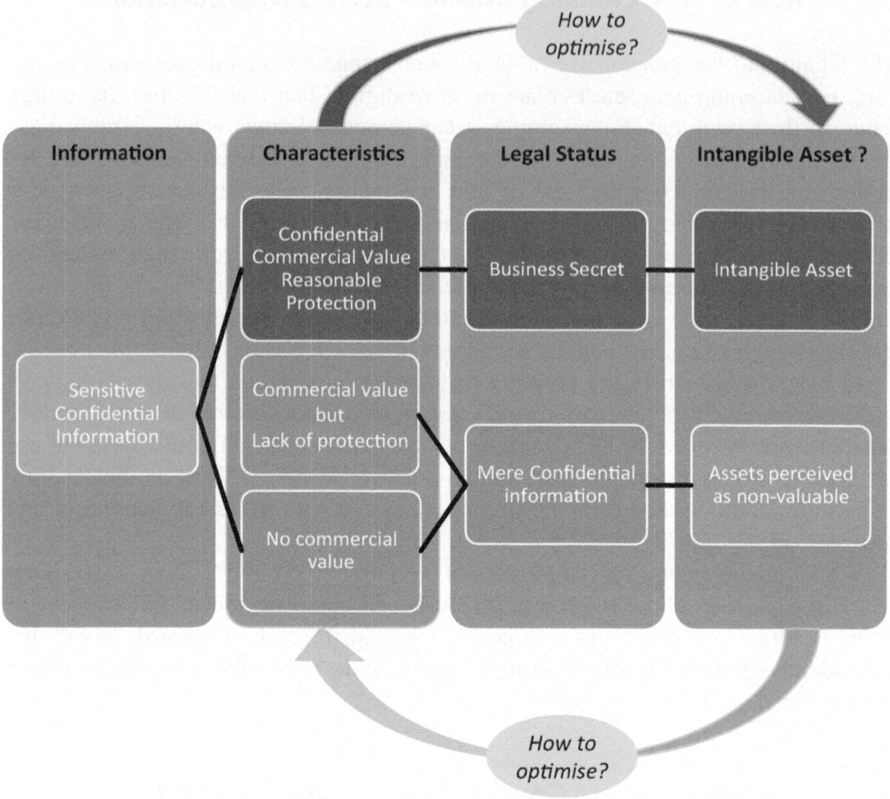

Fig. 1 From Confidential Information to Intangible Asset (credit: Véronique Chapuis & Pierre Ollivier)

An efficient **design of a governance programme** would therefore advantageously rely on a multi-facet legal business intelligence approach that combines strategic, business, financial, social, and legal views. This leads to asking oneself how information status can improve from "confidential" all the way to "Intangible Asset". It could advantageously show in practice the pros and cons of each key item with its associated financial value, hence helping the decision-making by managers and users (Fig. 1).

The question to ask is then: *"How can **Confidential Information** become a **business secret**, benefiting from legal protection and, as a consequence, how can its value and even therefore its recognition as an **Intangible Asset** be established to the benefit of the company (organisation) and of its users?"*

The following chapters develop these practical issues and the associated potential values captured by the company, addressing **topics and issues that business owners and managers deal with in their daily jobs**:

- WHAT?—Chap. 3 shows how confidential information **becomes a business secret**
- WHY?—Chap. 4 explains how business secrets **create value to a company** or an organisation
- HOW? (a)—Chap. 5 develops the **management practices** to actually protect confidential information and business secrets, and increase intangible assets portfolio
- HOW? (b)—Chap. 6 touches **contractual preventing strategies** that go hand-in-hand with prudential management practices
- HOW? (c)—Chap. 7 goes into some key managing details when addressing **legal protection strategies**

Confidential Information as Business Secret

Graham Bell, Pierre Ollivier, Philippe Simon, and Ferzana Haq

Abstract

This chapter explores the forms of business secrets, which include but are not limited to trade secrets and sensitive information, and compares them against other common forms of Intellectual Property such as patents. We compare the benefits of keeping business secrets vs. patenting innovations, with a particular interest in the innovation trends from Artificial Intelligence (AI), Machine Learning (ML), and Internet of Things (IoT). We also take a look at how the increased use of data—both personal data falling under General Data Protection Regulation (GDPR) and other regulations, and non-personal data—impacts how organisations must think about management of such assets.

Finally, this chapter considers the people involved in business secrets—as the originators of the secrets, as employees, academics, or individuals involved in the process. We look at the obligations of the individuals and the duty of care that the organisation has to them.

G. Bell (✉)
Cambridge, UK
e-mail: graham@cubicibuc.com

P. Ollivier · P. Simon
Paris, France
e-mail: pierre.ollivier@winnotek.com; philippe.simon@winnotek.com

F. Haq
Singapore, Singapore
e-mail: ferzanahaq@hslegal.com.sg

P. Ollivier et al. (eds.), *Business Secrets Management*, Management for Professionals, https://doi.org/10.1007/978-3-031-82512-5_3

1 Forms of Business Secrets

1.1 The Many Forms of Confidential Information

Confidential information can take many specific forms, depending on its nature. The form or source of the business secret is one important aspect, but business secrets may also have a time dimension—which is different from other forms of protection. Patents for example, if granted, have a life of 20 years (meaning the legal rights, if maintained, can be enforced over this period), but once published, patent documents are available in the public domain in perpetuity.

A business secret has no formal limit, and if kept secret may be maintained indefinitely; on the other hand, a business secret may have a very short life. AI or IoT solutions that derive value from real-world data, for example, may consider the data sources as extremely valuable information. A solution that combines traffic congestion data with weather data might need to protect that data for 12 to 24 hours, but the data may have little historic value. The data sets are also always changing, so any permanent record is unlikely to be highly sensitive beyond its useful time window.

Alternatively, the most important piece of information within a business may be the name of a target for acquisition. But immediately after the acquisition the information is public knowledge.

One can identify several types of confidential information that can pretend to a business secret status in various circumstances (Fig. 1).

1.2 Keeping Secret Rather Than Patenting Inventions

When an organisation develops a new invention, it has a choice whether to file for a patent to protect that invention, or to keep it as a secret.

The metadata surrounding a patent often provides signals to the market about trends and intentions in the organisation—such metadata becomes publicly available when a patent document is published.

The patent specification may also contain or point to business secrets. These may be unrelated to the invention captured by the patent in question, but inadvertently exposed in the text.

Organisations may therefore choose not to seek patents as this gives away too much information, and instead keep the invention as secret. When looking at this choice an organisation should consider:

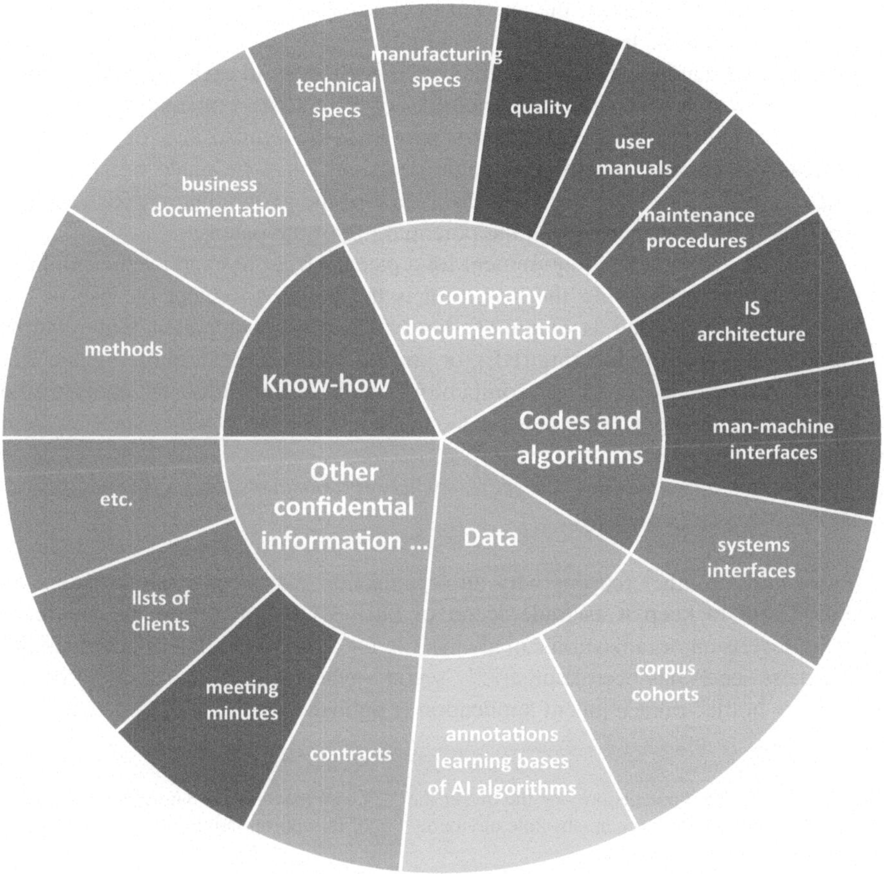

Fig. 1 Types of confidential information = potential business secrets (credit: Pierre Ollivier)

- *Is a patent even possible*? Some inventions may be in areas where patents are not allowed, e.g. pure algorithmic inventions,[1] if the claimed subject-matter is directed to a specific plant variety or specific plant varieties.[2]
- *Whether the invention meets the threshold for a patent*. It may be questionable if the particular invention meets the threshold for a patent—it may be questionable if it is novel over the known art—whether the filed application risks being rejected for absence of inventiveness, i.e. if the patent fails to be granted due to some objection by the patent office, the patent application is still published and remains

[1] European Patent Office. List of exclusions - > Programs for computers https://www.epo.org/en/legal/guidelines-epc/2023/g_ii_3_6.html.

[2] European Patent Office. List of exclusions - > Plant varieties https://www.epo.org/en/legal/guidelines-epc/2023/g_ii_5_4_1.html.

publicly available. Hence, the attempt to claim a monopoly on the invention is exposed without the benefit of the monopoly.

- *Cost.* Patents can be expensive, and must be applied for in each national jurisdiction, which can lead to significant multiples of filing costs. For small and medium enterprises (SMEs), budget constraints may limit the number and/ or geographic coverage of patents, meaning strategic decisions must be made on when and where to file. Since such decisions are linked to the geographic markets served, these must be assessed through the potential life of the patent.
- *Ease of detection.* A key requirement for a patent owner to exercise their right to restrict others from using the invention is the ability to detect the use of the invention. If detection is extremely hard, e.g. a product patent that requires complex Reverse Engineering (RE), or process patent not externally visible that would require access to a competitors facility (in order to analyse the manufacturing steps), there may be a consideration as to whether such a patent could ever be enforced.
- *A patent has a limited life—20 years*—whereas a business secret, if not exposed, is effectively in perpetuity.

There may be other reasons why an organisation may decide not to patent an invention, but to keep it as trade secret or business secret. Given the nature of business secrets an organisation can always file for a patent at a later date assuming the business secret has been kept strictly secret—whereas "the genie cannot be put back in the bottle" once a patent application is published.

	Patents	Secrets
Legal strength	Granted patents provide the owner the right to enforce an absolute monopoly on the invention	Legal recourse for damages in the case of misappropriation
Cost	High initial costs, depending on number of jurisdictions covered Ongoing maintenance costs (if maintained)	No cost to maintain appropriate physical and IT security measures and to protect any disclosure by appropriate confidential measures
Risks	No grant (patent too weak, opposed prior art…)	Detection of leakage or loss may be difficult
Timing	Can take 3 to 5 years, or more, to obtain a patent	Immediate
Scope of protection	Local in the countries where patent has been filed	No limit
Longevity	20 years after filing, and then becomes public domain	In perpetuity assuming secret is maintained
Market signalling	High—All information relating to patent applications are made public, regardless of whether patent is granted or rejected	None assuming secret is maintained
Other		Can be "converted" into a patent at a later stage should the organisation decide to do so

(continued)

	Patents	Secrets
Can be licensed?	Yes	Yes—If it has been valued and with suitable contractual obligations to maintain secrecy

There is a third option to organisations looking at the patent vs. secret decision—the defensive publication (sometimes called a defensive disclosure). This is an approach where an organisation decides that it does not want to pursue the legal approach of patenting, but does not want a third party to seek a patent either. Publishing the invention, i.e. releasing it into the public domain for defensive purposes can be an alternative route to providing freedom to operate (FTO). Ideally, if a third party attempts to file a patent for an identical or similar invention, it would be rejected by patent examiners as the defensive publication would be found during the patent search and act as prior art.

Often defensive publications are made in trade journals or at industry conferences. While such venues may have an interest in publishing positive innovations, and will do so faster and more cheaply that going the patent route, they may be less interested in publishing negative or incomplete concepts.

While defensive publications can act as prior art stopping third parties from acquiring potentially blocking patents, they also act as prior art against the organisations' own interests, and hence should be used with care if there are more potential future patents in the technology under consideration.

1.3 Other Creations Concerning Products and Processes

As suggested above an organisation may develop technologies that do not reach the threshold of patentability, but none-the-less represent a valuable business secret. Such technologies are often associated with production process optimisation given the particular context of the organisation.

Likewise, operating procedures within the organisation could be business secrets—Standard Operating Procedures (SOPs), training manuals, and quality control procedures are all potentially business secrets (and not necessarily Trade Secrets) as they potentially provide differentiation for the organisation.

1.4 Data—IoT / AI and ML

We define as Data—IoT / AI and ML the economic sector that deals with massive data handling (Data), Internet of Things (IoT), and Artificial Intelligence (AI).

Increasingly in sectors such as IoT / AI and ML, it is data that is the core asset used by the organisation to derive value. Such data comes from sensors that are installed in environments in industrial facilities (factories, oil rigs, and retail outlets) across wider environments (such as traffic monitoring / congestion monitoring within a city or district, pollution monitoring such as particulate detection) or globally (such as weather stations and atmospheric monitoring).

AI and ML systems are often referred to as "black box systems" suggesting that the actual content of the algorithm is unknown to even the developers. This is due to the nature of machine learning where the algorithms are trained with suitable data to allow the system to "learn". Hence, the actual final state of the trained system (the operating state) is unknown—it is a black box. Such systems are unlikely to be protected by patents, but more importantly the key to high performance / high accuracy systems is often the training data rather than the initial system. This data could be composed of thousands or millions of data points, e.g. photos or sounds, which themselves cannot be patented, but could potentially be covered by copyright.

Often in IoT systems the organisation(s) responsible for installing the sensors may not be the same as those performing analysis of the data. Indeed, big data analytics allows for new business models involving the aggregation and analysis of large data sets from disparate sources. The organisations performing the analysis therefore rely on the data sources as their main input and may have no tangible assets of their own. The use of ML or AI only compounds this, as the algorithms used may be black boxes, and as discussed above are not protectable by traditional approaches. Companies operating at the convergence of IoT and AI/ML are left with data as their only value drivers.

An important consideration for data-based business secrets is the longevity of the data. Training data sets may have a long life. Training data sets are typically composed of control data that have been selected, cleaned, normalised and labelled in some way. High-quality training data sets are key to train the AI/ML systems and hence have high strategic value. Actual operational data used in the analysis, coming from real-world IoT systems may have much shorter longevity. Although there may be other legal reasons for retaining the data, some systems have useful lives in the order of minutes or hours. An organisation generating value from a combination of real-time traffic congestion data with pollution data may have limited utility for data sets from 6 or 12 hours ago, particularly as traffic congestion has moved on; the same pollution data however may be of great interest for another organisation advising farmers on long-term weather patterns.

In such scenarios, keeping secure records of training data covered by suitable business secret procedures may be appropriate. Keeping long-term records of live data may not.

1.5 Personal Data

Due to digital massive use by individuals and to the social networks' significant developments, personal data has increasingly spread worldwide, which has created a number of issues when dealing with data related to individuals: private information, preferences, photos, etc. These issues have materialised in various laws, and especially in Europe with the EU General Data Protection Regulation (GDPR), which deals with privacy and security. This regulation, adopted in 2016 and enforced in

2018, recycled, revamped, and repurposed the principles of the 1995 data protection directive (see more details in[3]).

GDPR applies to any entity, even if this entity is not in the EU, and the fines may be quite significant. Therefore, it is important to carefully understand its concept and the related obligations. The main topics described in the mentioned EU website include concepts such as:

- *Personal data*: Any information that relates to an individual who can be directly or indirectly identified. Names and email addresses are obviously personal data. Location information, ethnicity, gender, biometric data, religious beliefs, web cookies, and political opinions can also be personal data. Pseudonymous data can also fall under the definition if it is relatively easy to identify someone from it.
- *Data processing*: Any action performed on data, whether automated or manual. The examples cited in the text include collecting, recording, organising, structuring, storing, using, erasing… so basically anything.
- *Data subject*: The person whose data is processed. These are organisations' customers or site visitors.
- *Data controller*: The person who decides why and how personal data will be processed. These are organisations' owners or employees who handle data.
- *Data processor*: A third party that processes personal data on behalf of a data controller. The GDPR has special rules for these individuals and organisations. They could include cloud servers like Tresorit[4] or email service providers like Proton Mail.[5]

The key objectives of GDPR can be defined as follows, to achieve "**better protection for personal data"** (Fig. 2 from Consilium Europa[6]):

- Clear consent required from data subjects to process data
- More and clearer information provided about data processing
- Right of data subjects to move data from one service provider to another
- Limits on the use of automated processing of data to make decisions, for example in the case of data subjects "profiling"
- Data subjects have the right to rectify and remove their data, including the "right to be forgotten" for data collected as a child
- Easier access given to data subjects to their personal data
- Stricter safeguards for transfers of personal data outside of the EU

[3] "What is GDPR, the EU's new data protection law? "https://gdpr.eu/what-is-gdpr/.

[4] https://tresorit.com/.

[5] https://proton.me/mail?ref=gdpreu.

[6] https://www.consilium.europa.eu/en/press/press-releases/2016/04/08/data-protection-reform-first-reading/.

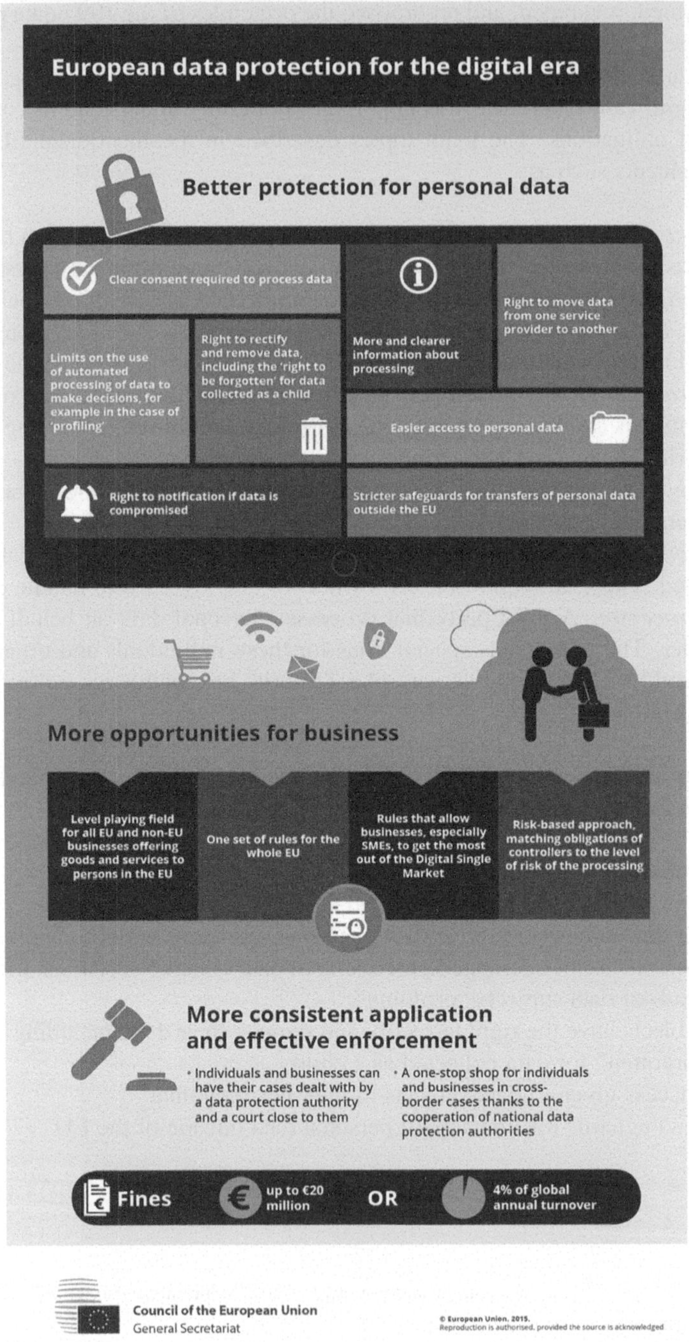

Fig. 2 Key objectives of EU General Data Protection Regulation (credit: Consilium Europa)

The law describes a number of principles relating to *accountability*, *data security*, and *data protection by design and by default*, *when it is allowed to process data* and the *rules about consent of a data subject to process their information*. It becomes mandatory, in certain circumstances, to appoint a *Data Protection Officer* (DPO). *Peoples' privacy rights* are also a key element of the law; privacy rights are the right to be informed, the right of access, the right to rectification, the right to erasure, the right to restrict processing, the right to data portability, the right to object, rights in relation to automated decision-making and profiling.

Under GDPR an individual is also able to ask an organisation what data it is holding on them. This means it is vital that the organisation knows what it holds, and maintains that data in such a way that it is able to respond to such requests, and when requested, erase part or all of the relevant data.

Due to GDPR, it becomes more and more a practice in businesses Worldwide to include a specific clause dedicated to these obligations in **non-disclosure agreements** (NDA), and more generally, in almost all contractual agreements between companies or between companies and organisations. Typically NDA clauses would include a clause mentioning the related law, a clause defining sensitive personal data that shall not be collected, a clause defining protection obligation by the parties, collection authorisation or collection prohibition of certain data, minimum protection measures for data collection and data processing, specifying who has the right to collect under what conditions, as well as location and duration of data storage.

2 Non-Business Secrets / Non-Trade Secrets—Exploring the Definition

2.1 Example of the Canteen Menu

The most commonly cited set of information that should be demonstrated to not be a trade secret is the organisation's canteen menu. While this is a mundane example it helps to demonstrate the tests as described in Sect. 4 in Chap. 2 apply.

Clearly the menu for the canteen is likely to meet the first element of the definition of business secret—it is known only to the organisation / within the organisation. A canteen menu is often compartmentalised into that instantaneous informational function, and is not widely known throughout the business ahead of time. We might describe that as a surprise—rather than a secret!

A canteen menu is also unlikely to be known to any entity outside of the organisation. While catering suppliers may know broadly what ingredients have been ordered they may not know the specifics of how those ingredients will be assembled (the internal "process")—or indeed if all the ingredients will be used together—a typical canteen may provide different "products" to suit vegetarians, vegans, and meat eaters—it is therefore unclear which dish an order of, say, onions may be heading for. This is similar to an electronics manufacturer who may order multiple components for a portfolio of consumer electronics products. Suppliers may see a broad set of components, but without a detailed product description (Bill of materials) will not know exactly what is been developed until the product is made public.

However, while the canteen menu is known within the organisation, and unknown to entities outside the organisation, we can probably agree that it fails the third test—a loss of value to the organisation or a gain of value to the third party in case of "loss". Should a competing organisation gain access to the canteen menu and offer the same menu in its canteen there is unlikely to be loss within the original owner or gain within the "infringing" party.

2.2 Other Forms of Non-Business Secret

Other forms of non-business secret might include lists of employees. While start-ups in "stealth mode" may hide their employee lists in order to hide their intentions, generally employee lists are not unknown outside of organisations. Social media use means that a large majority of people publish their employment status and identity of employer—LinkedIn for example.

Likewise, product specifications or documentation such as user manuals may be made available to the general public through websites. In such circumstances, this information should not be considered secret in any form. It may be held in confidence prior to the product launch, and it is not uncommon for early reviewers to be provided products and manuals with review embargos restricting what they can say or show prior to official launch dates.

2.3 Negative Results as Business Secrets

It is commonly understood that not all R&D is successful resulting in development activities that are followed through to products or services. Depending on technology and industry, a ratio of around 1:10 for successful R&D commercialisation is common. This figure would suggest that for every one project that successfully makes it "out of R&D" there are nine that are not pursued. There may be a number of reasons why an organisation decides not to pursue particular paths of research, and we recognise that not all result from "failure"—however we use "negative results" as short-hand for those projects that are not continued.

So assuming there is one path that results in success that it taken forward into a product or service, or further research, it may be that the organisation patents this success, or it may choose to keep this "success" a secret. Either way, the question is what to do with the nine others.

While the nine "negative results" may not have value to the organisation, **they may have value to others.** Consider a direct competitor, looking to duplicate the successful solution. With no prior knowledge of the nine other projects that were explored by the original organisation it is fair to assume that given a similar set of capabilities they too might require nine iterations to find the tenth successful case. If then, the information about the original companies' nine negative results is exposed this would benefit the competitor who could avoid the same mistakes, save the money in exploring research paths that were not taken and short-cut the time to find the successful route.

Alternatively one of the nine may not be the most optimal solution, but may still be a viable and commercially deployable option.

It follows then that the originating organisation should treat the information about the negative results as business secrets.

As always there may be reasons why an organisation may choose to share information relating to failure cases. The market may not be competitive, but may be an ecosystem of organisations looking to establish a common standard, or adopt a single technology. **Such negative research outcomes are valuable and therefore must be protected as business secret.**

3 Employees and Individuals' Relation with Business Secrets

3.1 "Creators" of "Business Secrets"

Business secrets are versatile in nature since by definition they include all types of information with tactical or strategic value to a company, whereby leaking, pilfering, unlawful capture, misuse, negligent disclosure, or other undue appropriation of such information would cause tangible damages to the company whatever the time horizon for said damages to appear.

Therefore, business secrets can originate in all major functions of an ongoing concern: R&D, manufacturing, finance, marketing, sales, communication, human resources, legal, and even corporate management. Intuitive examples include intellectual property assets (patents, trademarks, models and designs, software applications, databases, and know-how), decision support tools such as clients databases, financial simulation algorithms, target costing tools... They also may consist in preventive and/or predictive maintenance algorithms, manufacturing "sleight of hand", manufacturing processes, R&D testing protocols, quality control tools, etc.

Business secrets also arise, in many industrial contexts, along the product or process life in service: for example, FMEA (failure mode economic analyses) outputs and data during the design phase, actual field feedback under the form of "failure trees" relative to components, modules, systems, or processes, qualify as business secret because it embodies the reliability performance and ageing behaviour of the company's output under "normal" service conditions. The same can be said of consumer satisfaction studies which embody end users' perception of the company's image and reputation, or sales pitches and value proposal presentation which are designed to prompt a prospect's purchase decision. Such examples are naturally not exhaustive.

Consequently, "creators" of business secrets belong to a plurality of functions in the company: R&D engineers and technicians (a majority of patent inventors), manufacturing managers, quality assurance managers, data scientists, cost estimators, but also potentially communication managers, treasurers, corporate finance managers, sales managers and account executives, designers, credit managers, even HR executives.

These creators do not always need to be employees of the company: interns, contractors, and professional service providers (even consultants) may produce business secrets for the company as long as their contractual commitments ensure that ownership of said secrets reverts to the company itself, exclusively or not.

3.2 Obligation of Individuals in Relation to Business Secrets

Individual employees each must comply with two distinct but complementary policies of the company:

- Business secrets Policy, when it is specified as a distinct corpus.
- Security Policy, encompassing all activities of the firm.

Business Secrets Policy

A business secrets Policy spells out rights and obligations of employees concerning all information labelled as "business secrets" as well as confidential information that may qualify as business secrets. Their obligations are specified by their habilitation, itself dependent on their qualification, function, and "need to know" as determined in the company's own classification of secrets (typically 4 to 5 grades of confidentiality and protection).

For example, cost structures of products or systems which are key elements of competitivity are usually "off limits" to sales executives to prevent them from negligently disclosing such secrets to client's purchasing executives during negotiations.

The business secrets Policy should typically detail which employee profile has access to which kind of secret, and the degree of freedom the same profile enjoys with regard to using, sharing, and disclosing the secret, first within the company itself and then outside the company. These provisions closely mimic the "secret habilitation" of government employees with regard to "nationally sensitive" information.

Within the corporation, access to and freedom to use, share, disclose, secrets, are naturally correlated to the individual's need to manipulate such secrets in order to perform their functions efficiently: for example, FMEA results and "failure trees" embodying the quality level and field reliability of a product or system may be widely accessible to even lower ranking Quality Assurance employees, or R&D and manufacturing technicians best positioned to remedy observed defects in future generations of products. Contrarily, in the finance function, maybe only the CFO or his direct reports need to know about them in order to translate them into "costs of non quality", and in the sales functions only account executives and their superiors need to know in order to decide which product features to stress and which to be quiet about in their "value proposal" arguments.

Security Policy

All provisions of a security policy should apply to the protection of business secrets and be complementary rather than redundant with the business secrets policy. These provisions obviously apply to all employees even those who have no opportunity to access, use, or disclose secrets. They can usually be segmented into two domains:

- **Infrastructure and decision support tools policies**: Hardware and software locks on various internal IT networks, access rights to repositories of sensitive data including business secrets, data storage in real or virtual "safes", e.g. a cloud-based, services provider secured data centre. Screening and security measures on operational premises: Temporary confiscation of visitors' laptops and smartphones, continuous watch by cameras and/or drones, and malevolent intrusion detection. Overall cybersecurity infrastructure and tools, including biometric identification procedures and physical access control to premises, etc.
- **Behavioural policies**: Prudential measures for travelling collaborators, for example ban on holding business conversations in public places, whether on the phone or face to face, on openly working on laptop onboard a plane or train, in airports and train stations waiting rooms, etc. Continuous close escort of outside visitors on company premises, restriction on dissemination of company's documents (whatever their nature) during trade shows, scientific conferences and professional events, etc.

The above-mentioned measures (list non-exhaustive) apply to all hierarchical levels and all functions of the company: we can then consider that the specific provisions of the business secrets policy apply "over and above" those of the comprehensive security policy.

Beyond the intuitive risk of negligent disclosure of secrets by ignorant or insufficiently trained employees, specific risks are associated with specific types of collaborators. Outside collaborators like suppliers, contractors, distributors, multi-brand agents, consultants, even pro bono workers, will be addressed in Sect. 3.3 below. However, individuals much closer to the firm may jeopardise the protection of business secrets:

- **Student interns and visiting scientists**, or **visiting employees from foreign based** subsidiaries of the firm, where legal protection of business secrets is different: it is impossible to "clean up their brain" of all the sensitive information they may have had access to, once they return to their university, laboratory, or overseas subsidiary. They must therefore at least be required to sign NDA's in their own name or under their organisation's authority, just like common practice already provides that they relinquish all IP rights to any invention they may have contributed to during their presence within the firm, such IP rights reverting exclusively to the company.

- **Company shareholders, board members, and corporate advisors**: These are not salaried employees, but typically because of their function, they enjoy access rights to highly sensitive information. Although anti-fraud laws already punish negligent as well as malevolent disclosure or pilfering of secrets, for instance for stock price manipulation, hostile takeovers, etc., an efficient business secrets policy might add specific contracts to be signed by such stakeholders, providing for financial and professional sanctions—and termination of the business relationship with the firm—in case of any disclosure of secrets whatever the original intent. One of the most common instances being that of board members sitting on the boards of Connex-industries stakeholders, or even competitors: it may be legitimate to compel such individuals to sign "non competing agreements" covering all secrets their board seat gives them access to.
- **Employees about to leave the firm**, whether on their own or following dismissal. For the same reason as interns and visiting scientists, it is impossible to prevent their taking away potential or confirmed secrets when they leave. Corrective measures include at least signing of non-competing agreements—which in certain countries require a financial compensation to the employee in order to be enforceable-, nominal NDA's for a duration as close as possible to that of the potential competitive advantage embodied in the endangered secret, and if practically feasible, isolating the soon to leave employee from colleagues accessing and using already labelled "secrets" and cutting his access means to all repositories of such secrets. Consider putting the new employer on notice: i.e. sending a notification to the new employer that the new employee knows business secrets that should not be shared or exploited.

3.3 Contractual Partners Obligations

As mentioned above, we address here the case of outside contractual partners: suppliers, contract R&D laboratories, distributors, multi-card or exclusive agents, consultants, service providers such as patent counsels, law firms, CPA's (certified public accounting firms), and other industrial firms involved in collaborative projects, be it R&D, manufacturing, or other. All types of contractual partners are included, whether they operate on a one-to-one contractual basis or in the framework of a consortium, such as E.U. sponsored collaborative innovation programmes like Eureka, H2020, etc. This also includes the case of professional associations and syndicates which usually foster information sharing between members, whereas this legitimate process may lead to careless disclosures or unlawful appropriation of secrets by third parties.

Different protection frameworks are usually activated, each providing specific but non-exhaustive protective steps towards confidential information and business secrets:

1) **Non-disclosure agreements (NDA)**: Their validity is usually limited to a specific project, assignment, product, or technology range, and to a typology of

information "reasonably necessary for the execution of the contracted services or the completion of the collaborative project". Therefore, a technology consultant may not, as a general matter of course, be granted access to his client's cash management system; a patent counsel is not supposed to know about his client's M&A's plans, etc. At a minimum, most NDA's spell out that information sharing between partners is limited to the duration of the assignment, collaborative project, services contract, and the like but provide for a longer obligation of confidentiality than said duration (e.g. 2 years confidentiality vs. a 6 months consulting assignment): the competitive advantage intrinsic to the secrets potentially disclosed under the contract should therefore be preserved beyond successful completion of the project or assignment. Similarly, NDA's assess that no transfer of IP rights of any kind may result from sharing of confidential information or business secrets, even though their disclosure is necessary for successful achievement of contractual tasks. Moreover, stakeholders to the NDA are responsible for strict compliance of all their employees with the provisions of the agreement and for controlling dissemination of other parties' information through their own workforce on a strict "need to know" basis.

2) **Collaboration contracts**: Consulting assignments, professional services (law firms, patent counsels, CPA's, advertising agencies, ...), and collaborative R&D or manufacturing projects are commonly ruled by ad-hoc contractual agreements. The same is true for supplier/client contracts, including contract laboratories for externalised R&D work or subcontracting for prototype or pre-series manufacturing. Such frameworks are also relevant for selling patent licenses limited to manufacturing and selling without any right to engage in R&D around the licensed product or process. The strongest contractual framework may be that of a joint venture (JV) with equity investment: the JV's charter specifies the nature and range of confidential information shared by the partners within the JV perimeter, explicitly excluding from reciprocal disclosure any secrets unrelated to the JV's purpose and daily operating requirements. Violation of the JV charter with regard to protection of partners' secrets outside its perimeter constitutes a felony and a valid cause for legal punitive action.
Such contractual agreements commonly define the type of confidential information that could/should be disclosed by each party on a "need to know" basis, i.e. restricting their perimeter to elements strictly necessary to the successful execution of the contract, be it supplies, professional services, consulting, subcontracted R&D or manufacturing tasks, or collaborative scientific and industrial projects. For the latter, the agreement must detail the nature and sensitivity of all information to be shared between partners, in particular each stakeholder's "background" contribution: formal IP assets, business secrets, know-how... freely disclosed to the partner only for the duration of the project and only for completion of its contractual objectives. After termination of the contract—successful or not—continued access to the background by the partner is only possible upon signing a licensing agreement and paying subsequent royalties. Any abusive appropriation, misuse, disclosure to third parties, etc., of

background components constitute a violation of contractual commitments, a valid cause for cancellation and for legal action to collect damages in court.

It is further good practice that such collaboration contracts set out guidance over how foreground IP (including any know-how, knowledge, or potential inventions) will be shared post-collaboration. Ideally this will address ownership vs. usage rights.

3) For a majority of contractual agreements, another lever for protection comes from the partners' respective **deontology obligations as dictated by their professional status,** typically for "regulated" professions such as lawyers, CPA's, patent counsels, or **by their professional association,** typically strategy or management consultants, IT service providers, advertising and communication agencies … Such provisions cover in priority confidentiality obligations and protection of all client's proprietary information—including therefore business secrets—against careless disclosure to any third party and even to uninvolved employees of the supplier/service provider. Moreover, specific protection measures are often spelled out in a company's purchasing policies and specific buying conditions, and symmetrically in many suppliers' and service providers' general selling conditions. Depending on the relative strength of both parties, larger entities' purchasing policies may force extended disclosures of business secrets on the part of "weaker" stakeholders: e.g. many large industrial groups presently demand from their potential suppliers, as a prerequisite to qualifying them on their panel, a full disclosure of the IP condition relative to the product or technology offered for sale. The buyer's goal is to identify the respective shares of internal development (hence own IP assets), imported knowledge (licensing-in of third-party patents), and re-use of publicly available information in the genesis of the candidate supplier's offering. This prudential work step aims at reducing the buyer's risk of unknowingly infringing third parties' rights if the candidate supplier is a counterfeiter. It appears as a constraint from the candidate supplier's standpoint but in practice results in building mutual trust between the parties.

3.4 Disclosure to Governmental or Judicial Authorities, or Courts, Discovery

There are naturally several situations where the legitimate owner of business secrets becomes bound or may be constrained to disclose them. In most cases, the obligation is issued by a governmental authority or a court of law, for example (non-exhaustive list):

- **Governmental departments or agencies**: Defence, foreign trade control… for potential exporters of sensitive goods or materials, national defence contractors detaining strategic knowledge, etc., labour department for corporations owning and operating foreign manufacturing subsidiaries where employment conditions could be at risk to violate national labour laws.

- **Tax and customs authorities**: For any issue relating to tax evasion, transfer prices between parent company and subsidiaries, fulfilment of tax payments, fair use of government subsidies, infringement of country-specific export restrictions, compliance with "fair trade" regulations, export contracts with local compensation clauses, etc.
- **Courts of law**: For any litigation, whether between industrial stakeholders (breach of contract, counterfeiting ...), lawsuits from employees or trade unions, class action suits by NGO's (nongovernmental organisations), etc. Such litigations may lead to the court ordering a "discovery" process, whereby all supports and repositories of data owned and/or operated by a company may be legally seized and screened by prosecutors and by opponents' legal counsels. Since the perimeter of data to be seized and screened involves all digital information potentially relevant to the litigation, the amount of data to be disclosed becomes massive and the probability of inclusion of business secrets in the perimeter is quite high.

On this issue, it is useful to distinguish between "evidence" and "discovery":

- "**Evidence**" generically covers all types of data that can be used as argument and/or proof to support the case of one of the parties in the litigation, to confirm or dismiss suspicions of negligent, fraudulent, or criminal behaviour, for example a conflict between a corporation and a governmental agency including tax and customs authorities.
- "**Discovery**" is a process whereby such evidence is sought via identification, collection, and detailed screening of a company's data, whether already disclosed, readily accessible, or kept secret from outsiders and even segments of the company's own insiders (employees, executives, shareholders, etc.…). A discovery process aims at capturing specific categories of information—dictated by the nature of the law infringement or the litigation—but requires collecting and screening massive amounts of data, most of which probably bear no relevance to the case… although their relevance is an unknown at the start of the process.

Therefore, any discovery process is likely to collect and screen business secrets which are irrelevant to the case but nonetheless embody serious value for the company: their disclosure, even if strictly limited to a government authority or a court of law, may cause serious tangible harm to the interests and the wealth of their original owner. For example, in the framework of a patent infringement/product counterfeiting litigation, collection through discovery of a company's R&D projects, product designs, test results, pricing policies, etc., is likely to capture business secrets covering other products and patents than the strict object of litigation, yet if the plaintiff gains access to these secrets it may unduly acquire a competitive advantage beyond the range of its present claim.

"E-discovery" is the electronic version of the discovery process. It has recently evolved towards advanced methods of discovery, optimised for handling massive data with efficiency higher by several orders of magnitude than human screening, which is still widely practiced today, even in e-discovery. Instead of teams of reviewers working in parallel screening documents against a reference list of keywords or terms in order to decide YES or NO on their relevance, modern e-discovery leverages Artificial Intelligence via machine learning algorithms trained to identify logical relationships between words or segments of sentences within a given document, after a number of questions (or "prompts"), thus allowing the operator to decide relevance or irrelevance for the case with a high probability of accuracy. These algorithms similarly allow for early identification of correlations between unknown documents (based on querying their content) and thus for quick build-up of "clusters" of relevant "evidence" out of massive amounts of documents.

The issue for the original owner of business secrets thus becomes: "*Which data management policy should be designed and enforced, to minimise the risk of unnecessary—but harmful—disclosure of business secrets during a discovery whose issue they are irrelevant for, but which may capture them nevertheless*"? Part of the solution may lie in the classification level and labelling of business secrets as stored by the company itself: for example, if a company manufactures and trades in defence-sensitive goods and services, or masters technologies labelled by government authorities as "national strategic value", it may have a case to request exemption from disclosure of that particular range of secrets, should a discovery involving "less sensitive" data be engaged against it. The risk to national interests might indeed supersede the benefit of fulfilling the plaintiff's legitimate request.

Failing such a configuration, the company might request from the court, while complying with the demands of the discovery, protective measures against excessive disclosure of discovery results—potentially including business secrets of higher value than the estimated stakes of the litigation that triggered the discovery—: strict limitations to the court itself and the plaintiff's legal representatives, ban on any public release by any party towards any media; and—if applicable—leveraging of professional e-discovery expert consultants to provide a second opinion on real relevance of "raw discovery results" to the case. This might result on requalifying part of the business secrets included in the discovery as "irrelevant to the litigation", therefore exempting them from disclosure to even the plaintiff, let alone the media and public at large.

3.5 Talking to Employees of Confidential Information and/or of Trade Secret?

Many discussions take place in various professional events, particularly in the USA, whereby the question is raised whether or not employee contracts should refer to "Confidential Information" rather than "Trade secrets", the issue being that the latter denomination is not well understood. The positive argument states that employees better understand the concept of Confidential Information rather than that of Trade Secret. However, the drawback for using "Confidential Information" is that this embraces a too broad set of information so that corresponding company policies could be invalidated by courts, because they would prevent employees from openly sharing and using their own knowledge in their daily duties.

From another viewpoint, it should be noted that, trying to enforce protection of a very broad mass of information, be it legally or by any other means (internal procedures, hardware or software restricted access to repositories, etc., see Chap. 5 of this book), may endanger the company's business activity itself. If this enforcement hampers employees' everyday freedom to trade with third parties' information that normally leverages future business success, it might result in forsaking or even destroying company value by shrinking the scope and perimeter of business opportunities.

A medium path should therefore be found to reconcile these two legitimate management objectives: protection of confidential information and in particular trade secrets, vs. continuous enhancement of company asset value. Indeed, identifying and efficiently classifying data initially recognised as "Confidential Information" is a prerequisite for granting part of them, after screening, the status of trade secret and then deploy adequate protection measures. This also supposes a proactive employee training policy teaching the legal criteria for "trade secrets" labelling, the multiplicity of their sources within all functions of the company, and at a minimum a simple set of tools and KPI's to heuristically estimate their "value".

A prerequisite for the success of such programmes is the build-up of a company-specific classification for business secrets (3, 4, or 5 levels of secrecy and corresponding protective measures, physical and/or digital) and the detailed definition of access rights by hierarchical level, by function (field as well as staff) and if applicable by enrolment in specific projects or task forces requiring access to higher level secrets than the individual's rank and job description would normally warrant (see also Chap. 5 of this book, Section 6 "Implementing a Governance and business secrets Policy (Detection, Qualification, Protection)" for further details).

Once this stage is completed, formal training programmes for employees may be launched, covering both mastery of the classification and its vocabulary (the "bill of materials" of business secrets), and behavioural prescriptions, which might be summarised in a compact "vademecum" or "business secrets user's manual" providing efficient answers to employee's FAQ's (frequently asked questions) when confronted with confidentiality and secrecy issues in their daily duties. Training of newly hired collaborators in understanding the classification and learning behavioural "reflexes" should be an imperative in their integration roadmap.

Formally training employees in the classification designed by the firm for its business secrets and in the protective measures to be enforced for each "level" in the classification should help them draw the line, among all the data they routinely handle to fulfil their duty, between the data that may be freely exchanged, the one with restricted disclosure ("need to know" basis, etc.…), and the one they have no latitude to disclose to anyone without explicit authorisation from their hierarchy.

The result of this process should be a net positive contribution to creating and strengthening intangible assets, without negative impact on employees' freedom to use non confidential information to serve business development activities. Both processes simultaneously contribute to enhancing overall corporate value.

4 Confidential Information Vs. Employee Skill and Knowledge

Focusing on the many issues related to employees and confidentiality, where there is a potential breach of confidence by an employee or an ex-employee, the question remains to be seen whether or not the related information is part of the skill and knowledge of the employee (who hence cannot be prevented from using it) or whether it can be validly regarded as the company's confidential information.

In the example of the Clearlab case (Singapore) - which is summarized in Chap. 1 of this book, Sect. 3.7 "Case 7: Clearlab", and further discussed in Chap. 5, Sect. 2.7 "Protection Against Breach of Confidence in Singapore" - while the law of breach of confidence does not distinguish between types of confidential information, the Singaporean courts have taken care to distinguish between "skill and knowledge" belonging to an ex-employee and "confidential information" belonging to the ex-employer. While the law recognises that an employer's confidential information should be protected in a post-employment situation, the scope of protection should not unreasonably encroach upon the ex-employee's ability to utilise his skill and knowledge to seek alternative employment or to compete with the ex-employer in the same field.[7]

As a matter of public policy, an employee should be entitled to use his skill and knowledge, whether or not it is confidential to the employer at the time of acquisition. If the employer's right to restrain misuse of his confidential information collides with the public interest of allowing an ex-employee to freely use his acquired skill and knowledge, it is the latter which should prevail.

This is the correct approach because an ex-employee should not be restrained from entering into future employment or even engaging in a competing business simply because the ex-employee had been provided with or had access to his ex-employer's confidential information. Any other approach would restrain employee mobility and be anti-competitive.

Of course, it may not always be clear whether confidential information falls within the realm of "skill and knowledge" of the employee. However, in breach of confidence cases, plaintiffs are required to specify types of confidential information alleged to have been breached by the defendants with sufficient clarity. With this consideration in mind, the courts are able to reach a reasonable conclusion as whether the information is proprietary to the ex-employer (such as customer data or specific software programs owned by the ex-employer) or whether it is part of the skill and knowledge of the ex-employee or is simply information that is part of the public domain (in which case it cannot be protected as confidential information).

In any event, the use of an ex-employee's skill and knowledge may be restrained if the ex-employee is bound by a restraint of trade clause or restrictive covenants. But

---

[7] Clearlab *SG Pte Ltd v Ting Chong Chai and others* [2015] 1 SLR 163 paragraph 67.

such an action arises in contract and not from any duty of confidentiality. However, the courts, such as those in Singapore, may construe such clauses very strictly because of the strong public interest against restricting employee mobility and competition. A restraint of trade clause must be reasonable and should have a limited time period, geographical location, and scope. In general, a restraint of trade clause will be held to be invalid and unenforceable unless it is reasonable having regard to the interests of both parties as well as the public interest. Broad restraint of trade clauses will usually be struck down by the courts.

On the other hand, restraint of clauses may be a valid form of protection if the confidential information concerned is a trade secret, and by extension could also be—potentially—if it is a business secret from the company management's perspective. As stated by the Singaporean High Court in Clearlab:[8]

> *'It seems to me that "trade secrets" as understood in the second contract is used as a juxtaposition to "skill and knowledge". Restraint of the latter was unjustifiable because it unduly constrains competition and interferes with an ex-employee's right to depend on it to earn a living. In balancing between the interests of the ex-employer in protecting confidential information and the interests of the ex-employee to use his skill and knowledge, the law has to come down on the side of the ex- employee. This is less of a question on the degree of confidentiality necessary to grant protection and more of a question of whether a restraint of trade is reasonable and therefore justified'.*

Therefore, in breach of confidence cases, **the courts do not distinguish between the degrees of confidentiality** of information and an employer is free to protect all confidential information by contract, provided it does not form part of the ex-employee's skill and knowledge. As stated by the Singaporean High Court in Clearlab (see this Case 7 summary in Chap. 1 of this book):

> *"It seems to me implausible that the agreement should collapse at some point along the spectrum of confidentiality in spite of parties taking the trouble to define and agree what confidential information they would protect. On the other hand, it is important to recognise that confidential information could form part of an ex-employee's general skill and knowledge during the course of employment. To the extent that the restraint against the use of such knowledge and skill is unreasonable, it could be struck down"*

[8]Clearlab *SG Pte Ltd v Ting Chong Chai and others* [2015] 1 SLR 163 paragraph 74.

5 Addressing Global Strategies Means Facing Different Trade Secret Legal Complexities

Academic literature mostly refers to Trade Secrets as anything that is considered an intangible asset or any confidential information that is not formal or registered IP.

In a commercial context, the definition of Trade Secrets becomes a common target standard worldwide, **given at a high level by the three requisites: "confidential not known", "commercial value", and "reasonable protection measures"**, which came into practice through the TRIPS (Trade-Related Aspects of Intellectual Property Rights). It is indeed similar in Europe, UK, and in the USA (since the Trade Secret Act and also somehow before) and probably in many other countries.

> TRIPS already introduced trade secrets and test data,[9] mentioning specifically that "*Undisclosed information includes **trade secrets and test data**. Trade secrets must be protected against unauthorised use, including through breach of contract or confidence or other acts contrary to honest commercial practices. **Such protection is conditional upon the information being secret, having commercial value and reasonable steps** having been taken by its owner to keep the information secret. Test data submitted to governments in order to obtain marketing approval for new pharmaceutical or agricultural chemicals must also be protected against unfair commercial use and disclosure. Extended transition periods continue to apply to least developed country members (see section below on transitional arrangements)*".

But there are several jurisprudence details that show interpretation differences in how countries adapt their legal practices to these definitions. For example, European companies referring explicitly to "Trade Secrets" in writing agreements when US entities are possibly concerned, even with the new EU law of 2016, may still create some difficulties. There are indeed differences between the two regimes at the granular level[10] on some aspects:

- **Assessing the "reasonable measures":** EU position is a continuing requirement of protection: a trade secret shall be "*subject to reasonable steps under the circumstances, by the person lawfully in control of the information, to keep it secret*"; whereas US position is that "the owner … has taken reasonable measures to keep such information secret". The USA does not mention any "continuous protection", as does the EU.

[9] Intellectual property: protection and enforcement (https://www.wto.org/english/thewto_e/whatis_e/tif_e/agrm7_e.htm).

[10] https://news.bloomberglaw.com/ip-law/insight-a-comparison-of-the-new-eu-and-us-trade-secrets-regimes.

- **Composite information** as trade secret: EU position is that composite information (combination of information coming from different sources) can still be protected as a trade secret, even though aspects of it may be known or can easily be deduced (this will only be the case provided the precise configuration and assembly of the information is not already known, or cannot be easily deduced); whereas the USA is looking at the information secrecy as a whole: even if certain elements are known, it will not necessarily mean that a secret combination or assembly of bits of information loses its trade secret protection.
- **Proper means** of trade secret acquiring: EU position is that a trade secret is lawfully acquired when it is obtained by independent discovery or creation, or by "observation, study, disassembly or testing of a product or object that has been made available to the public or that is lawfully in the possession of the acquirer of the information who is free from any legally valid duty to limit the acquisition of the trade secret". US position is that information can be a trade secret provided it is not readily ascertainable by another person through proper means. Guidance for the meaning of "proper means" lies in the express acts that are not "improper means" under 18 U.S.C. §1839 (6)(B), including "reverse engineering, independent derivation, or any other lawful means of acquisition".

For example, in the Singapore context, as developed further in Chap. 5 of this book, Sect. 2.7, there is no specific definition of a trade secret whether by the courts or by statute. "Trade secrets" are viewed as a form of confidential information, which is protected from misuse through the common law of breach of confidence and through the laws of contract, amongst others. "Confidential information" is broadly defined as any information which is not in the public domain and provided that the owner of the confidential information has taken reasonable steps to preserve its confidentiality, the information will be treated as confidential. However, the more important and valuable the confidential information is, the more the owner should be under an obligation to take stringent steps to protect such information and to limit who has access to it. In this sense, it is reasonable to require that the owner of valuable trade or business secrets to take prudent steps to preserve the secrecy of such information.

6 Taking a Simplified Helicopter View Towards a "Business Secrets" Concept

The complexity described above is one reason, as explained in Sect. 1.2 "Consider Strategic Information as business secret" in Chap. 2, the authors chose to focus on a business level approach that allows some abstraction from the country specifics of legal issues related to Trade Secrets. **Evaluating the value of confidential information has to deal with moving the status from "confidential information"**—*better understood by employees*—towards **"business secret"** towards aggregated **"intangible asset"**—*better handled by management*—, which indeed characterises the actual value of that bucket of information.

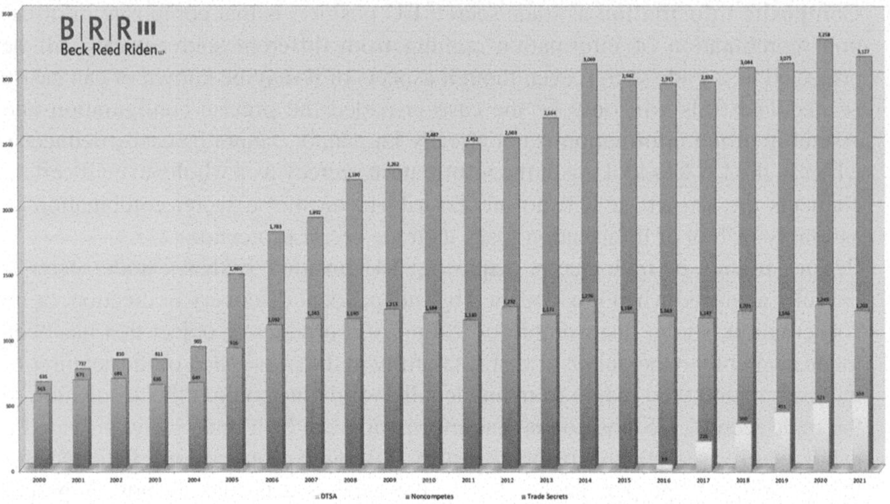

Fig. 3 Reported decisions on noncompete and Trade Secret Cases (survey graph, credit: Beck Reed Riden LLP)

Besides, in a commercial context, there is no defined roadmap on how and when more countries will join TRIPS or use applicable law on trade secrets, as in Europe, USA, and China, and all progressively align their practices: as developed in the above, several countries do not have the trade secret definition yet, and in case they used this term in their contracts, they would fall under the respective laws relative to trade secrets, which may cause operational and unexpected legal troubles to them. We indeed observe on the Westlaw platform for legal research a strong increase of trade secret litigations compared to noncompete situations, and now, very recently appearing, an increase of Defence Technology Security Administration (DTSA) litigations. This shows a clear increase of secret-related litigations reported by Westlaw (Fig. 3, chart issued from Westlaw, also reported by CMS 2022).[11]

For all these reasons, it is believed preferable to start a secrecy strategy by keeping these trade secret law related details out of scope first, to enable executives do take strategic business and management views, and then align their legal strategies according to their views. This also provides an interesting advantage, which is allowing management to design processes and protection measures, and then raise awareness and train employees around these practical measures.

In a LES Nouvelles article of Dec. 2021,[12] the authors noted that "*A key benefit of using the concept of business secrets is that it allows for a common understanding between enterprise managers, who are not necessarily legal experts,* ***to enable them***

---

[11] CMS cases comparison chart: https://faircompetitionlaw.com/2022/04/01/new-trade-secret-and-noncompete-case-growth-graph-updated-april-1-2022-no-not-a-joke/.

[12] Business secrets Are At The Heart Of A Good Intangible Asset Strategy For Company Executives (les Nouvelles—December 2021), PIERRE OLLIVIER AND VICTOR N. DE LEON — Page 316.

to build efficient and comprehensive strategies that can be shared across geographic borders*, such strategies being then validated by the legal teams, to be compatible with the related legal strategies. This also avoids endless discussions about not-yet essential legal details that would kill the creative thinking process needed to build strategies, which discussions should instead take place after setting high-level business strategies in order to adapt the latter to legal specificities. Building strategies has to first deal with determining the individual intangible assets and their contribution to company market value*".

In such an approach, "business secrets" means anything that meets, for the management, the three criteria of "*confidential not known*", "*commercial value*", and "*reasonable protection measures*" at the corporate level, and not necessarily at the country level. It is indeed important to address the subject first at a certain macro level that ignores the trade secret law technical specifics, easier to grasp for managers; and then close the loop with legal specifics for other details.

We then introduce this particular "business secret" related approach as a new interesting tool for executives and business managers, which goes together with concrete, global, practical, and executable company strategies.

Takeaways

Executives shall consider looking at the expected value of a "business secret" when dealing with trade secret issues together with their legal counsels or their legal departments on a global basis, and not only country by country: this might give innovative hints as to how to overcome challenges that derive from regional specificities, and thus focus on the value to the company.

Business Secrets Increase Asset Value

Graham Bell, Véronique Chapuis-Thuault, André Gorius, Aldona Kapacinskaite, Pierre Ollivier, Katarína Račková, and Philippe Simon

Abstract

In this chapter, we look at how business secrets, which include but are not limited to trade secrets and sensitive information, can create value to organisations, and we also look at how they increase value for them. We consider both monetary and non-monetary benefits. We consider the forms of business secrets that create value, and how organisations can identify and manage them.

We provide some example approaches for organisations to develop valuations for IP assets, including business secrets.

Finally, we also consider the associated downsides of business secrets—the associated costs to maintain, and potential costs of loss.

In this chapter, our initial focus is the corporate context, looking later to the context of Higher Education Institutes (HEIs) and Independent Research Organisations (IROs).

The original version of the chapter has been revised. A correction to this chapter can be found at https://doi.org/10.1007/978-3-031-82512-5_9

G. Bell (✉)
Cambridge, UK
e-mail: graham@cubicibuc.com

V. Chapuis-Thuault · A. Gorius · P. Ollivier · P. Simon
Paris, France
e-mail: chapuisthuaultveronique@gmail.com; andre.gorius@winnotek.com; pierre.j.ollivier@gmail.com; philippe.simon@winnotek.com

A. Kapacinskaite
Management and Technology Department, Bocconi University, Milan, Italy
e-mail: aldona.kapacinskaite@gmail.com

K. Račková
Technology Transfer Office of SAS, Slovak Academy of Sciences, Bratislava, Slovakia
e-mail: katarina.racko@gmail.com

P. Ollivier et al. (eds.), *Business Secrets Management*, Management for Professionals, https://doi.org/10.1007/978-3-031-82512-5_4

1 Introduction

In this chapter, we look at how business secrets increase value for organisations. We consider how business secrets can create value to organisations, monetary, i.e. give it a financial value and non-monetary in nature, i.e. strategic and qualitative value before any financial value can be identified; we look at the forms of business secrets that create value, and how organisations can identify and manage them.

We provide some example approaches for organisations to develop valuations for IPassets, including business secrets.

Finally, we also consider the associated downsides of business secrets—the associated costs to maintain, and potential costs of loss.

In this chapter, our initial focus is the corporate context, looking later to the context of Higher Education Institutes (HEIs) and Independent Research Organisations (IROs).

2 Business Intelligence / Competitive Information / Market Signals

2.1 Patents, Trademarks, and Other IP Assets Are Strong Value Creation Items

It is commonly agreed that intangible assets include intellectual property such as patents, trademarks, designs and models, copyrighted material such as works and software, etc. Trademarks are used to create product and firm identification by the market and allow for quality and reputation increase, which in return will create additional revenue to their users. Copyrighted material includes creative works such as texts, books, images, videos, games, etc., and also software.

Another type of asset becomes more and more visible and valuable in the digital era: data collected and used by algorithms, from sources that can be either public on the Internet or private as long as related data is kept secret.

2.2 Patents Are Particularly Valuable But Sometimes Reveal Competitive Issues

Among all types of IP assets, patents provide a particularly interesting IP right to their owners (patent holders). The right is often described as a negative right, in that the patent holder is granted a monopoly on the patented invention, giving them the right to restricts others from using the invention. A patent holder is free to limit or restrict others from using the invention, and if third parties do so without the patent holder's agreement (typically a license to use) the patent holder can seek legal remedies; alternatively, a patent holder may decide to license the invention to a third party either exclusively or non-exclusively (as agreed contractually in the license agreement)—which is a commercial agreement.

The granting of the patent monopoly is an extremely strong IP right, since it creates an efficient barrier to entry and is supported more or less uniformly by historically seasoned jurisdictions worldwide, and the tradeoff is that the patent is made publicly available. That is, all patents are systematically published by almost all patent offices, and once published are available for inspection openly: in fact, most of these patent offices provide open, free access to patent information.

A patent is a protection for a new invention that can be a product, a process, or a design. It is originally filed as "patent application" with a patent office, which means that this application is candidate for becoming a patent; once it has successfully passed all the examination procedure and subsequent changes, the last version receives the status of an official "granted patent". Since patent applications are published during their examination by the patent offices, there is much free to use and monopoly-free valuable information available in the patent applications: including patent applications which are abandoned or rejected—i.e. those patents that do not meet the necessary thresholds in terms of technical solution to a technical problem, novelty, inventiveness, as specifically defined by each national patent law. Further, many patent offices publish the prosecution histories—i.e. the documentation, discussions, and exchanges between the applicant and the patent examiner. This meta-data provides a further rich picture of why the patent was rejected, and perhaps how the applicant tried but failed to convince the examiner.

Failed patent applications are an extremely valuable information for anyone doing research and development, which helps assessing technology roadmaps and making strategic budget-related decisions involving key company resources. In the context of business secrets, we can describe such information as negative insights, or negative secrets—knowing what went wrong for one organisation can save another significant time and costs in avoiding the same mistakes.

2.3 Increasingly, Data and Meta-Data Can Create Value As Well

Data is sometimes referred to as the new gold of the digital era in virtually all business sectors.[1] We talk here of data and meta-data about IP assets as seen above such as patents, trademarks, and also about business secrets.

Data applies to the main assets—the patent for example. The meta-data is the data about that asset, for example the inventor, the technology taxonomy, or the filing date and grant date.

Both the data and meta-data can provide a rich picture of an organisation's R&D activities for both internal and competitive purposes. Big data analytics and AI developments in recent years have indeed proven the ability to identify key trends in terms of inventors, shifts in technology focus and intent.

[1] https://www2.deloitte.com/us/en/pages/real-estate/articles/future-real-estate-data-new-gold.html and https://www.forbes.com/sites/forbestechcouncil/2023/03/27/how-to-make-use-of-the-new-gold-data/.

Both the data and the meta-data act as market signals / business intelligence. For example, since patent data is freely available it is a rich source of information on the innovation trends within organisations. Sophisticated patent analytics tools are able to plot trends and, using AI techniques, predict future avenues for patenting, deriving competitive intelligence from this large data set.

In 2023, IBM announced that it was no longer interested in pursuing patent records—it had previously been the top filing company in the USA for 29 straight years. The raw numbers of patent grants are only one metric in considering a company's innovative activity. However, IBM regularly used its number one ranking in annual patent filings as a marketing tool. At the very least, IBM now has to explain why it is no longer the leader and why that is not a bad thing.

3 Business Secrets and Value Creation

Starting from an intellectual property (IP) perspective, IP generally supports four types of business objectives:[2]

1. Strategic positioning
2. Maximising income generation
3. Conflict avoidance / resolution
4. Cost reduction

Applying this analysis grid to business secrets leads to the following table:

Business objective	How business secrets (BS) create value
Strategic positioning	• Legal protection (if a trade secret) • No access by competition when it is kept secret • Competitive advantage, as long as used and kept secret • Barrier to entry
Maximising income generation	• BS are of value per se • BS enables strategic alliances • BS is strategic to suppliers / customers • BS can be licensed under certain conditions
Conflict avoidance / resolution	• Improved knowledge flows • BS can deter competition from legal disputes
Cost reduction	• Reputation / image / brand • Barriers to entry: Competitors do not access cost reduction hints that are kept secret

[2]Sullivan, P. and S. Harrison (2008). "IP and Business: Managing IP as a Set of Business Assets". WIPO Magazine(1).

4 Business Secrets Increase Value for Organisations

4.1 Business Secrets: A Major Source of Value

What Else Than Trademarks and Licensable Intangible Assets?

We live in a world where intangible assets are considered as the major source of value to companies. More specifically, one can say that "Unregistered intangible assets contributing to 50% market value would necessarily **be mostly composed of business secrets**".[3] In other words, business secrets could contribute to more than 50% of market value.

Research in strategic management traditionally argued that a "*competitive advantage grows fundamentally out of value a firm is able to create for its buyers that exceeds the firm's cost of creating it*".[4] In the past few decades, much of the value a firm creates has been deemed to stem from its intangible assets.

> **Case Study**
>
> In a study performed in 2015, Binder et al. analysed the details of company reports concerning share deals over the period 2000–2014.[5] Looking at profit split statistics, the results using third quartile (i.e. meaning that 75% of the occurrences were falling within the result of this quartile) were quite illustrative, using the example of trademarks profits as the most easily tracked intangible asset profit in public reports.
>
> Their data shows that:
>
> - The third quartile positions Profit Split (Fig. 1) value of licensable Intangibles in Percent of Enterprise Value at around 30% to 35%.
> - The third quartile positions Trademark Profit Split (Fig. 2) in Percent of Enterprise Value in the range 15%—20%, which is part of the above.

A principal advantage of business secrets to firms (and a disadvantage to researchers) is the lack of any requirements for systematic registration with authorities. Business secrets have frequently been referred to as "informal"

[3] Ollivier, P., & De Leon, V. N. (2021). Business secrets are at the Heart of a Good Intangible Asset Strategy for Company Executives (SSRN Scholarly Paper No. 3946562). https://papers.ssrn.com/abstract=3946562.

[4] Porter, M. E. (1985). Competitive Advantage: Creating and Sustaining Superior Performance. Free Press.

[5] Valuation Of Intangibles And Trademarks—A Rehabilitation Of The Profit-Split Method After Uniloc, C. Binder, A. Nestler, LES Nouvelles, 2015 pp. 203–212.

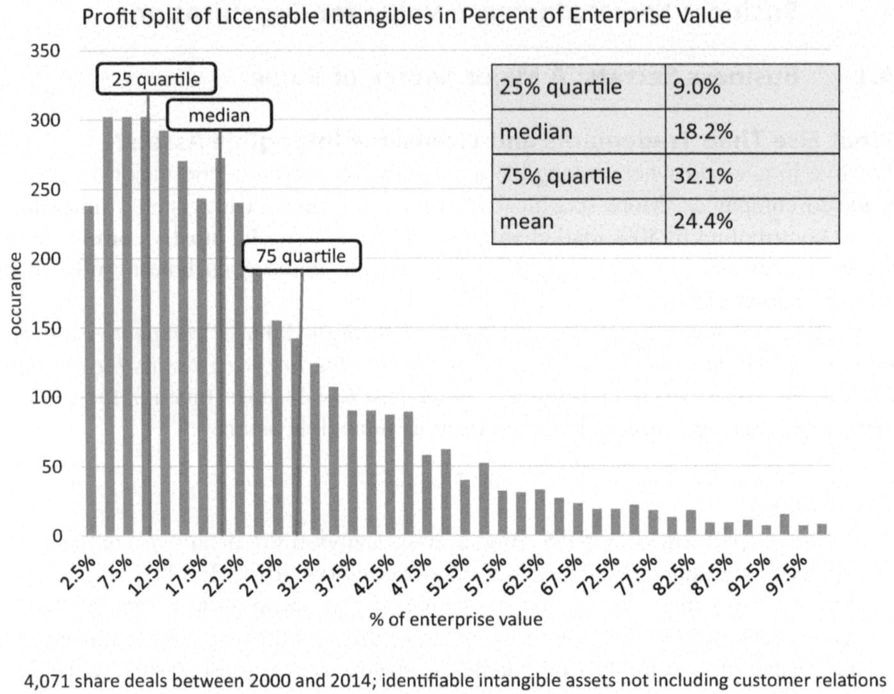

Fig. 1 Profit split of licensable intangibles in percent of enterprise value (credit: les Nouvelles, 2015, Uniloc, C. Binder and A. Nestler). Source: markables.net

intellectual property by social scientists, precisely due to their lack of registration.[6] Accordingly, other types of intellectual property, such as patents, trademarks, and copyright, due to being registered, have been considered more "formal". The line is arguably becoming thin, as scholars argue for the usefulness of treating trade secrets as a "true" intellectual property like any other[7] and as managers realise their importance for performance. In addition, lack of registration does not imply lack of codification within the firm, as well-organised entities often do keep records of their business secrets.[8]

[6]Hall, B., Helmers, C., Rogers, M., & Sena, V. (2014). The Choice between Formal and Informal Intellectual Property: A Review. Journal of Economic Literature, 52(2), Article 2. https://doi.org/10.1257/jel.52.2.375.

[7]Lemley, M. A. (2008). The Surprising Virtues of Treating Trade Secrets as IP Rights. Stanford Law Review, 61(2), 311–353.

[8]Criscuolo, P., Alexy, O., Sharapov, D., & Salter, A. (2019). Lifting the veil: Using a quasi-replication approach to assess sample selection bias in patent-based studies. Strategic Management Journal, 40(2), 230–252. https://doi.org/10.1002/smj.2972.

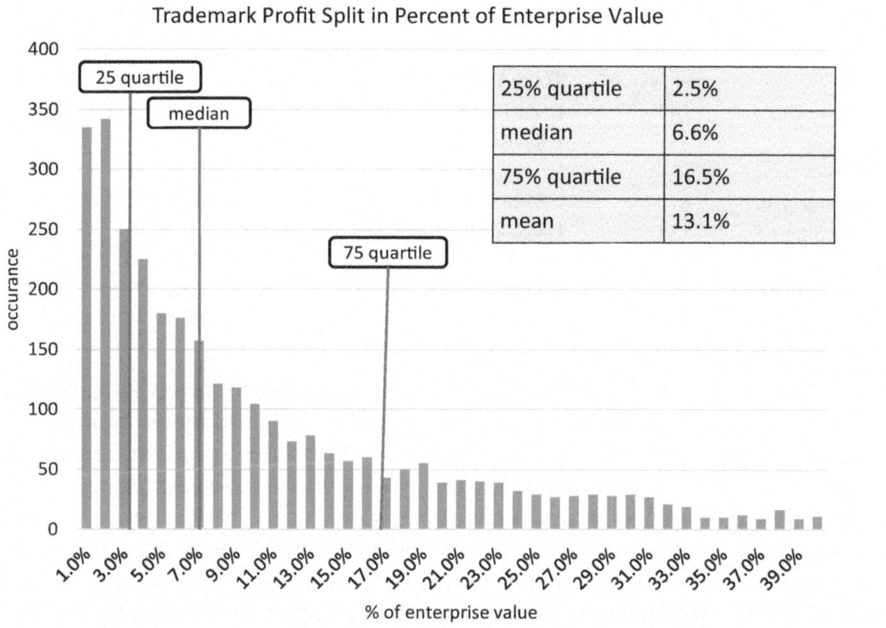

4,071 share deals between 2000 and 2014; identifiable intangible assets not including customer relations

Fig. 2 Trademark profit split in percent of enterprise value (credit: les Nouvelles, 2015, Uniloc, C. Binder and A. Nestler). Source: markables.net

Available Evidence—Towards an Absolute Value of Secrets

A related source of confusion stems from the fact that sometimes secrecy is considered a low-cost manner to protect innovation due to the lack of registration costs.[9] Although, as we will discuss later, this is perhaps not always true, and such an assumption can lead to organisations lacking the required dedicated and formal processes to manage business secrets which risks their leakage. Since business secrets rarely have readily ascertainable costs attached to them, firms also struggle to establish their value. The disconnect between secrecy driving the majority of all intangible value and having no readily ascertainable value is indeed vast.

[9] "Internally developed intellectual property such as trade secrets or ideas most likely are not recorded on the balance sheet because they have no directly associated costs or clear value. Patents, trademarks, and copyrights generally have associated costs and are capitalized as assets on the balance sheet". https://www.investopedia.com/ask/answers/061715/intellectual-property-considered-form-capital-asset-within-company.asp.

Table 1 Trade secret cases and associated values hereunder

Parties	Number of secrets	Total Awarded damages/Settlement	Value per secret
Kolon v. DuPont	149	US$919.9 M	US$ 6.2 M
Motorola v. Hytera	21	US$764.6 M	US$ 36.4 M
Waymo v. Uber	8	US$245 M	US$ 30.6 M
Merck Sharp & Dome v. Pfizer	134	US$—(settled in a different court with Merck as defendant)	–
Wyeth v. Natural Biologics	1	Company shutdown	US$ 500 M–2 B for annual drug sales

To obtain some absolute rather than relative value of trade secrets in particular, one way to proceed is sampling a set of trade secrets examined by the courts. This entails dividing the number of secrets identified in court cases against the amount of damages the offenders were ordered to pay. While this is a selected sample with likely considerably higher than average trade secret value, it does provide some insight into how trade secrets are valued under circumstances of contention and alleged misappropriation. In addition, assuming that the value per secret provides some relatively stable and reliable information, we can proceed dividing the number of US$ 5 trillion,[10] the estimate of the total worth of secrets in the USA by the average value of a trade secret, to understand what is probably the *lower bound of the number of trade secrets in the economy*. Indeed, there are likely many more, less valuable business secrets over which firms never end up litigating in court due to the difficulties associated with proving the existence of trade secrets and their misappropriation. In addition, firms may worry that public proceedings may further deteriorate the value of their trade secrets and of their reputation.

With these caveats in mind, proceeding to calculate some *upper limit of trade secret average value*, in Table 1 below "Trade secret cases and associated values":

While far from comprehensive or representative of the economy, these values give us some sense of what is at stake when trade secrets are leaked and the price tag put on them in court or in settlements (Table 1 **Trade secret cases and associated values hereunder**).

Relative to average patent value, the difference may at times be vast. For example, Motorola's trade secrets in the case against Hytera were valued at an average of US$ 36.4 M per secret, relative to a generous valuation of US$ 500,000 per patent Google was estimated to be paying in its acquisition of Motorola, supposing all Google was paying for in the Motorola acquisition was patents. The transaction involved US$ 12.5 B for Motorola's 24,000 patents at the time.[11] Taking the average of Kolon vs. DuPont, Motorola vs. Hytera, and Waymo vs. Uber cases

[10] https://www.uspto.gov/subscription-center/2017/one-year-developments-protection-trade-secrets.

[11] Hall, B. H., Helmers, C., Rogers, M., & Sena, V. (2012). The use of alternatives to patents and limits to incentives. Intellectual Property Office Newport, UK.

with clearly identified values per trade secret, the average absolute value of a trade secret was US$ 24.4 M.

Further, dividing the estimated value of trade secrets in the USA of $5 trillion[12] by the average value of a trade secret in our limited sample (US$ 24.4 M), we get around 200,000: a lower bound for the number of trade secrets in the US economy. Once again, this is a very coarse and imprecise calculation, but it does give an insight into the minimum number of valuable trade secrets held by firms.

In comparison, if we consider that there have been around 216,000 patents granted in the USA every year between 1991 and 2020,[13] and the average useful life of a patent is 10 years,[14] then we might assume there are 2.16 M US patents active on average in any given year, although it is commonly discussed that only a small fraction of them have value and contribute value to the US economy.

Generally, academic literature compares the relative value of patents and secrecy, and in many cases it determines that firms find keeping secrets more effective than patenting when trying to protect valuable knowledge. Patents, on the other hand, may serve several other purposes, such as serving as a highly visible signal in attracting finance.[15] In a nutshell, this brief overview shows that high profile trade secret court cases tend to exhibit a high price tag associated with the trade secrets.

4.2 Business Secrets: Management Approaches to Valuation

Increasing Company Attractiveness

The protection of business secrets makes it possible to **increase the attractiveness of a company while reducing the risks** of uncontrolled disclosure leading to plundering, counterfeiting, or plagiarism, as shown in Fig. 3:

A Few Examples of Business Secret Valuation in Different Sectors

This section demonstrates why formally identifying business secrets, drafting a protection policy for each key process, and then deploying it by using robust tools, e.g. recording it in the company's quality procedures, is a key practice to implement as often as possible.

We present here a few example case studies of business secrets valuation in different sectors, exhibiting some of the various facets and steps firms would take when valuing their business secrets.

---

[12] Castellaneta, F., Conti, R., & Kacperczyk, A. (2017). Money secrets: How does trade secret legal protection affect firm market value? Evidence from the uniform trade secret act. Strategic Management Journal, 38(4), 834–853. https://doi.org/10.1002/smj.2533.

[13] Average number of grants 1991 to 2020 as per data from https://www.uspto.gov/web/offices/ac/ido/oeip/taf/us_stat.htm.

[14] https://www.wipo.int/edocs/pubdocs/en/wipo_pub_941_2020.pdf.

[15] Hsu, D. H., & Ziedonis, R. H. (2013). Resources as dual sources of advantage: Implications for valuing entrepreneurial-firm patents. *Strategic Management Journal*, *34*(7), 761–781. https://doi.org/10.1002/smj.2037.

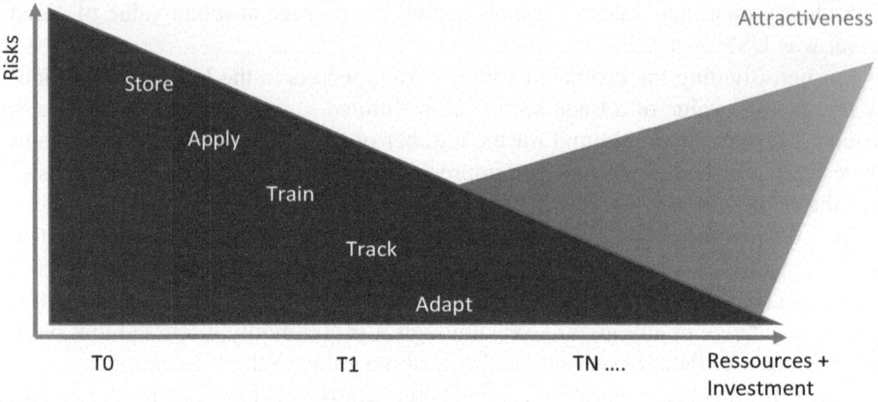

Fig. 3 Risks and attractiveness versus resources invested during the process of managing business secrets (credit Véronique Chapuis and Pierre Ollivier)

Case Study

Security and safety system, IT service trading platform

A company had developed and marketed a software system dedicated to safety systems control and management. The valuation task was to gather factual elements allowing the underlying know-how to be characterised (a process or product design, a quality control software, a certification design, etc.), and then positioning it in terms of competitiveness and control of future risks. These steps of gathering factual elements and assessing risks—mostly technical and operational—are essential for a valuation, especially when evaluating a know-how involving technical and operational details, which an economic analysis would not achieve alone.

As a result, the company found arguments and models enabling it to enter into negotiations with partners, clients, or investors on a positive basis which could be validly recognised.

Takeaway

Having a formalised valuation model will allow the parties in a negotiation to structure that negotiation. Models are typically a mix of factual data points such as time and material costs and assumptions and estimates such as future sales or market sizes.

However, a model where input assumptions can be adjusted in "real-time" during the negotiations allows both sides to explore their own position and that of the other party.

In the absence of such a model, the parties are left "plucking numbers from the air" which is unlikely to be justifiable.

Case Study
Energy production process
One company needed to evaluate its technological know-how within a European collaborative industrial project for the production of new generation bio-energy. The valuation task consisted in characterising and mapping the know-how, leading to the outline of a revenue model. After that, the valuation model was established, allowing the company to negotiate with the project's international partners, which led to identifying a number of strategic decisions that were good for the partners, e.g. for them to reallocate R&D resources, and useful to consolidate the respective contributions to the project.

Takeaway
It is valuable to map the know-how in order to take a number of strategic decisions that are potentially good for collaborative projects' partners. In the related example, it allowed for reallocating R&D resources and for better consolidating the respective contributions to the project.

Takeaway

Case Study
Power production process
Another company wanted to strengthen its ability to protect the sensitive information, i.e. confidential and strategic, that underpins most of its business, with patents being an important but not the majority contributor. The goal was to create a protection policy to enhance business secrets value.

A strategy was therefore established transversally between all company departments, in several steps:

1. An inventory of the company processes was drawn up by a restricted working group in order to identify and characterise the sensitive information, the documents and exchanges with third parties and the value they represent for the company.
2. Identification of a limited number of internal asset carriers, providing them with awareness training, then letting them train their colleagues all over the company; global training was managed in project mode by a member of the executive committee and with progress monitoring indicators.
3. Drafting of a protection policy for each key process, then recording it in the group's quality procedures.
4. Progress monitoring at the executive committee level and taking corrective actions.

(continued)

Takeaway

Having a company-wide project leading to better processes increases awareness about sensitive information across the various services and businesses, and ultimately strengthens the value of the company through securing its business secrets.

Case Study

Energy storage

A startup in the field of energy storage has set up its laboratory on the premises of a large group that has invested a part of its capital by contributing cash, equipment, and resources in kind, but without actually intervening in the R&D activities. Later on, the group had financed, beyond its initial contributions, scientific consulting services in which it had not intervened. However, due to this additional financing, the group claimed co-ownership of any IP resulting from this work, primarily know-how and methodology; this was not acceptable to the startup. In order to better negotiate the allocation of present and future IP rights, the startup performed a precise mapping of the activities, of their owners, and of the contributions of each party to the results.

It then became possible to provide the parties with clear elements documenting the negotiation.

Takeaway

In any collaborative project, the formalisation in real time of the confidential information and data (including trade secrets, know-hows, and personal data), its traceability as well as that of the patentable inventions and the mapping of the contributions of each partner are key. This practice ensures an equitable allocation of the "background" (previous knowledge) and of the "foreground" (knowledge resulting from the project,) while avoiding the risks of conflicting property claims on assets.

Case Study

Green fertiliser production

An inventor created a company to market a fertiliser device. In addition to the patents protecting the core of his technology, this inventor filed a number of detailed envelopes of know-how with a trusted third party. This know-how covered both the performance of the device and the quality of the fertiliser produced. It allowed for hybrid licenses to be granted to an industrial

(continued)

manufacturer, where royalties on sales were coupled with billable engineering hours to optimise the performance of the technology.

Takeaway
This example demonstrates that, when an invention includes a significant part of know-how beyond the patentable technology, the formalisation of this know-how multiplies the accessible economic models and maximises the potential of value creation.

4.3 Is it Possible to Determine the Value of a Business Secret, and How to Do It?

Multiplicity of Strategic Environments Dealing with Confidential Information

Prior to determining the economic value of business secrets, companies need to assess the—government sensitive—value of their Confidential Information that eventually could become a business secret.

Many countries put in place laws that control disclosure of sensitive information that falls under the regalian domain. For example, in France, the Strategic Information and Economic Security Department (SISSE) of the General Directorate of Enterprises—which is an administration with powers where the others are private organisation with the duty to help, as well as, French Association of Private Enterprises (Afep), the French Business Leaders Union (Medef), in collaborative mode, have produced a guide for companies to help them determine which data is likely to fall within the scope of the 1968 blocking law ruling the regalian reserve in France.[16]

Most of the time, determining a business secret economic value means valuing a broader element, the underlying intangible asset that results in a combination of identified business secrets (as described in Chapter 3 of this book, section 3.1 "Forms of business secrets"): a database, a software code, an algorithm, etc.

Determining the market value of a patent is a known task, once the contextual situation is clearly identified. Determining the contextual market value of a **non-patented asset other than trademark or copyright** is also possible, if a certain number of precautions are taken. The method consists of, in addition to a classical economic analysis, characterizing the underlying know-how and related business secrets to position its competitiveness and the organisation's control of future risks.

[16] Guide à usage des entreprises d'identification des données sensibles (Guide for companies to identify sensitive data), AFEP, MEDEF, 2022 (https://www.medef.com/uploads/media/default/0019/99/14409-guide-donnees-sensibles-mars-22.pdf).

These additional steps of gathering factual elements and assessing risks are essential for a solid valuation when evaluating a know-how or a trade secret.

Evaluating **technological know-how within an international collaborative project** is also possible. The basis of the evaluation is the characterisation and the cartographic formalisation of the know-how, which leads to sketching a revenue model. On this basis, the economic model of valuation can then be established using the same method as for an intangible asset (see Sect. 4.4 for more details).

Business Secrets' Value Is Actually Created Through a Relevant Policy

In the case of inventions and creations, when they include a significant part of know-how beyond a specific patentable technology, the formalisation of this know-how increases the business potential by multiplying the number of future accessible business models—i.e. new products and services and new revenue streams due to the resulting competitive advantage, which then maximises the potential value for the company.

It is possible to map the company's activities, their authors and the actors' contributions to their own knowledge and results. Such a map is essential to build a strategy for protecting and enhancing key confidential information, as well as to manage its deployment, since its objectivity facilitates negotiations.

At a corporate level, the steps to design and implement a policy for the protection of confidential information can be defined as follows (see Sect. 2 in Chap. 5 for more details):

- Inventory of the situation drawn up by a dedicated transversal working group (including project managers, lawyers, IP specialist, financial experts, marketing experts…). This group will characterise confidential information, select trade secret, if necessary identify sensitive information among these trade secrets subject to Export Control documents, the value they represent for the group.
- Present the criteria to comply with, for an information to qualify for this classification.
- Drafting of a protection policy for each key process. A possible practice would be to record the policy and its related progress indicators in the group's book of quality procedures.
- Monitoring and reporting of progress at the executive committee level.
- Deployment of corrective actions as needed.

Business Secrets, an Undervalued "Asset"

Companies traditionally manage the disclosure of their confidential information to third parties through "NDAs" (non-disclosure agreements) and by marking "confidential" the "confidential information" they want to transmit. "business secrets" are seen by many companies as being "already managed".

But on the field, some valuable assets are not protected or valued at their fair value. "A trade secret is basically anything you want to keep your competitors from knowing, because information assets are the lifeblood of the business today. It has become a commonplace to say that the capital of modern companies has become immaterial for a generation" underlines Jim Pooley, former Deputy Director General of WIPO—World Intellectual Property Organisation. In other terms, due to the digital era, many trade secrets can hide behind almost anything: thus revealing them is like unearthing a treasure!

As stated earlier at the beginning of this Chapter, business secrets might well represent around 50% of the value of companies. How can these estimates be linked to the company's official (accounting) reporting? Accounting standards require that these intangible assets be recorded on the balance sheet in the case of technology or company acquisitions (Purchase Price Allocation), and, for a marginal part, through the capitalisation of development costs (IFRS/IAS 38). As a result, published balance sheets generally recognise only a small portion of the IP and business secret as intangible assets actually used by companies, the rest—for example a clients' list—being drowned in "Goodwill", i.e. the difference between the amount of the asset shown on a company's balance sheet and the market value of its tangible and intangible capital.[17]

A Relative Value of Secrets

When considering secrecy as a mode to protect valuable information, one of the first issues managers as well as academics face is understanding what business secrets are, and how they can even relate to trade secrets (TRIPS Art. 39.2).[18] These are non-trivial requirements: proving in a court of law that a piece of information is in fact not generally known to the industry participants, demonstrating that there is value derived not just from the information itself but from the fact that it is secret and showing that reasonable measures have been put in place to maintain secrecy. Note that much confidential information is never ascertained to be a trade secret: it is simply not subject to the rigorous examination that an establishment of a trade secret status would require. Non-legal experts have frequently assumed that any valuable secret information or invention qualifies as a trade secret but this does not ensure the legal status of a trade secret nor allows to ascertain its value. Indeed, economists and strategy scholars typically do not differentiate between business secrets and trade secrets.

As mentioned above, how to value business secrets, or even more stringently, trade secrets, remains an open question. Some have argued that the value of such resources has increased over the years due to new technologies, a changing work environment, and an expanding scope of what trade secrets are understood to be (Almeling, 2012). The value of all intangibles reportedly increased from 17% of total assets in 1975 to 81% in 2009 for S&P 500 firms (Almeling, 2012). In addition, in the beginning of the 2000s, estimates for the US public firms valued their trade secrets at $5 trillion and two-thirds of all intangible assets, on average (Castellaneta et al., 2017). Thus, the value of trade secrets alone would constitute more than half of

[17] Revised IFRS 3 standard (https://eur-lex.europa.eu/legal-content/EN/TXT/PDF/?uri=CELEX:32009R0495&from=EN).

[18] https://www.wto.org/english/tratop_e/trips_e/intel2_e.htm.

the value of all intangibles (see also section 4.1 above). According to surveys, most firms rely on trade secrets when innovating: in a survey conducted in the UK, 70% of firms reported to rely on trade secrets to protect their innovations (Rogers et al., 2012). Another manner to gauge the value of trade secrets has been to estimate the cost of trade secret theft, with an estimated 1–3% of GDP in industrialised economies (Michel et al., 2014), although more recent reports revised the cost of cross-border theft misappropriation closer to 0.01% of GDP (Ciuriak & Ptashkina, 2020). While there is a consensus their weight in the economy is substantial, how to value individual business and trade secrets has been a difficult task.

Economists and strategy scholars often depict a firm's choice in creating novel products and processes hand in hand with considerations of the incentive to do so. If firms are to create new products and processes, they must estimate that they will see a satisfactory return, on average. Typically, academics consider a mutually exclusive tradeoff between different protection modes, except in a few cases where, for example, secrecy and patenting have been shown to be complementary (Crass et al., 2019). Usually, the following situation is depicted: a manager may choose to either patent (or otherwise obtain formal, registered protection such as copyright) or to keep an invention secret. Some scholars analysed this question developing mathematical models showing that when a firm chooses between different types of intellectual property protection forms, it may consider the "size", or importance, of the valuable piece of information or invention. Theoretically, researchers have shown that under some plausible circumstances, firms choose disclosure for their "little" patents while keeping "big" secrets undisclosed (Anton & Yao, 2004). The intuition behind the theoretical model is that when it is impossible to protect a disclosed invention perfectly from misappropriation—meaning filing a patent application prior to disclosing and having the means to detect and prove future infringements—it is more optimal to choose secrecy relative to patenting for more valuable inventions. Empirical studies have also hinted at a tradeoff, highlighting that inventors are less likely to patent when employee mobility-limiting Inevitable Disclosure Doctrine is upheld (Contigiani et al., 2018) and following the adoption of the Uniform Trade Secrets Act in the USA (Png, 2017b). However, the UTSA was also associated with higher R&D budgets, suggesting firms did innovate and kept more inventions secret relative to patenting (Png, 2017a). Direct evidence of sector-wide trade secret use has been scant, although recent research has uncovered methods to study trade secrets in industries with disclosure requirements (Cunningham & Kapacinskaite, 2022). However, one objection is that the choice between registered intellectual property (e.g. patents) and unregistered intellectual property (e.g. business secrets or trade secrets) is not clear-cut. However, research in this area is still lacking.

Taken together, studies across the USA and Europe confirm a consistent picture: secrecy is a highly important mode of value appropriation. **For instance, the Community Innovation Survey in the European Union queries managers from a representative sample of firms across different countries regarding the extent to which they introduced new products into the market, used new processes, and how effective they found different forms of protection to**

be. By a considerable margin, secrecy has long been reported as a more effective manner to protect innovation (Arundel, 2001; Arundel & Kabla, 1998). **Studying the Community Innovation Survey in the UK in 2012, Rogers et al. report that 31% of respondents using secrecy ("informal protection") achieved 25% or more of an increase in turnover following an introduction of a new product.** Among firms who did not use secrecy, 18% achieved such increase. Similar patterns have been found in an older survey in the USA (Cohen et al., 2000) but also more recently: firms find secrecy a highly valuable mechanism to protect valuable knowledge, for example, compared to patents (National Science Foundation, 2019). These findings are consistent with the theoretical reasoning that if secrecy was a more effective protection measure, then firms would be particularly more likely to use it for larger inventions where they have more to lose if the invention leaks to competitors. In summary, this overview shows that scholars have often tried to run a horse-race between different forms of IP and deduce the *relative* value of secrecy, rather than finding a manner to ascertain its value in *absolute* terms.

Valuation: Pragmatic Approaches—Art Not Science, and Dependent on Context

Here we consider pragmatic approaches to developing valuations for forms of IP including business secrets.

The value of any form of IP is dependent on context—who is asking the question and why.

We typically consider viewpoints from three perspectives (Fig. 4):

1. An insider looking in (someone within the organisation considering the context of the organisation).
2. An insider looking out (someone within the organisation looking at the external environment).
3. An outsider looking in (someone from the outside looking into the organisation).

The question of "why" may relate to function and / or intent. Typically, when we think of IP we think of the origins of the IP, and in the case of patents this may be an engineering department or product team. We will no doubt also think of the legal department; and since patents have a direct cost associated with them, we will think of a financial role. The "why" questions relating to patents are often:

- Should we patent this invention—what are the costs and benefits?
- Could we sell the patent to someone else or license it—and if so what price / what royalty?
- Are there other reasons for patenting, e.g. good marketing, employee motivations?

Business secrets, as discussed elsewhere, cover a much wider set of concepts than technical inventions. They have no "registration costs", but may have costs that the

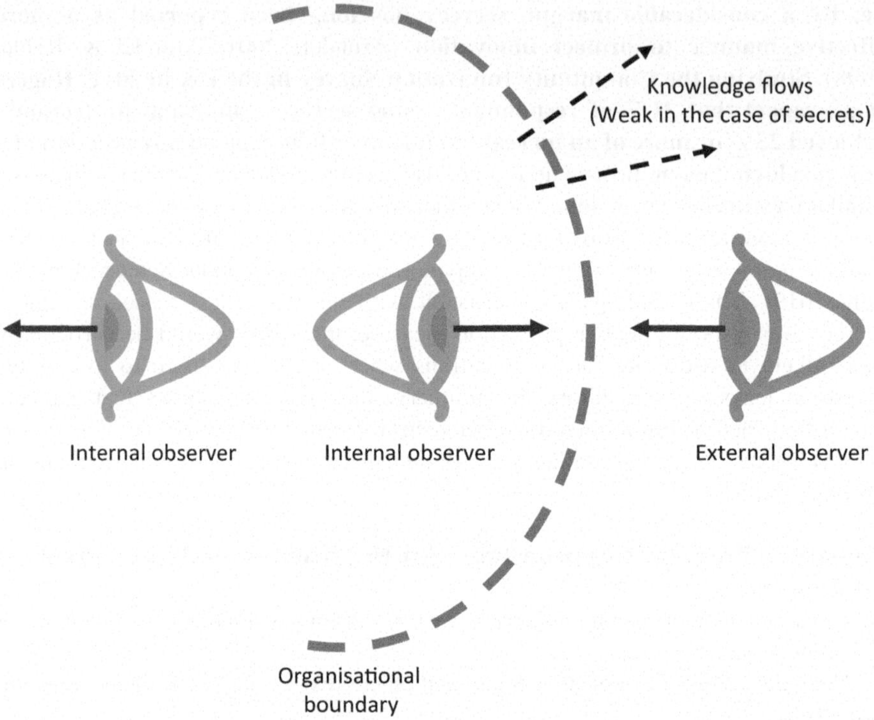

Fig. 4 Risks and attractiveness versus resources invested during the process of managing business secrets (credit Graham Bell, Cubicibuc)

business incurs as a result of maintaining the secrets internally—these may include indirect IT costs and HR costs. Importantly, if kept secret, they are not visible to external stakeholders, and possibly many internal stakeholders.

The set of "why" questions for business secrets are however similar to those for patents:

- Should we keep this a secret—what are the costs and benefits?
- Should we share the secret with other parties—and if so, should we require monetary compensation for doing so? And if so, how do we calculate that?
- Does keeping the secret align with organisation / employee culture and hence will it positively reinforce behaviours?

It should be noted that the value of business secrets is likely to be different depending on the viewpoint and the purpose.

There are typically three types of business secret value: using the IP methodologies:

1. Monetary value
2. Marketing value (external signalling)
3. Motivational value (internal signalling)

Additional practical benefits from protecting business secrets can be understood as including:

- **Reassure investors**: Mapping business secrets and assigning them a value shows that the company effectively protects its critical information and strategic advantages. Seeing value associated with a business secret can be an incentive for outsiders to invest in the company.
- **Be a trustworthy partner**: Potential partners will feel more secure because they will have confidence in your company's ability to take care of business secrets, including those arising from collaboration. They will be more willing to share their own confidential information.
- **Declare one's own background knowledge**: Knowing what you master and what it is worth strategically and financially makes it possible to list your own knowledge (and therefore your initial contribution) in collaborative research agreements with private or public partners. Such knowledge is necessary to build any strategy for exploiting the results and turn it into a contractual agreement.

Case Study

- Valuing your contribution to the project **SAFRAN H2**[19] (a programme designed by Safran, the French aeronautics industry global leader, towards startups to accelerate hydrogen adoption).
- Participate in the development of cybersecurity: France wants to encourage technology transfer between academics and industry in the field of cybersecurity (2022).[20]

[19] https://www.safran-group.com/fr/espace-presse/safran-lance-explore-h2-programme-identification-developpement-startups-specialisees-domaine-2022-06-22?utm_source=POC+Media&utm_campaign=93702148e3-EMAIL_CAMPAIGN_2022_05_02_09_37_COPY_01&utm_medium=email&utm_term=0_1d4d05f04c-93702148e3-411075069.

[20] https://www.usine-digitale.fr/article/la-france-veut-encourager-les-transferts-de-technologie-entre-academiques-et-industriels-de-la-cybersecurite.N2020577.

4.4 Monetary Value: Pragmatic Approaches

Reviewing Classical Valuation Approaches

The first conceptual valuation for business secrets is that of monetary value—how many dollars the business secret is worth, to the organisation as an asset or as a potential sale to a third party.

Typically, this consideration is made when an organisation is considering some kind of transaction—sale, license, or other collaborative arrangement—where a monetary equivalent for the IP in question is required.

This may be the insider looking out—an IP manager considering the licensing of some IP to an external party; or an outside looking in—a potential partner or acquirer looking to value the organisation's IP.

There are three commonly adopted approaches to business secrets valuation, each of which can be implemented in different ways:

1. **Cost method**—A good "anchor" for negotiations. The Cost Method bases the valuation on historic cost data traceable to the secret, indexed to take account of time, e.g. R&D engineering effort to develop the technical innovation embodied in the secret (including certification and standards compliance costs where applicable). Where cost data is not available proxies may be used.
2. **Market method**—This is a practical approach based on comparable transactions. Where recent data for similar IP package / portfolios exist such comparable values can be compelling. This data is difficult to find for business secrets. Data is available for patents and trademarks and could be adapted for secrets covering technical innovations (those kept secret rather than "graduating" to patents).
3. **Income method**—Discounted Cash Flow (DCF) of future licensing royalties. This model is typically employed where strategic fit within operating companies cannot be anticipated, but licensing royalties from a pure-licensing model can be determined. For business secrets/trade secrets an associated cash flow for licensed sales, or a cash flow due to the potential lost profits of the secret owner in the case of loss of secret could be utilised.

The following table cited by the OECD in a report on IP valuation[21] provides a good summary of the advantages and disadvantages of each approach as well as typical uses. It can be applied to business secrets as follows:

	Cost approach	Income approach	Market approach
Advantages	Objective and consistent	Theoretically superior to other approaches as focused on future	Practical approach which makes use of prices actually paid for

(continued)

[21] "Valuation and exploitation of intellectual property", OECD STI Working Paper 2006/5, 30 June 2006, table presented at page 27. http://www.oecd-ilibrary.org/docserver/download/307034817055.pdf?expires=1498582721&id=id&accname=guest&checksum=8D8DF0FC2C29A4855C77131F103A7637.

	Cost approach	Income approach	Market approach
	Reliability of historic cost data	earnings or cash flow Widely accepted and concept widely understood	comparable assets Variety of market-based approaches such as comparable companies, comparable transactions, or a premium price-earnings-multiple approach allows comparison
Disadvantages	No correlation between expenditure on an asset and its value Difficult to distinguish between "normal" operating expenses and investment expenditure leading to the business secrets Subjective nature of estimate of costs of replacement and business secrets may not be replaceable	Requires subjective cash flow allocation Translation of theory into practice requires assumptions which are limiting Relevant information is not always readily accessible from internal reporting systems	Given the uniqueness of intangible assets, third party arm's length transactions involving similar assets as the business secrets are infrequent
Typical use	Only used in limited circumstances (e.g. when the replacement cost can be estimated with a reasonable degree of reliability and confidence)	Primary valuation methodology and the most widely used where information of an appropriate quality can be obtained. The limiting nature of the assumptions needs to be understood and where possible scenario analysis should be performed.	Extremely important indicator of value, if information on recent transactions involving business secrets exists However, in practice sufficient information is rarely disclosed and this methodology is used as a cross check on other more theoretical approaches

Internal R&D Spend as Upper Bound Check

Since even formal trade secret laws do not generally restrict third parties from independently developing the secret, only providing measures to address secret misappropriation, it can be a useful starting point to consider the internal spend to originally develop the secret in the first instance. For example, if a technology company spends $10 M on developing a new innovation which it decides to keep secret it may be appropriate to assume a similarly skilled competitor could also develop the same, or similar technology given a similar level of investment. Should the original company decide to license their innovation (to license the secret) to that competitor, then a make/buy judgement might suggest $10 M is a maximum limit that such a license is worth.

Indeed, assuming the original organisation had a number of unsuccessful attempts along the way to the final solution, it could be argued that the IP for the final solution is worth significantly less than the full R&D investment. This also points to the potential value of "failed R&D" discussed elsewhere. The leaking of such information would potentially allow a competitor to short-cut some of this R&D and hence provide a benefit for them—the information of the failed R&D has value to the competitor.

As described above, any IP licensing deal often comes down to a commercial consideration, and often a Make / Buy decision. In the case of licensing or acquiring secrets, the potential cost of "Make" may set an upper bound on the cost of a potential "Buy" or licence decision.

In determining a useful valuation for IP it is often appropriate to combine two or more valuation methods. Being able to combine valuation approaches to reinforce a valuation range can be critical to negotiation success with external parties.

The income method is particularly suited to sensitivity analysis as the key input parameters can be adjusted to provide an overall valuation range. Sensitivity analysis involves building a set of possible scenarios and in doing so has the additional benefit of providing a mechanism to capture and evaluate risk.

Takeaways

A robust valuation with a transparent methodology allows the organisation to make informed decisions about the direction of IP creation, management, and exploitation. A clear valuation also allows the organisation to present the value of the IP to potential investors, partners, or acquirers.

However, where external stakeholders are involved, the external context may not be immediately known by the organisation, e.g. it may not be clear how a potential partner may want to integrate an organisation's technology. In such cases, there will be uncertainty in any valuation model.

Where stakeholders are sceptical about placing a reliable value on intellectual property, the income method can reflect this risk by, for example, varying the discount rate or by probability-weighting cash flows.

4.5 Non-Monetary Value: External and Internal Signalling

Observing Practices with Registered Forms of Business Secrets

Generally, business secrets have non-monetary benefits derived from signalling both internally to existing employees and externally to the wider market / eco-system. This is commonly found in the form of patents since they are visible in the public domain (see more above in this Chapter on patents versus keeping secret). Using patents as marketing collateral to signal that organisations are innovative is common practice, particularly among startups.

In research-oriented universities and Higher Education Institutes (HEIs), academics may have output metrics to measure the impact of research, typically based on publications such as journal articles, books, or conference proceedings,[22] which are forms of copyright IP.

These IPs are used as signalling within organisations / institutions as well as externally. Business secret can be used in similar ways, of course with care as the secret needs to be maintained in some way.

The counterargument may be presented by those in marketing functions looking to utilise the business secret for the benefits of the organisation. Again, we can point to examples such as the Coca-Cola or KFC recipes as examples of Trade Secrets (TS) that have been kept secret in the tech world, the Google Algorithm is another example of a well-known TS that is commonly deployed by the owner to demonstrate its technical prowess.

Business Secrets as Key Enabler for Open Innovation and Collaborative Projects

Open Innovation is seen as a key enabler for market growth, and in Europe in particular Open Innovation has been embraced at the level of the European Commission to promote cooperation in innovation. In contrast to the "Open" in Open Source, Open Innovation does not imply license free or royalty free access to innovation—while various definitions of Open Innovation exist[23] the central element is the concept of access to ideas and IP beyond organisational boundaries[24]—hence Open access. This access includes inflows (inbound) and outflows (outbound) of knowledge and IP.

In 2016, the European Union (EU) issued its vision for Europe on "Open Innovation, Open Science and Open to the World".[25] Since then, the European Commission has promoted Open Innovation as part of its digital single market and innovation policies. Europe's vision clearly recognises the role of IP for Open Innovation, stating that *"boosting cooperation on innovation entails putting in place adequate framework conditions and a level playing field, including fair and equitable treatment of intellectual property*".

[22] e.g., the UK's Research Excellence Framework—https://www.ref.ac.uk/.

[23] For a recent and comprehensive review and definitions of the OI research landscape, source: Bogers, M., et al., 2017. The open innovation research landscape: Established perspectives and emerging themes across different levels of analysis. *Industry and Innovation*. https://doi.org/10.1080/13662716.2016.1240068.

[24] Chesbrough, H., 2003. The logic of open innovation: managing intellectual property. *California Management Review*. https://doi.org/10.1177/000812560304500301.

[25] European Commission, 2016. Open innovation, open science, open to the world: a vision for Europe. Publications Office of the European Union, Luxembourg. www.ec.europa.eu/digital-single-market/en/news/open-innovation-open-science-open-world-vision-europe.

Case Study

A 2021 research project, the POINT project[26] provides for an empirical basis for existing Open Innovation models and the extent to which IP—including patents, utility models, designs, **but also trade secrets**, data and know-how—facilitates or hinders Open Innovation.

The POINT project collected evidence from case studies from seven value chains in Europe and further afield. This evidence demonstrated that soft-IP such as know-how, trade secrets, data and competencies account for more than 60% of the Foreground-IP created in Open Innovation projects, with patents reported as only 14%.

Hard-IP such as patents offers the advantage of showcasing ownership, protection and signalling innovativeness to the market and potential partners—a necessary step to enable knowledge flows from one entity to another; but it is evident from the case studies Open Innovation partners are often more interested in accessing the soft-IP of the other party. Such soft-IP may include data and know-how, linked to, but not directly available from the hard-IP.

The POINT project reported that for in-sharing of IP during Open Innovation collaborations nearly 70% of IP could be characterised as **soft-IP: Know-how account for 28%, competencies 19%, relationships / market knowledge for 13%, and data / test results for 9%.**

Likewise, POINT reported out-sharing of IP the same groups of soft-IP accounted for over 60% of IP: Know-how 24%, competencies 14%, relationships / market knowledge for 7%, and data / test results for 18%.

5 Business Secrets: Cost Implications

5.1 Cost of Identifying

Separate from the direct costs of developing the business secret itself, which may be R&D time and materials, or simply the cost of employee time generating specific business secrets; there is a non-trivial amount of time required to identify business secrets.

This can be thought of as equivalent to the invention capture phase of the patent process, and indeed where the business secret is a technical innovation that is kept secret rather than progressing to a patent application the step is the same. Whatever the secret, there must be policies and processes in place whereby the organisation systematically identifies a potential secret, makes a decision to keep it secret and then separates the secret from non-secrets.

---

[26] Building stronger Intellectual Property strategy capabilities: Supporting SMEs to succeed with Open Innovation. EASME/2019/OP/OO17. https://op.europa.eu/publication-detail/-/publication/3e42e795-353a-11ec-bd8e-01aa75ed71a1

This process will take management time and likely require the development of formal procedures—potentially requiring IT solutions to be put in place, which if developed in-house takes time and effort, and may distract from core business. On the other hand, if procured from a third party is likely to incur upfront and ongoing maintenance costs.

5.2 Cost of Maintaining

For many jurisdictions there is a requirement for trade secrets that an organisation should demonstrate it has taken reasonable steps to keep the secret. "Lite" solutions may include document identification / labelling or maintaining records (database or spreadsheet) of secrets.

Organisations with high reliance on secrets will often adopt IT-centric protection. Such approaches may include restricting access to employees to secrets, in extreme cases this may include physical barriers such as locked doors and secrets stored on non-networked infrastructure.

Case Study

The folklore around the KFC recipe tells that it is stored on a sheet of paper locked in a safe, and only one person in the world knows the combination to the safe (for the sake of business continuity planning, we hope that's folklore too!) –

Citation check: "Corporate Espionage; Secrets and lies". Brand Strategy. October 9, 2006; and / or https://gizmodo.com/this-is-the-vault-where-kfc-guards-the-colonels-secret-1650566046

In this category of costs, we also consider the indirect costs of building awareness within the organisation on the importance of secrets. This will vary from organisation to organisation, but for most will form part of a basic "on-boarding" for new employees and perhaps part of regular refreshers alongside other quality system training.

Where an organisation is also working alongside partners in Open Innovation collaborations it may be appropriate to on-board partner teams.

5.3 Cost of Loss and Leakage

An EC report (de Martinis et al., 2013) identified the following costs to business:

1. Direct loss of sales
2. Costs for internal investigation
3. Increased expenditure for protection

4. Costs for negotiating settlements
5. Costs for prosecuting and litigating

As discussed elsewhere, signalling to external stakeholders and the market is an important consideration for many forms of IP, and in the case of loss or theft of secrets an organisation must consider the implications.

An organisation must first consider whether to declare the secret theft at all. Doing so, even internally, may impact the performance of the organisation. There may be impacts on team morale, suspicions, and "finger pointing" or other matters to be dealt with by HR which will carry their own costs.

An organisation must also consider if a secret theft should be announced externally. In the case of loss of data, and particularly personal data, local regulatory policies such as GDPR may include obligations to notify / declare data breaches to oversight bodies, and individuals involved. Such a disclosure may have negative impacts on investor confidence or share price; it may impact market sentiment; reduce the attractiveness for partners, suppliers, and customers.

Case Study

Heathrow Airport Limited (HAL) has been fined £120,000 by the UK's data watchdog for the loss of an unencrypted USB memory stick reportedly containing airport security data.[27]

…

A member of the public found the stick, which was not password protected and the data not encrypted, on 16 October 2017 in West London. The contents were then viewed at a local library before being taken to a national newspaper, which recorded the data and returned the stick to HAL.

The Information Commissioner's Office (ICO) said today the stick contained 76 folders and more than 1000 files, which of "particular concern" included the names, birth dates, and passport numbers of ten individuals and details of up to 50 HAL aviation security staff.

5.4 Cost to Innovation

Impact on Internal Knowledge Flows and on Innovation

As we have touched on elsewhere, poor management of business secret may hinder knowledge flows—in terms of external signalling to the market place, internally within the organisation, and between the organisation and collaboration partners. Even where knowledge flows are supported the associated processes and legal contracting around business secrets may delay such collaborative partnerships.

[27] https://www.theregister.com/2018/10/08/ico_fines_heathrow_airport_over_lost_memory_stick/.

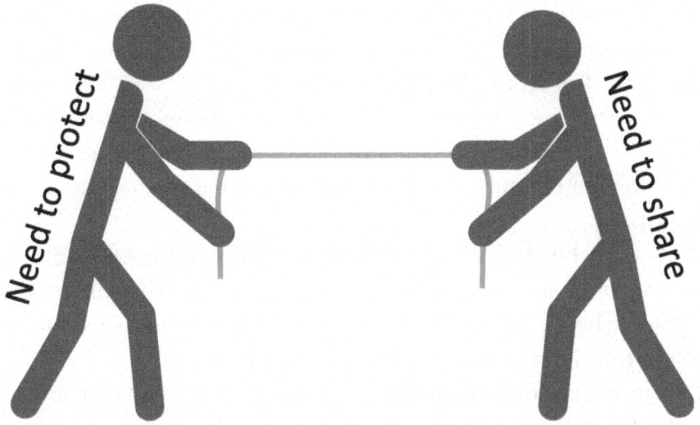

Fig. 5 Organisation tension—need to protect vs. need to share (credit Graham Bell, Cubicibuc)

Reductions in knowledge flows externally have an impact on an organisation's ability to demonstrate its knowledge which may manifest in a reduced ability to attract investors or innovation partners.

Reductions in knowledge flows within the organisation may manifest as a reduction in the organisation's ability to innovate. Innovation requires knowledge, and most innovation is incremental, building on previous developments. Restrictions on the internal flows of knowledge may have a detrimental effect on an organisation's ability to innovate. There is a tension between the need to protect, and hence keep secret, and the need to disseminate and share (Fig. 5); in the context of Open Innovation this is often referred to as the OI paradox.[28]

Additionally, organisational culture may be at odds with the needs of business secrets. Maintaining business secrets is often a matter for individuals—it is often employees that are the weak link in keeping secrets ("Most alleged mis-appropriators are someone the trade secret owner knows. Specifically, in over 85% of cases, the alleged mis-appropriator was either an employee or business partner"[29]), and hence any policies or processes put in place rely on employees "doing the right thing". However, it is evident that employees do not always share the same mindset which can affect company culture.

Highly secretive organisational cultures may have strong cultures of trust, but in the extreme may become siloed and uncooperative with other departments or even teams within the same department.

[28] The Open Innovation Paradox: Knowledge Sharing and Protection in R&D Collaborations, Marcel Bogers, Eindhoven University of Technology, Article in European Journal of Innovation Management · October 2010.

[29] Almeling, David & Snyder, Darin & Sapoznikow, Michael & McCollum, Whitney & Weader, Jill. (2023). "A Statistical Analysis of Trade Secret Litigation in Federal Courts". David S. Almeling.

Developers within the Open Source community by contrast typically have a mindset that nothing should be secret or proprietary and may take a suspicious view of any form of "protection" of knowledge.

It has been reported by some organisations that younger generations seem less interested in patents and indeed less interested in monetary rewards for innovation. They are more interested in publishing—getting their names "out there" and building a personal brand.

This mindset may be due to the transition from PhD / academic environment where such individuals are constantly encouraged to publish papers, into the commercial workplace where proprietary information is more the focus. Or it may simply be a generational trend derived from social network habits.

Where organisations become aware of such clashes between the needs of the organisation and the mindsets of the individuals, small changes to internal messaging can be effective in engaging with such employees. Publishing panels have a similar role to play as patent review boards, but since the emphasis is not on patenting younger employees are more open to engage with the process. During these discussions, the employee can be made aware of the need for trade secrets and the contractual obligations to disclose innovations, as would be the case in patent review board meetings.

Business Secrets Breaking the Double Virtuous Circle

While it can be argued that business secrets are essential for Open Innovation and collaborative projects, there is a downside to adopting secrets vs. other public forms of IP such as patents (noting that not all forms of IP may be available).

As discussed many times earlier in this book (e.g. Chap. 2, Sect. 3; Chap. 3, Sect. 1; Chap. 4 Sect. 2), the classic model of the patent system is based on the granting of a monopoly right in exchange for public disclosure. This then creates the double virtuous circle that allows internal private interests of business and the external public interest of society to co-exist.

Put very simplistically, where business identifies technical inventions to solve problems, the patent systems allow those inventions to be disseminated into the public for others to build on, thus becoming a social good.

Poor use, or poor management of secrets may disrupt both the internal circle and the external circle supporting the social good.

While business secrets do not grant the monopoly right, if protected correctly, the business is still able to benefit from the secret, diffusing the secret internally, and building upon it.

> **Case Study**
>
> "Trade secrecy and Covid19" by Mark Schultz, arguing that existence of trade secret laws enabled the creation of the vaccine before there were any patents for it.[30]

[30] https://geneva-network.com/wp-content/uploads/2021/09/Trade-secrets-and-Covid-19.pdf.

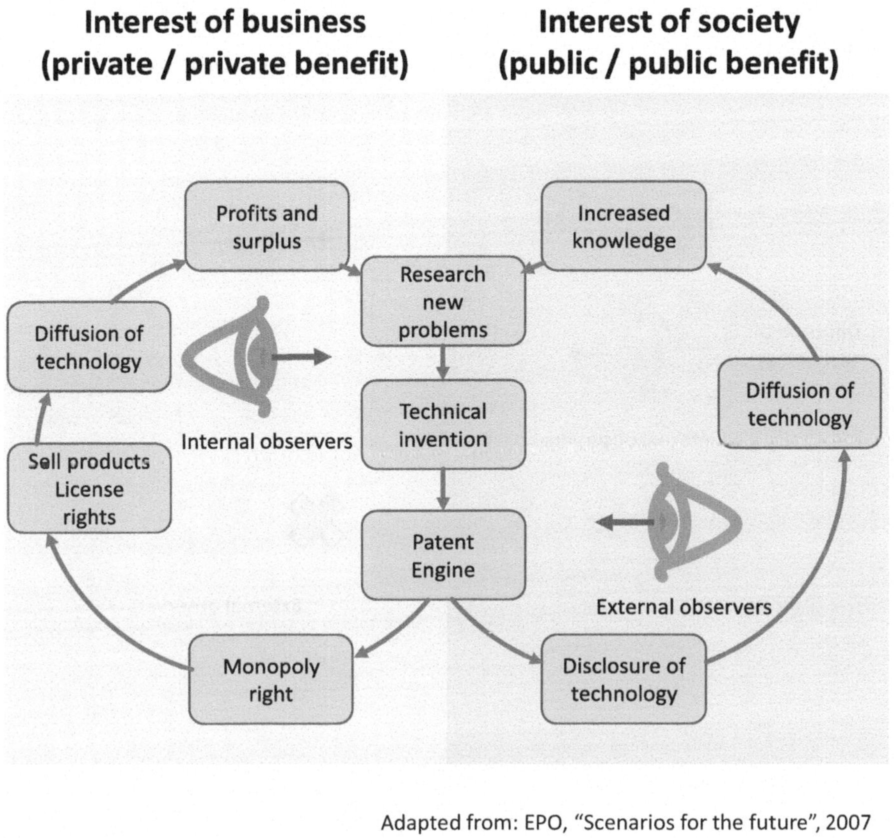

Fig. 6 Products or processes of a company (left): some of them (middle) are visible to the external world (right) (credit adapted from European Patent Office, EPO, "Scenarios for the future", 2007)

The only aspect visible to the external world, and society at large, will be the product or processes made visible (Fig. 6)—which may not directly contain the secret, nor imply the contents of the secret, although it may imply the existence of the secret (e.g. the general public knows that the Coca-cola recipe exists, because of the existence of Coca-Cola as a product … and some good marketing to boot.)

One challenge for an organisation relying on business secrets is its ability to signal to the market. Within the context of Open Innovation this lack of signalling means an organisation may find it harder to "attract" potential partners or investors (Fig. 7).

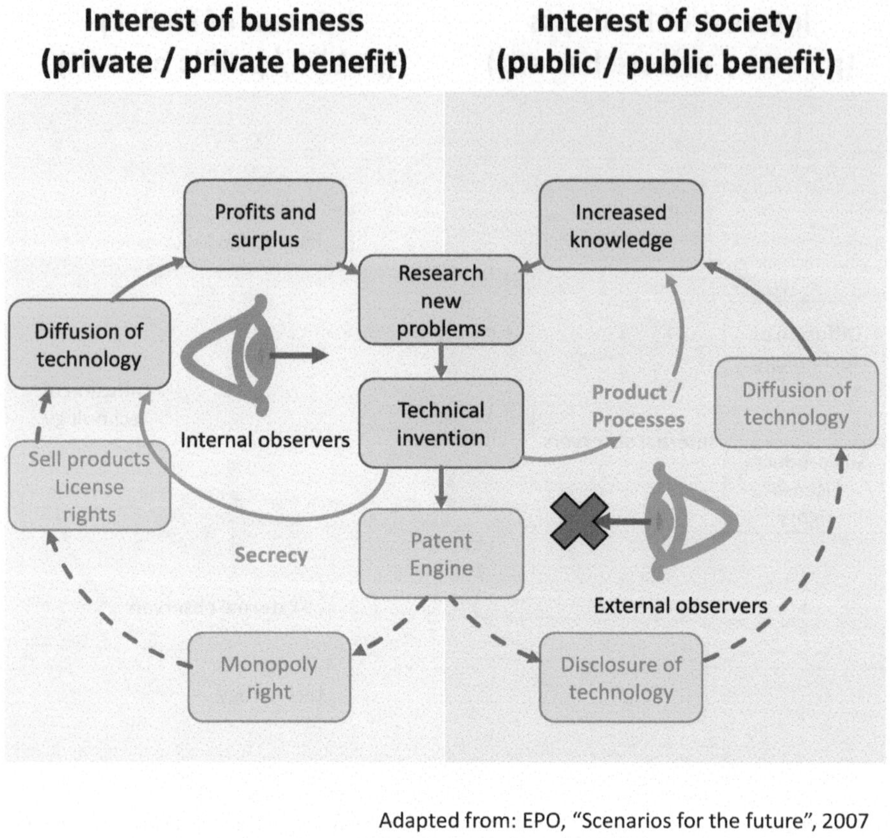

Fig. 7 Products or processes of an organisation relying on business secrets (left): only a smaller part of them (middle) are visible to the external world (right) (credit adapted from European Patent Office, EPO, "Scenarios for the future", 2007). This reduction in visibility may, in turn, reduce the "attractiveness" of business to investors, collaborators and other external parties that rely on such external signalling

Case Study

The case study interviews performed as part of the POINT project[31] demonstrate the importance of soft-IP for collaborations and Open Innovation initiatives. The project also looked at the challenges facing organisations, particularly SMEs when managing IP in the context of collaborative engagements.

(continued)

[31] Building stronger Intellectual Property strategy capabilities: Supporting SMEs to succeed with Open Innovation. EASME/2019/OP/OO17.

The primary challenge reported was the difficulty in contracting soft-IP forms, particular know-how, and data. This stemmed from the initial identification of the IP through to developing structures and contractual forms for sharing such IP.

Where initial identification and articulation of existing (background) IP was not performed, interviewees reported post-collaboration disputes over ownership and usage rights of soft-IP.

6 Business Secrets: In the Context of Research Organisations

6.1 Introduction

In this section, we consider the context of Research Organisations consisting of Higher Education Institutes (HEIs) and Independent Research Organisations (IROs).

Public research organisations such as research institutes and universities (hereafter referred to as research organisations), involved in a somewhat different situation than private businesses, may not have a direct financial incentive to protect their intellectual property, while private businesses often have a strong incentive to protect their intellectual property through patents, trademarks, and copyrights.

In addition, research organisations often experience situations whereby, due to the insufficient attention dedicated to results falling under business secrets, i.e. results that do not fall under formal protection (usually industrial rights), the research organisations lose out on value capture that directly or indirectly affects the worth of the organisation's intellectual property and thus the worth of the organisation itself.

6.2 Raison d'être

Although nowadays many research organisations do patent and have dedicated staff, they generally pay little or no attention to business secrets. Research organisations generally focus on advancing knowledge and understanding in their field, while private businesses primarily focus on generating profits. As a difference from the financial incentives of private companies, (public) research organisations have been mainly driven towards higher numbers of publications in Current Contents journals.[32]

[32] "Academic journals", "scholarly journals", and "scientific journals" are all commonly used terms to refer to journals that publish scholarly research articles in various fields of study.

"Current content journals" is another common term, but it could refer to journals that focus on publishing research in rapidly evolving areas or fields, where the content of each issue may be more closely tied to current developments or trends. Current Contents is database, ranking of journals. CC + "Impact Factor" scientific journal—that is the way of evaluating scientific outputs.

In an example case of Slovakia, in a recent performance evaluation of research organisations, business secrets were a very marginal chapter that has received almost no attention. Thus, the blank tables in the evaluation questionnaires filed by research organisations likely only illustrated the fact that the organisations did not have business secrets covered, rather than they did not exist in the organisations.

The main focus of such performance evaluation has of course been on publications, citations, projects, etc., but during the recent evaluations of research organisations some attention has also started to be paid to intellectual property and its transfer into practice. So far, the intellectual property concerned here involves those formally protected by a patent or utility model, mainly because of their good identifiability, traceability, and relatively straightforward commercialisation. This concludes the efforts over the last 10 years to establish rules, define processes and in some successful cases creating a support.

Hence, the research organisations do not have a direct incentive to engage in business secrets, especially as they did not have yet managed and established processes for transferring inventions and technological solutions into practice, including all related processes from identification, through increasing TRL, to collaborations and partnerships with industry.

One of the authors' personal experience shows that at least 50% of Research Organisations management in author's country have in their professional lifetime met with the loss of knowledge or know-how of the organisation/department due to movement of employees, whether because of a termination of employment, retirement, or death. Since insufficient attention is typically paid to early identification and recording/describing of the knowledge, it is not unusual, that emergence of such knowledge is realised belatedly (at which point it is usually already lost for the research organisation) and it costs months, or often years, to rebuild it again. This theme is perhaps similar to that observed in industrial organisations that they often do not know what they know.

In the environment of research organisations, the knowledge often involves know-how/skill to perform some (special) measurement/experiment/test, knowledge of the most appropriate parameters, approaches, implementation of the subject matter of the invention, etc.

This knowledge often does not qualify for patenting, but may ensure that the organisation is able to do better/unique research/service in its field, which has a direct impact on the name/credit of the organisation, and thus increases its worth. Also, the knowledge itself may be part of a commercialisation strategy, as an additional benefit, e.g., to granted licences.

6.3 Spin-Offs from Higher Education Institutes (HEIs)

A spin-off startup is a new company that is created by spinning off a specific business unit or division from an existing company. The new company is typically created to focus on a specific product, service, or technology that is different from the main business of the parent company.

A spin-off startup can be created for a variety of reasons, such as to allow the parent company to focus on its core business or to allow the new company to have more autonomy and flexibility to pursue new opportunities. Spin-off startups can also be used as a way to commercialise new technologies or business models that are being developed by the parent company.

In the context of research organisations, a spin-off startup can be created to commercialise the research and development done by the organisation. The spin-off startup can be created to develop and market new products, services, or technologies that are based on the research being done by the organisation. A spin-off startup can be a valuable way to turn their research into viable commercial products, services, and technologies and to attract investors.

It is becoming increasingly important for research organisations to position spin-off startups with a maximum asset value to attract investors. In order to achieve this, it is important for these organisations to focus not only on formal assets, such as patents and trademarks, but also on informal assets, such as business secrets.

Informal assets based on business secrets can be key to the future success of a startup. These assets often include proprietary processes, methods, and technologies that are not protected by patents or trademarks. They can be the foundation of the startup's business model and can provide a competitive edge in the market. For example, a startup that has developed a proprietary process for creating a new material may not be able to patent the process, but the knowledge of the process can be considered a business secret and can be used to attract investors.

It is important for research organisations to identify and document these informal assets early on, to establish processes for protecting them, and importantly to be able to present them in a structured form to potential investors demonstrating how the totality of the IP supports the startup business case. This can include implementing security measures to protect confidential information, as well as training employees on how to handle and protect confidential information.

6.4 Business Secrets: Supporting Organisation Prestige in HEI Context

An important "duty" of scientists in a public organisation is to publish their scientific results, which not only determines the evaluation of individual researchers, but also, as mentioned earlier, the evaluation of the given organisation.

Hence, we have scientific prestige and societal responsibilities on one side and earnings on the other. The prestige is to say, the scientific prestige within the scientific community. Because if an exceptionally interesting result is achieved, which is subsequently commercialised, prestige will be advertised among the general public through the media. However, this will be reflected only to a small extent in the scientific assessment. Therefore, it is necessary to find a balance between scientific and financial gain.

For this reason, it is necessary, as a motivating factor and a factor that will to some extent help stir up the creation and setting of new assessment rules (at least in a transitional period), taking into account also the financial interest of the organisation, to create such rules that will "compensate" for scientific workers' losses in scientific assessment. For example, if it were minor financial benefits, a specific scientist would suffer significant losses in the annual internal evaluation if he did not publish, which could lead to serious problems after some time (under the current arrangement in many research organisations).

Here, if we again take the example of Slovakia, we are talking about a transitional period in order to start a proper and balanced mechanism—a cycle that requires high quality people who would receive incentive-based remuneration, which requires the commitment of financial resources, which in turn requires quality outputs, which requires quality equipment and high quality people back-and-forth and so on. Here, the "high quality people" is meaning primary exceptional specialists, i.e. employees that possess all kinds of "je ne sais quoi" qualities including well-trained, gifted, experienced workers, great individuals, committed employees, and so on.

Or, when it turns around, a financial approach to dealing with intellectual property will bring finances from which the organisation can pay for high quality people and quality equipment, which will bring top results, for example, also in basic research, which can be linked to applied research, which will bring results suitable for commercialisation.

6.5 HEI & Independent Research Organisations (IRO) Context—The Technology Transfer Office (TTO)

Therefore, it is often the Technology Transfer Office (TTO) who helps the research organisation with these activities. However, they too may face challenges in attracting investors due to a lack of understanding of the research or a lack of interest in their products, services, and technologies.

Besides, according to the employment conditions in one of the authors' countries, establishing a spin-off startup from a public research institution is not an easy process (formally or content-wise), therefore, to be fair, there are several "transitional stages" to verify the viability before initiating the spin-off startup.

In conclusion, for research organisations, it is becoming more and more important to position spin-off startups with a maximum asset value to attract investors. While formal assets such as patents and trademarks are important, informal assets based on business secrets can be key to the future success of a startup. It is important for research organisations to identify and document these informal assets early on and to establish processes for protecting and transferring them to spin-off startups.

For these reasons, business secrets should be given more attention than they have received so far, also within the research organisations.

Takeaways

In addition to adjusting the assessment of scientific organisations and individuals, research organisations should also establish processes for transferring (in an ideal case) these formal and informal assets to spin-off startups.

This can include identifying which assets have commercial potential and working with the startup to develop a strategy for commercialising the assets. This can help to increase the value of the startup and make it more attractive to investors.

Research organisations are often focused on internal efforts and lack external vision of the market and external stakeholders. In order to maximise the value of potential startup we recommend:

- Research organisations should establish processes or procedures for identifying and protecting informal assets such as business secrets as early as possible and build awareness within the academic community on the importance of protecting such assets.
- Research organisations need to build internal capabilities or gain access to experience in commercialising their research, particularly in presenting their IP in a structured form that aligns with a clear business case.
- Research organisations may not have the necessary expertise or resources to develop and market new products, services, and technologies and should consider how to engage with external support services.
- Research organisations need to access networks and build connections to attract investors.

References

Almeling, D. S. (2012). Seven reasons why trade secrets are increasingly important. *Berkeley Technology Law Journal, 27*(2).

Anton, J. J., & Yao, D. A. (2004). Little patents and big secrets: Managing intellectual property. *The Rand Journal of Economics, 35*(1), 1–22. https://doi.org/10.2307/1593727

Arundel, A. (2001). The relative effectiveness of patents and secrecy for appropriation. *Research Policy, 30*(4), 611–624. https://doi.org/10.1016/S0048-7333(00)00100-1

Arundel, A., & Kabla, I. (1998). What percentage of innovations are patented? Empirical estimates for European firms. *Research Policy, 27*(2), 127–141. https://doi.org/10.1016/S0048-7333(98)00033-X

Castellaneta, F., Conti, R., & Kacperczyk, A. (2017). Money secrets: How does trade secret legal protection affect firm market value? Evidence from the uniform trade secret act. *Strategic Management Journal, 38*(4), 834–853. https://doi.org/10.1002/smj.2533

Ciuriak, D., & Ptashkina, M. (2020). Quantifying trade secret theft. *SSRN Electronic Journal.* https://doi.org/10.2139/ssrn.3706511

Cohen, W. M., Nelson, R. R., & Walsh, J. P. (2000). Protecting their intellectual assets: Appropriability conditions and why U.S. manufacturing firms patent (or not). NBER working paper no. 7552.

Contigiani, A., Hsu, D. H., & Barankay, I. (2018). Trade secrets and innovation: Evidence from the "inevitable disclosure" doctrine. *Strategic Management Journal, 39*(11), 2921–2942. https://doi.org/10.1002/smj.2941

Crass, D., Garcia Valero, F., Pitton, F., & Rammer, C. (2019). Protecting innovation through patents and trade secrets: Evidence for firms with a single innovation. *International Journal of the Economics of Business, 26*(1), 117–156. https://doi.org/10.1080/13571516.2019.1553291

Cunningham, C., & Kapacinskaite, A. (2022). Keeping invention confidential. *Academy of Management Proceedings, 2022*(1), 14792. https://doi.org/10.5465/AMBPP.2022.14792abstract

de Martinis, L., Gaudino, F., & Respess, T. S., III. (2013). *Study on trade secrets and confidential business information in the internal market*. Prepared for the European Commission. sn.

Michel, M., Stronberg, C., & Geday, P. (2014). *Economic impact of trade secret theft: A framework for companies to safeguard trade secrets and mitigate potential threats*. Center for Responsible Enterprise And Trade and PricewaterhouseCoopers.

National Science Foundation. (2019). Annual business survey: 2019 (data year 2018). https://ncses.nsf.gov/pubs/nsf22315

Png, I. P. L. (2017a). Law and innovation: Evidence from state trade secrets Laws. *Review of economics and statistics, 99*(1), article 1. https://doi.org/10.1162/REST_a_00532

Png, I. P. L. (2017b). Secrecy and patents: Theory and evidence from the uniform trade secrets act. *Strategy Science, 2*(3), Article 3. https://doi.org/10.1287/stsc.2017.0035

Rogers, M., Helmers, C., Hall, B. H., & Sena, V. (2012). The use of alternatives to patents and limits to incentives (SSRN scholarly paper no. 2710628). https://doi.org/10.2139/ssrn.2710628

Protecting Business Secrets to Improve Value Creation

Pierre Ollivier, Véronique Chapuis-Thuault, Ferzana Haq, Katarína Račková, Victor De Leon, Graham Bell, and Sylvain Roy

Abstract

This chapter aims to provide an in-depth review of the strategies and practices necessary to protect business secrets and thereby enhance business value. Our discussion will cover the legal principles governing breach of confidence, as well as the management processes and best practices in security that practitioners should implement to safeguard their business secrets from breach. Throughout this chapter, business secrets refer to trade secrets and any sensitive information.

The original version of the chapter has been revised. A correction to this chapter can be found at https://doi.org/10.1007/978-3-031-82512-5_8

P. Ollivier · V. Chapuis-Thuault
Paris, France
e-mail: pierre.ollivier@winnotek.com; chapuisthuaultveronique@gmail.com

F. Haq
Singapore, Singapore
e-mail: ferzanahaq@hslegal.com.sg

K. Račková
Technology Transfer Office of SAS, Slovak Academy of Sciences, Bratislava, Slovak Republic
e-mail: katarina.racko@gmail.com

V. De Leon
Manila, Philippines
e-mail: vnlllb@gmail.com

G. Bell
Cambridge, UK
e-mail: graham@cubicibuc.com

S. Roy (✉)
Montreal, Canada
e-mail: sylvain@sroy.ca

P. Ollivier et al. (eds.), *Business Secrets Management*, Management for Professionals, https://doi.org/10.1007/978-3-031-82512-5_5

The digitalization of business processes and the explosion of digital services amplify the challenges associated with protecting data, confidential information in general and especially business secrets. A general trend in the protection of business secrets, by effect of substantive law or case laws, is to place greater responsibility on the recipients of information (and employees in particular) not to take or misuse confidential information, provided that the owners of such information take reasonable steps to protect it.

We describe in Chap. 5 the regulation and case law applicable to business secrets and breach of confidence in each of the USA, Europe, and the UK. To further aid in illustration, examples are provided in Singapore and the Philippines, respectively. Additionally, this chapter describes how companies can implement a governance and business secrets policy addressing the physical, human, and IT elements necessary to reduce the overall risks of business secret leakage and loss of value.

Finally, this chapter looks at mechanisms that can be deployed during negotiations and deal-making. We consider when and how to use non-disclosure agreements (NDAs), and where memorandum of understanding (MOUs) can capture details of business secrets.

1 Introduction

This chapter aims at providing an in-depth review of the strategies and practices necessary to protect business secrets and thereby enhance business value. Our discussion will cover the legal principles governing breach of confidence, as well as the management processes and best practices in security that practitioners should implement to safeguard their business secrets from breach.

The broad discussion of Chap. 5 will lay the groundwork for additional analysis in the following chapters: Chap. 6 focuses on contractual strategies for protecting business secrets, including agreements with employees and entities, and Chap. 7 details defense and litigation strategies, including how to respond to breaches.

2 Legal Protections Against Breach of Confidence; by Law, by Contract, by Employee Contract

2.1 Breach of Confidence: A Key Issue for Secret Protection Strategies

Breach of confidence occurs when a party discloses or uses another party's business secrets without authorization. While some breaches may have minimal impact, many result in significant, permanent, and detrimental damages. Consequently, laws are essential to delineate the obligations of parties who receive or have access to confidential information and provide effective remedies for mitigating the damages resulting from a breach.

National laws address breach of confidence through various mechanisms. Most jurisdictions implement a general legal framework, supplemented by specific rules applicable to contractual agreements and employment contracts. Despite similarities, national laws vary considerably, and the extent of protection against breach of confidence differs widely across countries. This variation presents additional challenges for protecting business secrets in the context of international operations.

The following sections will discuss the protection against breaches of confidence, by law, supported by specific national examples, and by contract in various types of transactions.

2.2 New Protection Practice Trends Observed

The digitalization of business processes and the explosion of digital services amplify the challenges associated with protecting data, confidential information in general and especially business secrets. A general trend in the protection of business secrets, by effect of substantive law or case laws, is to place greater responsibility on the recipients of information (and employees in particular) not to take or misuse confidential information, provided that the owners of such information take reasonable steps to protect it.

Within this trend, however, there exist two sides of a spectrum in terms of the protection given to business secrets. On the one hand, there are jurisdictions with a codified system of laws, regulations, and precedence giving specific protection to business secrets. On the other hand, there are jurisdictions with emerging legal systems that have yet to adopt these systems. To aid in illustration, prominent examples of both sides of this spectrum are provided in Singapore and the Philippines, respectively, after a brief review of the relevant legal framework in each of the USA, Europe, and the UK.

2.3 Protection Against Breach of Confidence in the USA

In the USA, legal protections against breach of confidence are primarily governed by common law principles and statutory regulations from the Uniform Trade Secrets Act (UTSA) at the state level and the more recent (2016) federal Defend Trade Secrets Act (DTSA).

The UTSA

The Uniform Trade Secrets Act (UTSA)[1] defines trade secrets, provides remedies for their misappropriation, and creates a uniform standard for the protection of trade secrets across the USA. It was first drafted by the National Conference of Commissioners on Uniform State Laws (NCCUSL), now known as the Uniform Law Commission (ULC), in 1979. Prior to the UTSA, each state had its own set of rules and definitions regarding trade secrets, leading to inconsistent protection and legal uncertainty. The UTSA has been adopted by all US states except North Carolina and New York (where it has been introduced but not yet adopted). The act has influenced both the development of case law and legislative reforms.

[1] https://www.uniformlaws.org/committees/community-home?CommunityKey=3a2538fb-e030-4e2d-a9e2-90373dc05792.

The UTSA defines a trade secret as information that (i) derives independent economic value from not being generally known or easily ascertainable by others who can obtain economic value from its disclosure or use and (ii) is the subject of efforts that are reasonable under the circumstances to maintain its secrecy.

Misappropriation is defined in the UTSA as the acquisition, use, or disclosure of a trade secret through improper means or in violation of a duty of secrecy. Improper means include theft, bribery, misrepresentation, or breach of a duty to maintain secrecy. The UTSA emphasizes the importance of taking reasonable measures to maintain the secrecy of information. Businesses are expected to implement policies and practices to safeguard trade secrets, which may include confidentiality agreements and secure information handling procedures.

Remedies under the UTSA for trade secret misappropriation include injunctive relief (a court order issued to prevent further disclosure or use of the trade secret); monetary damages including direct damages suffered due to the misappropriation and any unjust enrichment gained by the misappropriator; and exemplary (punitive) damages which the courts can award in cases of wilful and malicious misappropriation. Additional damages related to attorney's fees may also be awarded to the prevailing party if the case is deemed exceptional.

While the UTSA itself is specific to the USA, the act has a broader impact on how trade secrets are protected internationally. Its principles and definitions have been referenced in discussions about global standards for intellectual property protection. The principles underlying the UTSA have also been incorporated into prominent international trade agreements and treaties, such as the World Trade Organization (WTO) Agreement on Trade-Related Aspects of Intellectual Property Rights (TRIPS).[2] Countries looking to develop or reform their trade secret laws often look to the UTSA as a model or reference point.

The DTSA

The Defend Trade Secrets Act (DTSA),[3] enacted in 2016, provides federal-level protection for trade secrets. Complementing the UTSA, it enables trade secret owners to bring civil actions in federal court for misappropriation. The DTSA also provides remedies including injunctions, monetary damages, and the possibility of treble damages in case of wilful and malicious misappropriation.

Case Law: Takeaways From US Decisions

US courts have developed a significant legal framework relevant to breaches of confidence and have provided further guidance by interpreting the UTSA. Below are some takeaways from US case law on breach of confidence and business secrets, highlighting the importance of proactive measures, and the broader implications for corporate conduct and industry standards.

(continued)

[2] WTO website at https://www.wto.org/english/tratop_e/trips_e/trips_e.htm.

[3] 18 U.S.C. § 1836.

These takeaways are classified by theme for easier reading. The case law corpus is extensive, and our references are by no means exhaustive. Readers interested in US cases will benefit from consulting specialized reference works.[4]

Definition of trade secrets[5]

To qualify as a trade secret, information must possess economic value derived from its secrecy. The information must not be accessible or easily ascertainable by others and must be subject to reasonable efforts against disclosure. Courts evaluate whether the information's economic advantage hinges on its secrecy and if it has been appropriately shielded from public access.

Reasonable efforts to maintain secrecy[6]

Effective protection is crucial for maintaining the trade secret status of valuable business information. Secret holders must implement and maintain reasonable protective measures to safeguard their business secrets. These measures include restricting access to sensitive information, employing strong security protocols (both physical and electronic), and using legal agreements such as non-disclosure agreements (NDAs). The efforts must be commensurate with the value of the information and the competitive advantage it provides. The determination of what constitutes reasonable efforts depends on the context, including industry practices and the nature of the information.

Misappropriation of business secrets[7]

Misappropriation can manifest through various means such as theft, deceit, or violations of confidentiality agreements. The core issue in cases of misappropriation is whether the trade secret was obtained or used without the owner's authorization, thus violating its protected status. To establish misappropriation, it must be demonstrated that the information was confidential and that its unauthorized use had a tangible impact on the owner's business interests. Courts analyse various factors in determining whether misappropriation has occurred. Among these factors are the manner in which the trade secret was obtained, the presence of confidentiality agreements, the economic impact on the owner, and the efforts made to protect the information.

(continued)

[4] Milgrim, Jerome. *Milgrim on Trade Secrets*. LexisNexis, 2022, is an example of reference work.

[5] E.I. du Pont de Nemours & Co. v. Christopher, 431 F.2d 1012 (5th Cir. 1970); Kewanee Oil Co. v. Bicron Corp., 416 U.S. 470 (1974).

[6] Id. E.I. du Pont; Waymo LLC v. Uber Technologies, Inc., 2018 WL 2266163 (N.D. Cal. 17 May 2018).

[7] Id. Waymo.

Legal remedies and enforcement[8]

Effective enforcement of trade secret protection relies on the ability to properly establish misappropriation and quantify damages. Remedies for trade secret misappropriation include injunctions to prevent further misuse, monetary damages for losses incurred, and punitive damages for particularly egregious conduct.

Injunctions are a primary remedy for trade secret misappropriation, serving to immediately halt the unauthorized use or disclosure of the trade secret. Courts may issue preliminary injunctions if there is a strong likelihood that misappropriation has occurred, and the plaintiff is at risk of suffering irreparable harm. The mere appearance of misappropriation could be sufficient to justify a preliminary injunction against an ex-employee, if it is likely that trade secrets were improperly used.

Monetary damages are awarded to compensate the trade secret owner for actual losses suffered due to misappropriation and any unjust enrichment obtained by the party responsible for the misappropriation. Courts may calculate damages based on the economic impact on the trade secret owner, such as lost profits or diminished market position, and the gains realized by the defendant from using the misappropriated information.

Pre-emption and legal boundaries[9]

State trade secret laws may be pre-empted by federal laws under specific circumstances, especially when trade secrets intersect with other forms of intellectual property. For instance, if a trade secret becomes publicly known through patent disclosures, state law protections are effectively overridden. This necessitates that companies carefully delineate their trade secrets and other intellectual property to ensure robust and non-conflicting protection.

Impact on corporate conduct and industry practices[10]

Ethical practices and rigorous trade secret protections are of primary importance, especially in competitive environments such as the technology sector. High-profile trade secret cases can significantly influence corporate conduct and industry practices. In response to recent cases, companies are increasingly adopting stringent internal controls, including access restrictions,

(continued)

[8] Id. Waymo; Martinez v. Gilead Sciences, Inc., 444 F. Supp. 3d 581 (N.D. Cal. 2020); PepsiCo, Inc. v. Redmond, 54 F.3d 1262 (7th Cir. 1995).

[9] Id. Kemanee; Cree, Inc. v. Rinehart, 2018 WL 4323830 (W.D. N.C. 2018).

[10] Id. Waymo; American Needle, Inc. v. National Football League, 560 U.S. 183 (2010).

employee training, legal agreements, and monitoring and auditing. Additionally, companies are also increasingly recognizing the value of integrating ethical guidelines into their corporate policies. Encouraging employees to adhere to high ethical standards can prevent the temptation to engage in or condone trade secret misappropriation. Finally, case law drives the development of industry standards for trade secret protection. Industry associations and professional organizations often respond to such cases by issuing guidelines and best practices to help companies navigate the complexities of trade secret management.

Criminal statutes and trade secret theft[11]

The interaction between trade secret law and criminal statutes becomes particularly evident in cases of deliberate misappropriation or deceit. The Economic Espionage Act (EEA) of 1996, which criminalizes the theft or misappropriation of a trade secret to benefit a foreign power, serves as a primary tool in combating industrial espionage.[12] Additionally, domestic theft of trade secrets for commercial advantage or financial gain is also prosecutable under the EEA, underscoring the severity of legal repercussions faced by violators.

Moreover, the Computer Fraud and Abuse Act (CFAA) often complements the EEA in cases involving unauthorized access to computer systems where trade secrets are stored.[13] Judicial interpretation of the CFAA has evolved, particularly around the concept of "exceeds authorized access", which has significant implications for employees who may access employer's digital files and misuse confidential information.[14] This interpretation plays a crucial role in defining the scope of lawful access and criminal liability in the digital age, where trade secrets are increasingly stored and managed electronically.[15]

2.4 Protection Against Breach of Confidence in the Context of the EU Trade Secrets Directive

The legal provisions most relevant to trade secrets in the European Union (EU) include the Agreement on Trade-related Aspects of Intellectual Property Rights

[11] United States v. Nosal, 676 F.3d 854 (9th Cir. 2012).

[12] 18 U.S.C. § 1831–1832 (Economic Espionage Act).

[13] 18 U.S.C. § 1030 (Computer Fraud and Abuse Act).

[14] United States v. Nosal, 676 F.3d 854 (9th Cir. 2012).

[15] J. Pooley, Trade Secrets § 8.02 (2023) [analysis of EEA enforcement and its impact on trade secret protection].

(TRIPS),[16] and the Trade Secret Directive 2016/943 (TSD), the later adopted on June 8, 2016 by the European Parliament and the Council of the EU.[17]

Pursuant to Article 39 of the TRIPS, member states have the obligation to protect undisclosed information in the broader context of protection against unfair competition, as outlined in Article 10bis of the Paris Convention (1967). Although TRIPS does not explicitly reference trade secrets, it mandates that natural and legal persons have the possibility to prevent information from being disclosed to, acquired by, or used by others without their consent, in a manner contrary to honest commercial practices. To qualify, such protection must satisfy three criteria: (a) it is secret, (b) it has commercial value because it is secret, and (c) it has been subject to reasonable measures to maintain its secrecy.

The TSD aims at standardizing the national laws in EU countries against the unlawful acquisition, disclosure, and use of trade secrets. The TSD provided a coherent legal framework and had a profound impact by enhancing legal certainty for businesses operating in multiple member states. The TSD's primary objective is to ensure the smooth functioning of the internal market, particularly to enhance competitiveness in the fields of research and innovation, by deterring the unlawful acquisition, use, and disclosure of trade secrets.[18]

The main provisions of the TSD include the following:

Definition of Trade Secrets

The TSD defines a trade secret as information that: (i) is secret meaning it is not generally known or readily accessible to individuals within the circles that normally deal with this type of information; (ii) has commercial value precisely because it is secret; and (iii) has been subject to reasonable steps by the person lawfully in control of the information to keep it secret. The "commercial value" requirement threshold is low and includes potential value, which does not need to be actual. Additionally, value may be determined if the unlawful use of the information would harm the interests of the information holder (harm test).[19]

Unlawful Acquisition, Use, and Disclosure

The Directive clearly outlines what constitutes unlawful acquisition, use, and disclosure of trade secrets. This includes: (i) acquisition by unauthorized access, copying, or theft; (ii) use or disclosure in violation of a confidentiality agreement or any other duty to maintain secrecy; or (iii) acquisition, use, or disclosure by a third party who knew or ought to have known that the trade secret was obtained unlawfully.

[16] ID. WTO.

[17] Directive (EU) 2016/943 of the European Parliament and of the Council of the EU dated 8 June 2016, on the protection of undisclosed know-how and business information (trade secrets) against their unlawful acquisition, use, and disclosure.

[18] Id. Recital 21.

[19] Id. Recital 14.

Lawful Acquisition, Use, and Disclosure

The Directive specifies circumstances under which the acquisition, use, or disclosure of trade secrets is considered lawful, thereby distinguishing legitimate activities from breaches of confidence. Legitimate activities include independent discovery or creation, reverse engineering (unless contractually prohibited), and exercise of the right to freedom of expression and information.

Remedies and Enforcement

Member states are required to provide effective remedies for trade secret misappropriation. These including cessation or prohibition of use or disclosure of a trade secret (by injunctive relief), corrective measures such as the recall or destruction of infringing goods, and prohibition of production, offering, placing on the market, or use of the infringing good. Additionally, damages may be awarded to compensate the trade secret holder for the losses suffered due to the misappropriation.

Protection of Confidentiality in Legal Proceedings

To prevent disclosure of trade secrets during legal proceedings, the TSD provides for further safeguards, including restricting access to documents containing trade secrets, limiting the number of individuals allowed to participate in hearings involving trade secrets, and issuing non-disclosure orders for parties involved in the proceedings.

Limitation Period

The period for bringing actions related to trade secret misappropriation is generally set at no more than six (6) years from the date when the trade secret holder became aware or ought to have become aware of the unlawful act.

Exceptions and Defences

The Directive recognizes certain exceptions and defence against claims of trade secret misappropriation, including "whistleblowing" disclosures made for the purpose of revealing misconduct, wrongdoing, or illegal activity, provided that the respondent acted in the public interest. Under the "Legitimate use of rights" exemption, a party may also use or disclose trade secrets to exercise the right to freedom of expression and information, or to protect a legitimate interest recognized by Union or national law.[20]

Case Law under the EU TSD Directive

Numerous cases have been brought to courts across the EU under the TSD, with a significant volume related to issues of former employment, particularly in the manufacturing sector.[21] The TSD is interpreted by national courts in member states. The claim most frequently litigated involves breaches of

(continued)

---

[20] Id. Article 14.

[21] "Trade Secret Litigation Trends in the EU", EUIPO 2023. The authors have identified 695 proceedings and 586 unique cases from 01.01.2017 to 31.10.2022.

confidence under confidentiality agreements (NDAs). While defences based on lawful conduct or exceptions are relatively uncommon, claims of unfair competition by defendants are frequently encountered.

A prevailing trend in case law suggests that general steps for protecting secrets, such as a broad NDA, are deemed insufficient. Instead, specific and targeted measures are required to effectively protect information.

Key takeaways from selected cases

Secrecy requirement

For information to qualify as trade secret, it must not be generally known among or readily accessible to persons within the circles that normally deal with information. The assessment of what is known should be from the perspective of an average person in the sector, not from specific individuals like former employee.[22]

Complex information configuration

In cases where the configuration of information is crucial, such as customer lists or business processes, the "secret" requirement is met even if individual components are publicly known. The unique configuration must not be easily obtainable through reverse engineering.[23]

Accessibility of information

The term "readily accessible" does not imply that information must be directly or immediately available. It may still require some effort to acquire, such as through reverse engineering.

Reasonable steps for secrecy

The courts adopt a flexible approach, taking into account the specific circumstances of each case. This includes evaluating both physical and cybersecurity measures. However, the protective measures must be "more than minimal".[24]

(continued)

[22] Id. Kevlar bv K.D.V., Elano nv, Finance 4 You bv, S.V.D.K., Finaid bv, Business Court Brussles, (29 July 2020) [Business Court of Brussels (2020)].

[23] Id. Higher Regional Court of Düsseldorf docket No 15 U 6/20 (11 March 2021) [Dusseldorf Regional Court (2021)].

[24] Id. Sadepan Chimica S.R.L., Sadepan Chimica NV v Two natural persons (31 March 2021) [Tribunal of Milan (2021)].

Evaluating reasonable steps

When assessing whether a company has taken reasonable steps to protect its trade secrets, tribunals consider factors such as the type of trade secret, circumstances of use, the value of the trade secret and its development costs, the nature of the information, its importance to the company, company size, customary confidentiality measures, labelling of information, and contractual provisions with employees or partners.[25]

Awareness of secrecy

Persons accessing information must be made aware of the holder's intention to keep said information secret.[26]

2.5 Protection Against Breach of Confidence in the UK

In the UK, trade secret protection is governed by a combination of the common law doctrine of breach of confidence, and statutory measures under the Trade Secrets (Enforcement, etc.) Regulations 2018.[27]

Trade Secrets Regulations

The Trade Secrets (Enforcement, etc.) Regulations 2018 aligns with the EU Trade Secrets Directive, providing clarity on unlawful practices and defining trade secrets as information that: (i) is secret, (ii) has commercial value because it is secret, and (iii) has been subject to reasonable steps to keep it secret.

Unlawful activities under the Regulations include unauthorized access, theft, or other illicit means of acquiring trade secrets; breach of confidentiality agreements; and the acquisition or disclosure of trade secrets by third parties aware of their illicit origins.

Lawful (authorised) use of trade secrets include independent discovery, reverse engineering (unless contractually restricted), and acts under the freedom of expression or information.

The regulations establish a wide range of remedies available for breach of confidence, subject to a prescriptive limitation period of six (6) years. The limitation period for bringing a claim is reckoned from the date when the breach occurred or when the claimant became aware of the breach. This limitation period can be extended in cases of fraud, concealment, or mistake.

[25] Id. Higher Regional Court of Düsseldorf docket No 15 U 6/20.

[26] Id. Italian Supreme Court of Cassation, No 34337 (27 December 2019) [Italian Supreme Court (2019)].

[27] UK Statutory Instruments 2018 No. 597.

Common Law Doctrine and Principles

The common law doctrine of breach of confidence has been shaped through landmark cases and establishes a robust legal framework against the unlawful acquisition, use, or disclosure of confidential information. The fundamental principle of this doctrine is that a person who receives information in confidence should not take unfair advantage of it. Underpinning the common law are equitable principles, focusing on fairness and justice, enabling courts to issue injunctions to prevent further misuse of confidential information and award damages for losses incurred.

Definition of Confidential Information

For information to be protected under the breach of confidence doctrine in the UK, it must satisfy three key criteria:

1. Quality of confidence: the information must not be generally known or readily accessible to the public. It should be specific and sufficiently valuable to justify its protection.
2. Obligation of confidence: there must be an obligation to keep the information confidential. This obligation can arise from a contractual relationship, such as an employment contract or a non-disclosure agreement (NDA), or it may be implied by the circumstances under which the information was shared.
3. Unauthorized use or disclosure: the information must have been disclosed or used without authorization, resulting in potential or actual harm to the party who shared the information in confidence.

Legal Remedies

UK courts addresses breaches of confidence with the following remedies:

- Injunctions: the most common remedy is an injunction, which can prevent the further use or disclosure of the confidential information. Depending on the urgency and the specifics of the case, injunctions can be interim (temporary) or permanent. An interim injunction is typically granted swiftly to prevent immediate harm, while a permanent injunction may be issued following a comprehensive trial, ensuring long-term compliance.
- Damages: to compensate for the financial losses incurred due to a breach, the injured party may seek damages. The assessment of damages will consider the actual losses suffered by the claimant, such as lost profits, lost business opportunities, or the diminution in the value of the trade secret. In certain situations, courts may also order an account of profits, compelling the defendant to surrender any profits gained from the unlawful use of the confidential information.
- Delivery or destruction: to prevent ongoing or future misuse of the confidential information, courts can order that documents or other material containing the confidential information be either delivered up to the court or destroyed. This remedy is crucial when physical or digital copies of the information exist and could pose continued risks.

- Declaratory relief: courts may issue a declaratory judgement stating that the defendant has breached their duty of confidence. This declaration is instrumental for the claimant to affirm their legal rights, which can be crucial during negotiations or in subsequent litigation.

Defences and Exceptions

Further, UK law recognizes several defences to a claim of breach of confidence:

- Public interest: a disclosure of confidential information made in the public interest may be justified. For example, whistleblowers who disclose information about illegal activities or serious wrongdoing may be protected from liability if they act in good faith. The public interest defence is, however, narrowly construed, and the defendant must show that the disclosure was necessary and proportionate.
- Consent: if the party who shared the information consents to its disclosure or use, no breach of confidence has occurred. Consent can be express or implied, depending on the circumstances.
- Information in the public domain: if the information has already entered the public domain through no fault of the defendant, then the duty of confidence may no longer apply. However, if the information was wrongfully disclosed by a third party, this does not necessarily absolve the original recipient of their duty of confidence.

Protection of Confidentiality in Legal Proceedings

UK courts have discretion to implement specific protective measures during legal proceedings to prevent the further disclosure of trade secrets and confidential information. These measures may include:

- Restricting access: limiting access to sensitive documents and evidence to designated individuals, such as the legal teams, the judge, and key witnesses.
- Closed hearings: conducting parts of the proceedings in private (in camera) to safeguard confidential information from public disclosure.
- Anonymization: redacting names or specific details from court documents to protect the identity of the parties or the nature of the confidential information.

Breach of Confidence in Employment Relationships

Employees often have access to sensitive information, and the law imposes a duty on them to protect their employer's confidential information. This duty continues even after the employment relationship ends, though it is typically limited to trade secrets or information that the employee is contractually bound to keep confidential. The courts have emphasized that general skills and knowledge acquired by an employee during their employment are not protected, but specific trade secrets or highly sensitive information are. The nature of the information and the steps taken by the employer to protect it are key factors in determining whether a breach has occurred.

Case law: Takeaways from the UK's Approach to Managing Breaches of Confidence

Quality of confidence

UK law protects trade secrets, proprietary business information, and any sensitive data disclosed in circumstances implying confidentiality. Information must meet a three-part test to receive legal protection: it must have the necessary quality of confidence, it must have been imparted in circumstances importing an obligation of confidence, and there must be an unauthorized use of that information to the detriment of the party communicating it.[28]

Circumstances of disclosure

The obligation of confidence can arise from various circumstances, including contractual relationships, fiduciary duties, and situations where confidentiality is implied by the nature of the relationship, the circumstances of the disclosure, and the expectations of the parties involved. Particularly, an obligation of confidence could exist independently of a contract, based on the nature of the information and the expectation that the information would be kept confidential.[29]

Reasonable steps to maintain secrecy

Both common law and statutory regulations in the UK emphasize the importance of taking reasonable steps to maintain the secrecy of confidential information. This can include implementing physical, technical, and organizational measures. Particularly, courts held that the protection of confidential information does not require the information to be novel, but the information must be of a confidential nature and its holder has taken steps to protect it.[30]

Balancing interest

In cases involving breaches of confidence, UK courts often engage in a balancing act between protecting the rights of the information holder and considering the broader public interest. This is particularly relevant in cases involving whistleblowing, where the disclosure of confidential information may serve the public good. Courts weigh the necessity and proportionality of such disclosures against the potential harm to the party whose information has been disclosed. This balancing approach ensures that the law is applied fairly and justly, protecting both private and public interests.

[28] *Coco v A N Clark (Engineers) Ltd [1969].*

[29] Attorney General v Guardian Newspapers Ltd. (No 2) [1990].

[30] Saltman Engineering Co Ltd. v Campbell Engineering Co Ltd. [1948].

2.6 Protection Against Breach of Confidence in the Philippines

While the Philippines does not have a specified codified law protecting trade secrets, said protection exists in bits and pieces through various applicable laws, procedural rules, administrative issuances, and Supreme Court decisions, which when put together provide quite the bird's-eye view.

The Philippines is bound by international law to protect "undisclosed information" through its ratification of the Agreement on Trade-Related Aspects of Intellectual Property Rights (TRIPS Agreement) in 1995,[31] which binds member states to protect "undisclosed information".[32] The definition of "undisclosed information" under the TRIPS Agreement is similar to the definition of "trade secrets" as defined hereafter in this chapter. This is in relation to "ensuring effective protection against unfair competition as provided in Article 10bis of the Paris Convention".[33]

The Intellectual Property (IP) Code of the Philippines includes "undisclosed information" (an umbrella term which covers trade or business secrets) as part of the definition and coverage of "intellectual property rights",[34] but does not provide the procedures and substantive provisions on the protection of undisclosed information.[35]

The landmark Supreme Court decision regarding trade secrets in the Philippines is the case of *Air Philippines Corporation, Inc, v. Pennswell, Inc.*[36] where the Supreme Court of the Philippines affirmed that trade secrets are considered privileged and confidential information and outlined a list of then-applicable laws recognizing said privilege.

The Court also adopted the following factors in American jurisprudence in determining whether certain information constitutes trade secrets (in the context of an employer-employee relationship):

"American jurisprudence has utilized the following factors to determine if an information is a trade secret:

(a) the extent to which the information is known outside of the employer's business;
(b) the extent to which the information is known by employees and others involved in the business;
(c) the extent of measures taken by the employer to guard the secrecy of the information;

[31] Cabilo, Zuraida Mae D. "Philippine Intellectual Property Rights under the World Trade Organization, 1995–2005: Implementing the Flexibilities under a TRIPsPlus Commitment", Philippine Journal of Third World Studies 24 (2009).

[32] The Agreement on Trade-Related Aspects of Intellectual Property Rights, Art. 39 (1).

[33] *Id.*

[34] Republic Act No. 8293 (the Intellectual Property Code of the Philippines), Section 4(g).

[35] Fitts v. Kimes Food International, Inc., Intellectual Property Office (IPO) Appeal No. 10-2016-0003, 30 October 2017.

[36] Air Philippines Corporation, Inc. v. Pennswell, Inc., G.R. No. 172835, 13 December 2007.

(d) the value of the information to the employer and to competitors;
(e) the amount of effort or money expended by the company in developing the information; and
(f) the extent to which the information could be easily or readily obtained through an independent source."[37]

Philippine laws and regulations granting protection to confidential information, trade secrets, and business secrets include the following:

- Philippine procedural rules on Evidence and Civil Procedure recognize the privileged nature of trade secrets. They provide that a person cannot be compelled to testify about any trade secrets "unless the non-disclosure will conceal fraud or otherwise work injustice".[38] Even if disclosure is compelled, the court is mandated to take protective measures to protect the interests of the trade secret owner.[39]
- The Philippine Revised Penal Code (RPC) in Article 291 penalizes "any manager, employee or servant who, in such capacity, shall learn the secrets of his principal or master and shall reveal such secrets".[40] Article 292 thereof focuses on trade secrets specifically, using the term "industry secrets". It penalizes "the person in charge, employee or workman of any manufacturing or industrial establishment who, to the prejudice of the owner thereof, shall reveal the secrets of the industry of the latter".[41]
- Proceedings before the Securities and Exchange Commission (SEC) also provide protection for trade and business secrets. The SEC is not authorized to require the revealing of trade secrets or processes in any application, report, or document filed with it.[42] Further, the Securities Regulation Code (SRC) by explicit includes trade secrets under confidential information, allowing the exclusion of trade secrets in certain reports, applications, or documents.[43]
- The Revised Corporation Code (RCC) of the Philippines[44] provides for trade secret confidentiality rules in relation to the Intellectual Property (IP) Code of the Philippines and the SRC, among other laws.[45]
- The Philippine Competition Act (PCA)[46] explicitly recognizes agreements protecting trade secrets as valid and not anti-competitive,[47] continuing on from

[37] *Id.*
[38] Philippine Rules of Court, Rule 130, Section 26.
[39] *Id.*
[40] Revised Penal Code of the Philippines, Article 291.
[41] Revised Penal Code of the Philippines, Article 292.
[42] Republic Act No. 8799 (The Securities Regulation Code).
[43] Amended Implementing Rules and Regulations of the Securities Regulation Code, Rule 66.3 (2).
[44] Republic Act No. 11232 (The Revised Corporation Code of the Philippines), Section 73.
[45] *Id.*, Section 73.
[46] Republic Act No. 10667 (The Philippine Competition Act), Section 15(e)(2).
[47] *Id.*, Section 15(e)(2).

the Consumer Act of the Philippines[48] which prohibits the revealing or taking advantage of trade secrets outside the context of administrative or judicial proceedings.[49]

- Philippine laws have slowly begun to modernize and adapt to the era of digitization, in response to the growing concerns of data breaches and possible leaks or disclosures of confidential data such as trade secrets. Personal data protection is governed by the Data Privacy Act of 2012,[50] while offences relating to computers such as hacking, forgery, and interception are governed by the Cybercrime Prevention Act of 2012.[51]

Valid Practices in the Protection of a Company's Business Secrets Related to Labour and Employment

An important subsection of Philippine laws and regulations to highlight in relation to trade and business secrets are those relating to labour and employment, since, as highlighted above, the general trend of the modern digitization age is to place responsibility upon the recipients of confidential information, with one of the most prominent examples being employees. There have been multiple cases decided by the Philippine Supreme Court which give an insight into the methods companies employ to protect their business secrets, and whether these methods are lawful.

The case of *Duncan Association of Detailman-PTGWO v. Glaxo Wellcome Philippines, Inc.*,[52] revolved around Glaxo Wellcome's policy requiring its employees to disclose to management "any existing or future relationships by consanguinity or affinity" with co-employees or employees of any of its competitor drug companies. The Supreme Court upheld the validity of this policy in light of the need to protect the company's business secrets and economic interests. The policy was "aimed at preventing a competitor company from gaining access to [Glaxo Wellcome's] secrets, procedures and policies".[53] The Court emphasized that the protection of a company's economic interests is rooted in no less than the Philippine Constitution, which "recognizes the right of enterprises to adopt and enforce such a policy to protect its right to reasonable returns on investments and to expansion and growth".[54]

The Court in *Molina v. Pacific Plans, Inc.*,[55] further emphasized the obligation of a managerial employee to protect the employer's trade secrets:

---

[48] Republic Act No. 7394 (The Consumer Act of the Philippines), Article 40(f).

[49] *Id.*, Article 40(f).

[50] Republic Act No. 10173 (The Data Privacy Act of 2012).

[51] Republic Act No. 10175 (The Cybercrime Prevention Act of 2012).

[52] Duncan Association of Detailman-PTGWO v. Glaxo Wellcome Philippines, Inc., G.R. No. 162994, 17 September 2004, 438 SCRA 343, 352.

[53] *Id.*

[54] *Id.*

[55] G.R. No. 165476, 10 March 2006.

> An employee's skill, aptitude, and other subjective knowledge obtained in the course of employment are not the property of his employer. However, an employee occupying a managerial position or office is obliged to protect the trade secret of his employer consisting of formula, process, device or compilation which it uses in its business and gives it an opportunity to obtain an advantage over competitors who do not know of such trade secret.[56]

Trade secrets are also protected in Philippine Labor law via the recognition of the validity of an employment contract containing a ***non-compete clause***. A contract with a non-compete clause is "a contract by which an employee agrees to refrain for a given length of time, after the expiration of the term of his employment, from engaging in a business, competitive with that of his employer".[57] The case of *Tiu v. Platinum Plans Philippines, Inc.*,[58] upheld the validity of the non-compete clause (also known as non-involvement clause) in employment contracts. In that case, the Court noted that petitioner, who was the company's Senior Assistant Vice-President and Territorial Operations Head, was involved in confidential and highly sensitive marketing strategies. The Court used the confidential nature of trade secrets in explaining the rationale of the validity behind the non-compete clause, stating:

> To allow her to engage in a rival business soon after she leaves would make respondent's trade secrets vulnerable especially in a highly competitive marketing environment. In sum, we find the non-involvement clause not contrary to public welfare and not greater than is necessary to afford a fair and reasonable protection to respondent.[59]

Other contractual clauses granting some form of protection to trade and business secrets have also been recognized as valid in Philippine Labor law. A ***confidentiality and non-disclosure clause*** ensures that the employee "will not use or disclose to any person, firm or corporation any information concerning the business or affairs of his employment for his own benefit or to the detriment of his employer".[60] This clause applies both during and after an employee's employment.[61] Similarly, a ***non-solicitation clause*** is a prohibition upon employees from soliciting or accepting business from any person or entity who during his employment has been "(a) a client, talent, producer, designer, programmer, distributor, merchandiser, or advertiser of the Company, (b) a party or prospective party to an agreement with the employer, or (c) a representative or agent of any client, talent, producer, designer, programmer, distributor, merchandiser, or advertiser of the employer"[62] in order to offer goods or services similar to that of the employer at termination.[63] A ***non-recruitment or anti-***

[56] *Id.*

[57] Alfonso Del Castillo v. Shannon Richmond, G.R. No. L-21127, 9 February 1924.

[58] Daisy B. Tiu v. Platinum Plans Philippines, Inc. G.R. No. 163512, 28 February 2007.

[59] *Id.*

[60] Chan, Joselito Guianan, *Bar Reviewer on Labor Law, 4th Revised Edition* (Pasig City: ChanRobles Publishing Company).

[61] *Id.*

[62] *Id.*

[63] *Id.*

piracy clause prohibits the recruitment of the employer's personnel by the employee for a limited time after the cessation of the latter's employment.[64]

All of the aforementioned clauses (and by extension, all practices enumerated) serve the purpose of protecting the legitimate business interests of the employer,[65] and to an extent, protecting trade secrets which an employee may become privy to through the course of his or her employment. All of these are thus options which businesses may consider implementing and incorporating in their employment contracts in order to not only give their business secrets the appropriate protection, but also ensure that a breach of said protection may be validly punished.

Digitization and Trade Secrets

On the other side of the spectrum is Singapore, a jurisdiction with numerous laws, regulations, and precedence on the protection of business or trade secret. This is an area of great concern for businesses in Singapore, particularly in this era of rapid communications and fast-paced technology. However, the protection is not maximized to its fullest potential, as many businesses have not taken adequate steps to protect their trade secrets. In an inaugural trade secrets event held in July 2022 by the Intellectual Property Office of Singapore (IPOS) and co-organized by the Singapore Business Federation "*Keep your secrets: protect your trade: How to Effectively Protect and Manage Trade Secrets for Business Growth*",[66] most participants indicated their company had valuable trade secrets, but less than one-third (1/3) had said that they had taken adequate steps to protect them.

2.7 Protection Against Breach of Confidence in Singapore

Business secrets or trade secrets are protected as "confidential information" in Singapore. There is no statutory definition of "confidential information", but it has been defined by the Singapore courts broadly to mean information which is not within the public domain. Confidential information is protected in Singapore mainly through the **law of breach of confidence**. Confidential information may also be protected **by contract**, through the **law of copyright**, or through the **doctrine of breach of fiduciary duties**.

In addition, there are certain *sui generis* statutes that protect specific types of confidential information. The criminal misuse of computers and cybercrimes are specific offences under the Computer Misuse Act[67] and the Cybersecurity Act.[68] The

[64] *Id.*

[65] *Id.*

[66] Keep Your Secrets, Protect your Trade: How to effectively protect and manage Trade Secrets for Business Growth: 6 July 2022.

[67] Cap. 50A, Rev. Ed. 2007, Sing.

[68] Cybersecurity Act 2018 (No 9 of 2018).

protection of personal data is also governed by the Personal Data Protection Act[69] which is a baseline data protection law that comprises various rules governing the collection, use, disclosure, and care of personal data. A brief outline of these laws is set out in the next section below.

However, this section is focused on the law of breach of confidence as the key form of legal protection of confidential information. "Confidential Information" should therefore be understood to encompass business secrets or trade secrets, which are specific types of confidential information.

Three Limbs to Prove: The "Coco" Test and the I-Admin Case

The law of breach of confidence in Singapore has developed through common law and has largely followed the position taken by the **UK courts**, including the three steps test to determine the existence of breach of confidence.[70]

Under Singapore law, businesses seeking remedy against breach of confidence must prove the following: (a) existence of confidential information; (b) an obligation of confidence on the part of the recipient of information; and (c) but the unauthorized use of that information.

In most cases, the first two elements can be established without much difficulty, as there would typically be a relationship or arrangement between the parties which implies an obligation of confidentiality (whether by employment, contract, or implied confidentiality). In the case of the first element (a), as long as the information concerned is not publicly available or was not legitimately obtained by the recipient from other sources, it would prima facie be deemed to have the necessary quality of confidentiality. The second element (b) would likewise be established if there was an *employer–employee relationship*, a *non-disclosure agreement*, or a *contract or communication* between the parties that the information of the business should be treated as confidential.

However, many cases fail to satisfy the third element (c). Even if the business is able to show that the recipient had access to and copied the confidential information without its permission, it is often difficult to prove that said recipient made unauthorized use of said confidential information to the detriment of the business. This is because the plaintiff has the burden of providing evidence of unauthorized use or misuse of the confidential information by the defendant, which is evidence that the plaintiff may not have access to.

The following sections analyse the three requirements of a breach of confidence claim in greater detail to provide further information on how businesses may satisfy all three requirements.

---

[69] Personal Data Protection Act 2012.

[70] Coco v A N Clark (Engineers) Ltd. [1969] RPC 41, already discussed Case 6 of the introduction, and Sect. 2.5.

First Element: Whether Information Has Necessary Quality of Confidentiality

The first element involves an assessment of whether the information that was disclosed to the recipient was *confidential*. There is no trade secret if the information is not confidential. As stated above, Singapore courts have taken a broad interpretation of "confidential information" to mean any information which has not become public knowledge. The law does not distinguish between degrees of confidentiality.[71]

For example, there are some types of confidential information that may only **require protection for a limited period of time** (e.g. data or know-how which by its nature will form part of public knowledge in a few years) or information which, while being "confidential", **may not be of critical value to the business**. These types of confidential information may be protected by a lighter set of restrictions (such as a general obligation of confidentiality in an employment contract or a non-disclosure agreement which expires after a set period of time).

Apart from **contractual restrictions** on the disclosure and use of such information, the organization should also **place controls on who has access** to such information and **when they can access it**, such as implementing password protections and time logs of when the information was accessed.

Employees who require access to business secrets should also be required to **sign specific non-disclosure agreements (NDAs)** which apply both during employment and indefinitely after employment. These requirements may either already exist as obligations under law or else should be written as clauses included in an employment contract.

Case Study

Singapore Clearlab case (see case description in Chap. 1 "Book reference terms, definitions and cases")

The plaintiff Clearlab relied upon an express confidentiality clause binding its ex-employees to protect and not disclose or use any confidential information. The confidentiality clause was very broad and included all information belonging to Clearlab or its group companies which was marked "confidential" or which the recipient knew or ought to have reasonably known was confidential, including information concerning the operation and methodology of the business, trade secrets, know-how, processes, research activities, data, manuals, customer and supplier lists, and so on. The confidentiality clause covered almost every type of information that may be disclosed by the plaintiffs to its employees.

(continued)

[71] Clearlab SG Pte Ltd. v Ting Chong Chai and others [2015] 1 SLR 163 paragraph 66.

The court was prepared to enforce such a wide clause, subject to whether any of the information should be regarded as part of the ex-employee's skill and knowledge which the plaintiff was not entitled to protect as its own.

Takeaways

Businesses should therefore ensure that their employees are bound by express confidentiality clauses whether in an employment contract or in a separate non-disclosure agreement. The obligation of confidentiality should be drafted to apply even after the employment comes to an end or is terminated.

Businesses may also draft wide confidentiality clauses to ensure all information of the business (other than information which is publicly available or which may be legitimately obtained by the employee from other sources) is treated as confidential. The issue of whether the information was in fact confidential information at the time of disclosure to the employee would then be a matter for the courts to decide.

Second Element: Whether There Was an Obligation of Confidence

Under the second limb of the Coco test, the business must show that the recipient was under an obligation of confidence. The basis for imposing an obligation of confidence may lie either in contract or in equity.

This element is usually satisfied in employer/employee cases because most employees are under a contractual obligation of confidence both during and post—employment, either via their employment agreement or a specific NDA. This was the case in both ***Clearlab*** and ***I-Admin*** (discussed further below) where the primary defendants were ex-employees who were bound by express obligations of confidentiality.

Even if the employee is not bound by an express obligation of confidentiality, the ***obligations of good faith and fidelity*** impose on the employee an ***implied*** contractual obligation to keep in confidence the information of his employer during and after the term of employment. However, it should be noted that once employment comes to an end, the employee no longer owes an obligation of good faith or fidelity to his ex-employer and the obligation of confidentiality may be more limited in scope. Therefore, it is prudent for an employer **to include an express confidentiality clause in its employment agreement or non-disclosure agreement, which extends beyond the term of employment**.

Takeaways

The key takeaway from these cases is that even if a recipient had not signed an agreement containing express obligations of confidentiality, the courts would still consider the relationship between the parties and the surrounding

(continued)

circumstances to assess whether there was implied term of confidentiality or if the recipient was under an equitable duty of confidentiality to the business.

However, it is advisable for businesses to ensure that any recipient of its confidential information is bound by an express confidentiality or non-disclosure agreement. Once this is established, then the threshold test of whether the recipient is bound by a duty of confidentiality of the business' information would be easily satisfied.

The Third Element: Unauthorized Use

Under the classic test in ***Coco***, even if the first and second limbs of the test are made out, there will only be a breach of confidence if the plaintiff satisfies the third limb of the test which requires evidence that there was an unauthorized use of the confidential information by the defendant to the detriment of the plaintiff. As stated above, this is often difficult for a business owner to prove, and in most cases this element is not satisfied.

However, in 2020, the Singapore Court of Appeal in its landmark decision in ***I-Admin (Singapore) Pte Ltd v Hong Ying Ting and others***[72] (the "**I-Admin**" case) introduced a **modified version** of the Coco test which in practical terms provides **greater protection for business owners** (hereinafter referred to as the "**Modified Approach**") by *relieving the businesses of the evidential burden of providing the third element of the test* and *shifting the burden onto the recipient to prove that there was no unauthorized use of the information*. The **Modified Approach** adopts the first two limbs of the test in Coco but *modifies the third requirement that there must be unauthorized use of the confidential information to the detriment of the party disclosing it.*

Case Study

The I-Admin case (see case description in Chap. 1 "Book references, terms, definitions and cases").

The Court of Appeal recognized that the third element of the Coco test posed the following dilemma:

> *….. the requirement that plaintiffs must show unauthorized use of their materials and resulting detriment has come under increased scrutiny. There may often be circumstances where defendants wrongfully access or acquire confidential information but do not use or disclose the same. Nevertheless, their actions compromise the confidentiality of the information in question. In such circumstances, why should the courts not have power to grant relief?*

(continued)

[72] I- Admin (Singapore) Pte Ltd. v Hong Ying Ting and others [2020] SGCA 32.

The Court of Appeal held that the test needs to be modified to recognize that the unauthorized "taking" of information by a defendant can result in a "wrongful loss" to the plaintiff, whether or not the defendant used the information to the plaintiff's detriment.

Further, the Court held that the mere taking and copying of such information (which results in the loss of the confidential nature of such information) should create a presumption of breach of confidence. However, this presumption may be displaced if the defendant proves that its conscience was not affected in the circumstances.

Takeaways

1. In essence, as long as the business can show that the information was confidential and that the recipient was bound by an obligation of confidentiality, **the mere access and capture of the information by the recipient will raise an inference that the recipient made unauthorized use of the information to the detriment of the business.**
2. To emphasize, under the third element of the test in I-Admin, the evidential burden is reversed, and **it is up to the recipient of the confidential information to prove that its conscience had not been affected** by the unauthorized taking the business's confidential information. This provides relief to businesses who would otherwise have difficulty in obtaining evidence that their confidential information had been misused by the recipient of the information.
3. It is **no longer necessary to show that the defendant profited from the use of the plaintiff's confidential information** if the plaintiff claims that he suffered a "wrongful loss". Such a task was difficult because it was often difficult to pinpoint what was used and what was gained by the recipient.
4. It is **possible that a former employee (or contractor) could breach a duty of confidentiality and find themselves liable for damages simply by taking confidential information**, without using or disclosing the confidential information.
5. **Plaintiffs who have suffered a wrongful loss may claim equitable damages**. In I-Admin, the Court was prepared to consider the additional costs which would have been incurred if the former employees had created their own software program without any reference to the former employer's programs.
6. **Employees (contractors) are at high risk when they leave with valuable data or software of their former employer** (even if they do not end up using it).

3 Legal Protections Other than Breach of Confidence

This section refers to specific statutes in Singapore but it shows legal provisions and practices where civil and criminal penalties apply and that could be beneficial for businesses to be aware of in jurisdictions following Common Law. As stated in the introduction above, apart from the overarching law of breach of confidence, there are also sui generis statutes in Singapore which protect particular types of confidential information and impose criminal and civil penalties for misuse. Similar statutes would also exist in other countries and businesses should be aware of such legislation which can both protect their business and also impose legal obligations on them to ensure that sufficient safeguards are taken with respect to the protection of personal data and cybersecurity threats.

These are summarized below.

3.1 Computer Misuse

The Computer Misuse Act ("**CMA**")—The CMA was enacted in 1993 to criminalize unauthorized access or modification of computer material and other computer crimes. The CMA contains many offence provisions that apply to both unauthorized and authorized uses of computers. The CMA also criminalizes the use of stolen data even if the offender did not steal the data himself. Further, the CMA has extraterritorial reach. Computer misuse involving computers or data in Singapore, even if committed from outside the country, nonetheless falls within the scope of the CMA.

Computer misuse cases in Singapore often simultaneously involve crimes of dishonesty, intimidation, and conspiracy as well as intellectual property infringement offences. The offences charged under the CMA are often used as the "foundation crime" to bring charges against the perpetrators.

This covers scenarios for example where ex-employees access a company's servers to obtain files or information for their own benefit. Offenders may face fines or imprisonment or both and be made to compensate the business if damage is done to the business' computer program or data.

3.2 Cybersecurity

The Cybersecurity Act ("**CSA**")—The CSA is administered by the Cybersecurity Agency of Singapore. The CSA provides a legal framework for the oversight and maintenance of national cybersecurity in Singapore. It strengthens the protection for critical information infrastructure (CIIs) which are computer systems that are directly involved in essential services such as water, energy, aviation, healthcare, defence, and media, among others. Owners of a computer system which are designated as a CII must put in place cybersecurity measures to ensure their systems are cyber resilient and protect them against cyberattacks. Following a review by the (CSA) and public consultation on a draft bill between December 2023 and January 2024, the Cybersecurity (Amendment) Bill was passed in 2024 to broaden protections for Singapore's digital economy and infrastructure. The amendment widens the scope of critical systems covered and increasing regulatory oversight to strengthen essential digital infrastructure and guard against evolving cyber-threats to the country's security, economy, and public services.

3.3 Personal Data Protection

The Personal Data Protection Act 2012 (PDPA)—The PDPA requires all organizations that collect personal data to put in place measures for data protection. Such measures include the appointment of a data protection officer (DPO) to oversee the organization's compliance to the PDPA, to put in place reasonable security arrangements to protect personal data from unauthorized access, collection, use, disclosure, or similar risks, and to notify PDPC and affected individuals of a data breach that is likely to result in significant harm or impact to individuals, and/or is of a significant scale. For breach of PDPA obligations, the PDPC will commence investigation against organizations and may take enforcement actions such as directions, undertaking, or imposition of financial penalties.

4 Securing Key Business Processes

4.1 Observed Limits of Current Situation in Many Companies

"Intangible assets" are not limited to known and formalized assets such as market intelligence, CRM files, decision-making tools (target costing and price estimation tools, etc.), and patent and trademark portfolios. They also include any unpatented invention (technical memo leading to patent application filing or remaining after a decision not to file), algorithm, method, know-how, compilation of data, etc. that provides or could provide a competitive advantage to the company.

In fact, regarding patents, the decision to patent or not is complex, and there are multiple mechanisms for the output not patented—to keep secret, to defensively publish, etc. But for those innovations that enter the patent process, the process is well established and well understood by those IP professionals that deal with patents.

As seen in Chap. 3, the origins of business secrets are much more complex; the authors believe this is one of the main contributing factors to the lack of best practice processes and policies around business secrets management. Some business secrets relate to those R&D innovations that an organization determines should not be patented but maintained as a secret; however, the vast majority of business secrets come from other functions within an organization.

We described in Chap. 3 how business secrets can include information such as mergers and acquisitions (M&A) targets, customer lists, internal data, customer feedback, and bug reports. These data may relate to functions such as finance, human resources (HR), manufacturing, and customer support, but may be irrelevant to R&D and product-related functions.

Importantly, and again unlike the patent process, there may be no immediate need within the organization for a centralized aggregation of business secrets. To the extent that business secrets originate within one particular function, it is highly likely that there is no benefit for this to be shared outside that function, or managed centrally within the organization. Indeed, broad dissemination within an organization may be counter to the nature of the secret itself—again touching on the topic of compartmentalization as a process to protect secrets.

Compartmentalization (see details in related box below) is typically understood to mean limiting access to specific information to persons on a **need-to-know** basis. Where need-to-know relates in some way to a utility to perform a job or function, meaning that even where an individual may be senior enough to access the information, they may be restricted from doing so because of a lack of need.

Compartmentalization

Compartmentalization is a security mechanism that can be used by organizations to maintain their secrets and protect sensitive information. It involves dividing an organization into smaller, discrete compartments or function, each with its own set of access controls and information boundaries. If one compartment is compromised, the damage can be limited, and the rest of the organization can remain secure.

One of the main advantages of compartmentalization is that it allows organizations to control access to sensitive information on a need-to-know basis. This helps to reduce the risk of accidental or unintentional data breaches and limits the damage that can be caused by an insider threat. Additionally, compartmentalization can help to improve efficiency by enabling different teams to focus on their specific tasks without being distracted by information that is not relevant to their work.

However, there are also some drawbacks to compartmentalization. For example, dividing an organization into smaller, discrete compartments naturally create silos within the organization. Siloed organizations are generally seen to impede collaboration and knowledge sharing. Additionally, it can be difficult to ensure that all necessary parties have access to the information they need, without compromising security.

Legal challenges can arise if an organization's compartmentalization practices are seen as discriminatory or if they violate privacy or data protection laws, for instance, compliance with data protection laws such as GDPR, which require organizations to ensure that personal data is processed in a lawful and transparent manner. Compartmentalization can potentially impede access to information that is legally required to be disclosed.

(continued)

Finally, compartmentalization can make it difficult to hold individuals or organizations accountable for their actions, which can further complicate legal issues. In 2015, the German automaker Volkswagen was caught cheating on emissions tests for its diesel vehicles. Engineers and executives involved in the scheme kept information about the cheating in small, isolated groups, making it difficult for regulators to detect the fraud. The resulting scandal led to significant legal and financial penalties for Volkswagen.

4.2 A New Initiative: The Singapore Intangible Disclosure Framework

An example of how companies are encouraged to better secure their business secrets is given by the recent initiative from the Singapore IP Office and the Accounting and Corporate Regulatory Authority of Singapore (ACRA), as described below.

In order to assist and encourage businesses to recognize, identify, and commercialize their valuable intangible assets (including its business secrets), the Singapore IP Office and the Accounting and Corporate Regulatory Authority of Singapore (ACRA) announced an Intangible Assets Disclosure Framework (referred to herein as the "Framework"), a public–private initiative believed to be among the first of its kind in any jurisdiction.[73]

The Framework provides a systematic and consistent way to disclose and communicate businesses' intellectual property and intangible assets such as brand value, patents, or registered designs. Enterprises are also encouraged to disclose intangible assets beyond those recognized under the accounting standards (e.g. human capital and/or internally generated intangibles) under the voluntary framework.

The Framework aims to encourage and assist businesses in developing a proper strategy to identify, measure, and manage their intangible assets, also with a view to enabling valuation and commercialization. One category of intangible assets recognized under the Framework is of course a subset of company's business secrets. The challenge of identifying and commercializing business secrets is that they are by nature confidential, and a company must ensure sufficient safeguards before making any disclosures under the Framework.

However, one of the outcomes of this exercise is that a company would be forced to consider what business secrets it owns as part of its business strategy and to rethink whether it has the necessary safeguards in place to preserve its confidentiality.

[73] https://www.ipos.gov.sg/manage-ip/intangibles-disclosure-framework.

4.3 Business Processes Are Essential to any Business Secrets Strategy

Information processing is at the heart of day-to-day activities in companies; it involves relational actions between employees, including company management, and between employees and third parties: suppliers and subcontractors, clients, partners, etc. Therefore, information is the very basic element exchanged during a specific process: purchasing, marketing, sales, accounting, research, development, logistics, etc. The table below (credit: Véronique Chapuis-Thuault) shows examples of information that is usually considered as key to protect:

Executive committee	* Decisions	* Organizational chart	* Planning	* Company's objectives
Commercial department	* Method of calculation of prices	* Commercial proposals	* Margins	* Customers list
Manufacturing and quality department	* Products technical specifications * Acceptable quality tolerance levels	* Manufacturing processes * Quality methods	* Production volumes * Quality levels targeted	* Target costs structure, ppm delivered, total quality performance, client satisfaction, KPIs
R&D department	* R&D programs	* R&D partners, make vs buy arbitrages	* R&D roadmaps, milestones, and results	* Unpatented inventions, new markets targeted, new patents volume
Purchasing department	* Expression of needs	* Pricing policy	* Suppliers' list	* Panel reduction, supplier qualification criteria
IT department	* IT security measures	* Codes and algorithms	* IT processes	
Legal, IP, and conformity department	* Board of directors meeting minutes	* Contracts	* Disputes	* Attorneys' list
Financial department	* Change policy	* Banks' list	* Loans conditions	* EBIT targets
Human resources department	* Employees' list	* Declaration of accidents	* Minutes of meeting with employees' representatives	* Employees turnover Salaries growth rate

4.4 Human Behaviour Is the Keystone of any Process

Most of the time, leakage of secrets and of value happens during a known process. Due to the habits and regular repetition of actions, no one is asking themselves the basic questions when receiving or disclosing an information, such as (this is a non-exhaustive list of examples):

- "Is this information confidential"?
- "If yes, who has ownership?" (my company, a given division or service, a third party, etc.)
- "Am I supposed to receive it"?
- "Am I supposed to disclose this information?"
- "Shall I mention that I received it, and to whom?"
- "Is my contact legitimate to give it to me?"
- "Shall I mention that I disclosed it to this contact, and to whom?"
- "Can I drag this information from this server to this folder"?
- "Is this information subject to specific protection measures? Which ones?"
- "What am I supposed to do to provide such protection measure at my level?"
- "Who should tell me what action is allowed with respect to this information"?

To ensure protection for key confidential information, it is important to implement reasonable protection measures throughout all processes, the first one of all being human resources related.

This will be all the easier to acculturate after a first level of confidential information, as trade secrets are in fact a subset of confidential information to which specific legal rules apply.

Takeaway

Here are some examples of good practices observed within companies to reinforce the culture of sensitive data in companies, starting from the simple concept of confidential information:

1. Include a clause in the employment contract regarding the protection of confidential information. Possibly attach a list of confidential information that the employee will be entitled to know.
2. Train employees on how to identify and protect confidential information and update the training regularly.
3. Conduct regular awareness sessions for employees on how and why it is important to identify and protect confidential information: what the impact of a breach of trust is on the company and what the potential legal consequences are for the perpetrator.

When an employee leaves, conduct an exit interview, reminding the employee of his or her obligations after leaving and having a list of

(continued)

confidential information at hand, especially information that has been the subject of confidential agreements with third parties. Have a checklist of items to be returned to the company and have the employee sign a certificate of destruction of documents and files before leaving.

4.5 Protecting Other Processes

Non-employee third parties are also important to consider in controlling data leakage because they are involved in many company processes. Prominent examples of these non-employee third parties include customers, suppliers, third parties, consultants, partners, and collaborative contracts, among others. For these third parties, confidentiality clauses equivalent to those for employees will be necessary, for example, adding clauses regarding trade secrets, mentioning the competent courts, and recalling. Training and awareness sessions can be provided for all contractors who work on company premises or who regularly exchange information with employees as part of company processes.

Processes other than those directly related to human resources should certainly be subject to specific protection measures, which should be put into perspective with regard to the company's strategy, as not all processes can be 100% protected. For example, the processes of R&D, innovation, collaborative platforms, software development, technology transfers, licensing contracts, and mergers and acquisitions could be the subject of a specific policy if the stakes are confirmed for the company. The corresponding information will be classified according to their **degree of sensitivity**, at least on a **minimum of three levels** (see also Sect. 4.2 *Identifying and classifying business secrets* for more details):

1. *Restricted (limited-criticality):* for information that should not be disclosed unchecked outside the company, part of the company, or a given scope.
2. *Confidential (very serious)*: when the consequences would be very serious or of great importance to the company, an entity, or an ongoing contract.
3. *Secret (vital):* when the consequences would be vital for the company, a legal entity, or an ongoing contract.

5 Situations and Business Practices Favouring Business Secrets Monetization

5.1 The Innovation Cycle in Data and Digital Environments

The digital era is accelerating innovation and at the same time fundamentally changing the game for innovation processes. This is because information, originally largely secret to begin with, flows immediately from one place to another and is then

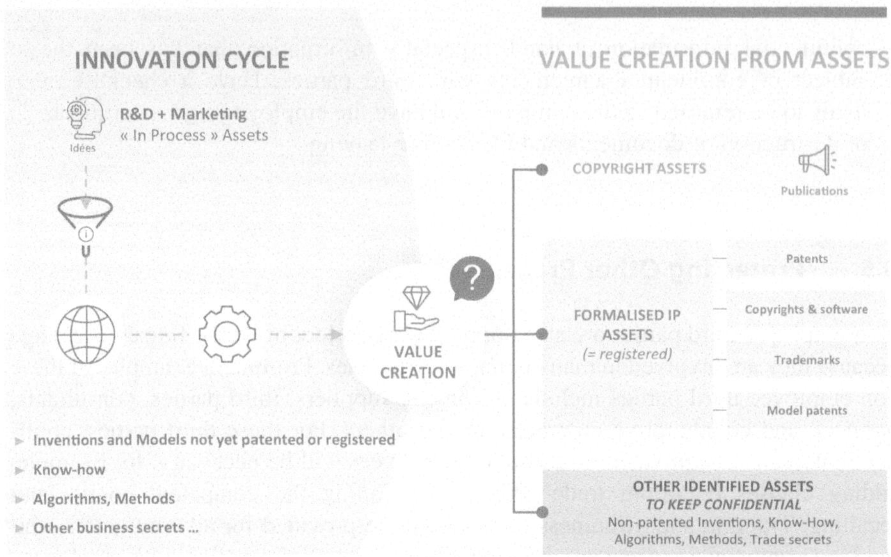

Fig. 1 Method for valuing secrecy in an innovation process (credit Pierre Ollivier, Winnotek)

reused in different contexts to create added value. But at the same time, this secret information may be—and actually will be—simultaneously accessible to a very high number of people, which is not a desired situation and is irreversible. Even if only disclosed once by mistake, erasing publicly disclosed information is virtually impossible.

The innovation cycle becomes a key process which can be seen as a broadly used practice, since it is used in many business situations, such as but not limited to: (1) R&D where ideas are filled from marketing in many cases; (2) product and service innovation; (3) open sciences, and even open platforms used for software development; and (4) more generally, IA data corpus development. Such a variety of situations put the innovation process at the heart of many business secret-related issues.

In such situations, Fig. 1 suggests a method for valuing secrecy in the innovation processes:

In this chart, the innovation cycle input and processed data must be secret; otherwise they do not add any competitive value. They include inventions and models not yet patented or registered, know-how, algorithms, methods, etc.

At the end of the innovation cycle, some of that data will be used to produce "intangible assets" such as publications, patents, software and other copyrighted works, trademarks, models, and patents. Of course, these various assets are favouring business secrets monetization through patent, trademark or software licensing, and company reputation.

But part of this resulting information will still have to be **kept secret** as such, because management evaluates that its secrecy adds value to the company as long as it is kept secret. In other words, this is when the management believes that it should have the potential to be monetized through methods such as licensing, providing new services or developing new products or features. This information is the type of business secret that needs the most attention from the management to ensure the value is not thrown out the window. For this, and due to the digital context, the following aspects should be taken into account to continuously maximize business secrets value potential and secure company's reputational capital:

- *Knowledge management*: impacts and strategies of data management and of confidential information marking
- *Cybersecurity*: ensure that prevention and recovery from cyberattacks will preserve business secrets, especially the most valuable ones
- *Personal data protection*: ensure this is correctly taken into account
- *Practical tools*: methods, and IT tools that allow a good business secrets management
- *Legal by design*: ensure, at the design stage, that projects and their results will be legal respecting laws, regulations, and standards all the way down the chain, towards product manufacturing, product and service commercialization, and even product recycling
- *Analyse context*, in light of new emerging business design situations:
  - How various intellectual asset types and their protection can impact strategy.
  - How enhancing certain asset types can impact supply chain design.
  - How the use of business secrets could be a key pillar in those designs.

5.2 Public Research Organizations: Creating a Practical Business Secrets Policy

A significant part of the financing of public research organizations (PROs) comes from collaborative partnerships with private companies. Conversely, PROs also finance start-up incorporations created from promising R&D projects. Therefore, it becomes necessary for company executives to understand how PROs organize their business secrets, and how both should align their respective strategies and policies. Thus, this section, although particularly dedicated to public research organizations, can easily be replicated in its near totality for small and mid-sized enterprises (SMEs) and corporations.

The first step towards managing business secrets is **their identification**. Ideally, the person who has the knowledge or skill should identify the business secret and then proceed according to the adopted policy, describe the "know-how", and inform the designated person about its creation.

In reality, however, this often does not work, especially in PROs such as research institutes and universities. If the knowledge is the result of a project and if its creation is expected, it is then usually identified by scientists because it is a necessary condition to meet the criteria of a successful project. These results are even protectable by industrial property protection (invention patents, trademarks, utility models, and design patents).

However, when the results may have commercial potential but do not have the potential to be protected by formal type of protection, the business secrets usually sit idle in limbo. They are in such cases often identified either as related to results protected by a formal method or as knowledge that has been acquired from long-term experience. Even worse, they may just be identified as know-how only after the fact, and thereafter chanced upon (e.g. in interviews or targeted brainstorming).

Another common situation is that know-how can also be created by non-scientific workers. Unfortunately, management often comes across a typical "reason why this knowledge is not considered interesting from a business perspective" because scientists and people working in research organizations, by nature, have objectives pointing in different directions and they **use criteria that lead often far from the financial perspectives** geared towards monetizing their job results.

It turns out that, in the scientific world, popularization and discussions take place at many different levels and in many forums and that, in such places, targeted brainstorming mostly focuses directly on identifying the know-how that has arisen, which helps eventually identifying the know-how that is a candidate to become a business secret.

When management identifies know-how that is believed to have the potential to be used for commercialization and monetization, it is necessary to **identify it and describe it** as accurately as possible to be able to grasp its key valuable elements. The more detailed and comprehensive the description is, the better the know-how can be handled and be considered a business secret.

The description does not necessarily have to be in written form. It can be done, for example, in the form of an audio or video recording. It is nevertheless important to record it in detail, so that it becomes self-explanatory, easy to understand, and replicable. The related activity should be described chronologically, step by step. If it is also necessary to **show how decisions are made in a technical process,** to explain and state the criteria under which a decision is to be made, how this decision should be made, and what may be its consequences.

The description should also be as objective as possible. Parameters should be given whenever possible and known in intervals of values, quite similar to those defining patent claims (e.g. descriptions such as "under these conditions it works ideally, at these intervals not so well, but it is possible to implement it, and above/below this value it no longer works").

When specifics are known, they should clearly be mentioned. Indeed, it should be kept in mind that an external partner/person may carry out the described activity. The description should then correspond to the expected activity.

In order to secure the information, it may be worth ensuring that the description's digital form is always encrypted with a password. Several tools are available and can be implemented for managing encryption and passwords. When the printed form is mandatory, it is a good practice to label it with at least the word "confidential"; this can also be done on the recording digital form. It is likewise practical to add an "identification number" to both forms. The explanation can be found in the following text below which concerns the recording of the information related to the subject know-how.

The created description/record needs to be **stored in a secure place**, with an emphasis on "**secure**". It is necessary to realize that know-how is far more sensitive to information leakage and disclosure than other inventions or technical solutions that have been protected by a formal type of protection (usually by a patent).

It is a good practice to choose the storage area depending on the form of the description; having multiple places might increase security, one for each form. The following are examples of good practices on security based on the form of recording/ description/ documentation:

- **Digital**—Find protected encrypted data storage with access limited to precisely defined individuals. Ideally, a disk/PC on a secured network that is not connected to the Internet. By implementing the above, at least a two-stage protection is ensured. The first level of protection is access to the storage, and the second is access to the encryption. It is key to encrypt the digital documentation using strong encryption algorithms to ensure that the data cannot be accessed by unauthorized individuals. Here are some safety criteria for securely saving digital documentation:
  - *Access control*: Access to the digital documentation should be controlled by a system that allows only authorized personnel to access it. This can be achieved through the use of usernames, passwords, biometrics, or other access control measures.
  - *Backup and recovery*: It is crucial to have a backup system in place to ensure that the digital documentation is not lost in case of system failure or other disasters. Regular backups should be taken and stored in a secure location.
  - *Physical security*: The storage location for the digital documentation should be physically secure, such as in a data centre or server room with safety and security access controls, security cameras, and other physical safety/ security measures.
  - *Data integrity*: The digital documentation should be protected against unauthorized modification or deletion. Measures such as digital signatures or checksums can be used to ensure the integrity of the data.
  - *Regular updates and patches*: The software and hardware used to store the digital documentation should be regularly updated with the latest security patches and updates to prevent vulnerabilities from being exploited.
  - *Disaster recovery plan*: A disaster recovery plan should be in place to ensure that the digital documentation can be recovered in case of natural disasters, cyberattacks, or other catastrophic events.
- **Paper**—Using a safe is recommended. Here are some safety criteria for securely saving documentation in paper form:
  - *Secure storage*: The first and foremost criterion for securely saving documentation in paper form is to ensure secure storage. The storage area should be secure from unauthorized physical access, such as a locked cabinet or a safe.
  - *Controlled access*: Access to the storage area should be limited to authorized personnel only. This can be achieved by issuing keys or access codes only to authorized employees.

– *Fire safety*: The storage area should be fire-proof or equipped with fire extinguishers to prevent documents from being damaged or destroyed in the event of a fire.
– *Water damage prevention*: The storage area should also be protected against water damage. For example, it should not be located in a flood-prone area or near pipes that could burst.
– *Organized storage*: Documents should be organized and labelled clearly for easy retrieval. This can be done through a labelling system or a document management system.
– *Regular backups*: Regular backups of important documents should be made to ensure that they can be recovered in case of any loss or damage.
– *Monitoring and auditing*: The storage area should be monitored and audited regularly to ensure compliance with security policies and procedures.
– *Disposal*: Documents that are no longer needed should be properly disposed of to prevent unauthorized access or use. This can be achieved through shredding or other secure disposal methods.

For practical reasons, it is good to **record the information related to the subject know-how** in a clear and structured manner. If such a registration system does not yet exist in the organization, it is good to create one. It can take the form of a database, but a table format (such as an Excel document) is also sufficient. The responsibility for filling in and managing it would be entrusted to the person responsible for managing intellectual property in the organization. If the organization does not have such a person, these services can sometimes be centralized (especially in research organizations). For example, in the case of the Slovak Academy of Sciences (SAS), individual organizations of SAS often do not have a special person managing the intellectual property of the given organization, and this task is taken over by the Technology Transfer office of the SAS.

The registration system should contain basic information related to each recorded know-how, but of course, each organization can expand the list of monitored data according to its needs. Basic metadata information about know-how may include:

• *Serial numbers.*
• *Title and/or keywords*—If the organization has multiple results falling under business secret in one area, well-defined keywords significantly help with orientation. Not only when searching for a specific result that you know is recorded in the system, but also in the case of searching for business secret related to a particular topic.
• *Identification numbers (labels)*—Used for unambiguous identification of the subject of business secret (e.g. in agreements). Its format can be arbitrary and may have several parts separated by a slash (e.g. OGBT/JK/INNOGLY/CA18103/2023/001). Ideally, the format and individual items of the identification number should be defined in advance, at least roughly.
• *Storage location*—In the case of a digital format, it is easier to define the path to the file (if possible).

- *The creator of the given know-how*—It is good to record who created the given business secret for at least two reasons. First, the person is likely to have the most complete knowledge about the related result, and in case complementary information or clarification is needed, it becomes quite simple to find whom to contact in this regard. Second, in case the given know-how leads to monetizing, it gives some clues about who is entitled to a potential reward.
- *List of persons with authorized access*—To limit the risk of information leaks, it is a good practice to precisely determine who and ideally to what extent (read-only, full access, etc.) this person has access to the know-how. The person responsible for the registration system should have a clear confirmation of authorized persons' permission to access the business secret. Confirmations may be part of the registration system, or if they are in paper form, they should be stored in a suitable place.

Additional information may include:

- *Commercialization strategy* (part of the service price, separately priced service, part of the granted licence/sale, etc.)
- *Valuation of the know-how (internally or by an expert witness)*
- *Data related to the monetization of the know-how* (when, to what extent, or if the know-how was part of a closed License Agreement, etc.)

The ability to access the registration system (not to be confused with ability to access business secrets!) should be granted not only to persons responsible for intellectual property management, technology transfer, and commercialization, but also to those preparing and managing technical projects within the organization.

To protect business secrets within the organization, it is good practice to prepare and implement a policy. This way, all employees will be aware of how to behave towards business secrets and how to handle them (and not just this "type" of intellectual property). They will also consider the consequences that a negative behaviour can have for the organization. These consequences could subsequently be transferred, at least partially, to the employee when legally possible and if acceptable from a global human resources management strategy perspective. The policy can, of course, be part of a more comprehensive document on how the organization handles intellectual property.

6 Implementing a Governance and Business Secrets Policy (Detection, Qualification, Protection)

6.1 Protecting Business Secrets in an Intensifying Economic Warfare

"Prevention is the key". Economic warfare is a reality that opens the way to all forms of plundering. The only way to protect your company is to anticipate by identifying your business secrets among your confidential information. General Eric Bucquet,

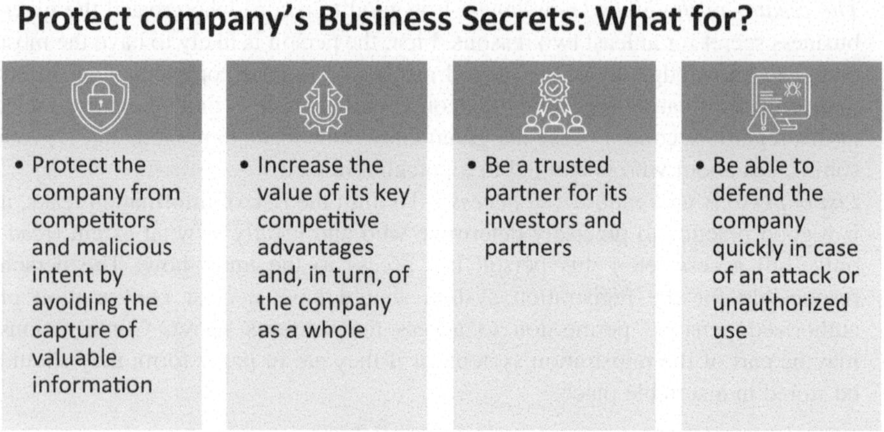

Fig. 2 Key reasons for a company to protect its business secrets (credit Véronique Chapuis & Pierre Ollivier, Winnotek)

French Director of Defence Intelligence and Security, states this recommendation in an interview on economic warfare.[74]

Protecting confidential information, and subsequently business secrets, will provide companies a number of advantages (see Fig. 2):

- Protects the company from its competitors by avoiding the capture, misappropriation, or misuse of valuable information
- Increases the value of its competitive advantages and consequently the value of the company as a whole
- Become a reference company for its investors and partners
- Be able to quickly organize its defence in case of aggression or malice

6.2 Identifying and Classifying Business Secrets

Identifying the confidential information that holds value allows a company to protect this information in case of a problem, but above all to better value the company in the eyes of investors and partners. The World Intellectual Property Organization (WIPO) stated in a recent publication[75] that "trade secrets have been part of commercial transactions for centuries, as a common and practical way for a business

[74] La Tribune, 6 July 2021, Entreprises et Finance, Michel Cabirol: "Nous sommes dans la guerre économique" (Général Eric Bucquet, directeur de la DRSD) (https://www.latribune.fr/entreprises-finance/industrie/aeronautique-defence/nous-sommes-dans-la-guerre-economique-general-eric-bucquet-directeur-de-la-drsd-888386.html).

[75] Secrecy: the IP right most often used by SMEs. WIPO Magazine, March 2021, Stefan Dittmer and James Pooley (https://www.wipo.int/wipo_magazine/en/2021/01/article_0001.html).

to maintain a competitive advantage", and that "Protecting an SME's competitive advantage by using secrecy requires awareness of what information needs to be protected to retain that advantage, and of the measures available to reduce the risks to its secrecy".

Business secrets concern **valuable confidential information** (cf. 2016/943 Directive European Law 2016) such as know-how, methods, strategic plans, and databases, which can in many countries—and since 2016 in Europe, and under certain conditions, benefit from legal protection under their specific laws (example of the French "business secrets Law of 2018"). More precisely, business secrets can constitute a competitive advantage for the company, and are labelled as:

- "*sensitive*" (in the sense of the common language, also the French Blocking Act of 2022)
- "*dual*" (which can be used for civil and military purposes in the broader sense)
- "*other*" (in terms of scientific and technical, assets of the nation; see above).

The following table will aid in asking the right questions about the protection of business secrets:

	Yes	No	Maybe
Do your business secrets contribute to:			
• Sustaining your business models?			
• Attract investors, clients, or partners?			
• Keep competitors at a respectable distance?			
• Engage in collaborative R&D projects?			
Could their capture by a third party:			
• Cause you significant harm?			
• Cause significant damage to your suppliers, partners, clients?			
• Prevent your technology or your start-up from emerging or growing?			
Can your business secrets be part of the **scientific and technical assets of the nation**? (PSTA or PPST in French)?			

If you answer Yes or "Maybe" to any of these questions, you have a good reason to start thinking of protecting, managing your business secrets, and valuing them.

6.3 Issue with People and Third Parties: Practically Managing Business Secrets

Beware of traditional practices: **Do not limit business secret protection to cybersecurity.** It must be fully deployed into five areas of protection: human (behaviours), physical (access, assets, information media, visits, risks of capture, etc.), organizational, legal IP, and IT (cybersecurity).

A number of good practice policies and measures can advantageously be implemented in SMEs, PROs, and global companies. These practices would rely on the different laws mentioned in the Singapore example by wisely generalizing the related takeaways when it comes to management strategy and protection measures. In a recent article,[76] Ollivier et al. define how to implement a business secrets policy in organizations; this article is reproduced below *with a few add-ons or edits in Underlined Italics*:

a) **Specify a group policy**: Despite the variety of laws applicable to a company or group, the company governance can be built on the basis of the highest applicable legal standard, and then adapted to local laws and regulations where necessary with a chart comparing legal definitions and processes.
b) **Deploy the policy over 3 fields**: Any company's efficient secrecy policy should be audited and enforced among all critical partners and stakeholders in the supply chain. The key performance indicators (KPIs) chosen to validate compliance and identify dysfunctions should be shared by at least all "critical" stakeholders as shown in Fig. 3 (Fields of business secret governance).

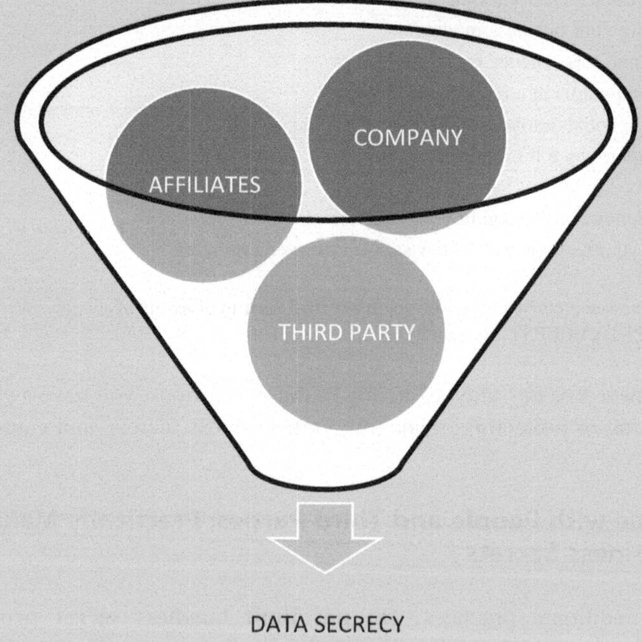

Fig. 3 Fields of business secret governance (credit: Véronique Chapuis)

(continued)

[76]Business secrets, High Potential Assets Under Development (les Nouvelles—September 2021). PIERRE OLLIVIER, ANDRÉ GORIUS, PHILIPPE SIMON, AND VERONIQUE CHAPUIS — Page 169.

Executive committee	Commercial department	Manufacturing and quality department	R&D department	Purchasing department	IT department	Legal, IP, and conformity department	Financial department	Human Resources department
Decisions	Method of calculation of prices	Products Technical specifications Acceptable quality tolerance levels	R&D programs	Expression of needs	IT security measures	Board of directors meeting minutes	Change policy	Employees' list
Organizational chart	Commercial proposals	Manufacturing processes Quality methods	R&D partners, make vs buy arbitrages	Pricing policy	Codes and algorithms	Contracts	Banks' list	Declaration of accidents
Planning	Margins	Production volumes Quality levels targeted	R&D roadmaps, milestones, and results	Suppliers' list	IT processes	Disputes	Loans conditions	Minutes of meeting with employees' representatives
Company's objectives	Customers list	Target costs structure ppm delivered, total quality performance, client satisfaction, KPIs	Unpatented inventions, new markets targeted, new patents volume	Panel reduction, supplier qualification criteria		Attorneys' list	EBIT targets	Employees turnover Salaries growth rate

c) **Organize cross-cultural collaboration** between several functional departments and business units (cf. Table above). It involves the legal and intellectual property department, all departments producing or receiving information, IT, security, HR, and insurance: in a nutshell, the whole company. Only the combination of inputs from these departments and business units makes it possible to build up a consistent policy meeting all legal criteria. Besides, it also suggests new management behaviours, an evolution of the ethics charter, new data management rules, new IT hardware, and software policy.

d) **Detect secrets**: verify their status as business secrets as per the company policy (and trade secrets as per the applicable laws by country when available) or as mere confidential information, *as per the relevant potential status attribution. This verification would be done by dedicated meetings gathering BU managers, support functions, and key information owners. At this stage, this confidential information status is only known by a few in the company: its value is still only guessed and not established yet*.

e) **Map the business secrets**, starting with know-how and key algorithms and formulas. The mapping should be made in forms that can be used to support operational decisions for protection or disclosure. An efficient knowledge management system, which provides an obvious "repository", eases the management of such data and therefore their protection. Some digital tools or methods available on the market help to set up this governance. Several are easily adaptable to fit the decision support of any specific company process. Specific methods, such as the CLAIRE® method by LEX Colibri, can be used to map the innovations, their components, history, and logical links, particularly in collaborative research and development programs where the traceability of ownership and exploitation is a critical issue with high-value stakes. The following steps should be followed:
   - *Define a typology* (e.g. classify know-how into a logical and understandable hierarchy).
   - *Classify past, present, and future confidential information.*
   - *Specify levels of criticality*: as the stock of data can be quite substantial, it is useful to pay attention first to confidential information holding substantial value. It is advised to request from each company's department to ***list their top ten business secrets and the top ten of their stakeholders***. Then an analysis can be made as per the relative criticality levels. Depending on companies' strategy, adopting a gradual approach, one can select business secrets characteristics and countries of operation using 3 types of criticality levels with varying degrees of impact, value, and life cycles:
     1. **Vital and essential data**. The disclosure of which can have irreparable impact and result in companies' destruction or in significant loss leading to bankruptcy

(continued)

2. **Competitive advantages**. The loss of which can have costly, but not irreversible, consequences
3. **Non-vital secrets**. Secrets which still need protection because their disclosure or exploitation by third parties could still be detrimental to the company

Thereafter, a check must be made of the consistency of protective measures with the level of criticality of business secrets.

f) **Organize traceability**: census or mapping (creation of a typology) for management and traceability purposes, using the criticality levels in particular by formalizing key know-how and ensuring that all work and inventions produced are stored on company's data management system rather than on employees' computers. Ensure that the same is made with deliverables from contractors.
g) **Estimate the actual value creation potentials** that can be achieved from identified business secrets, and then act accordingly at the right time, knowing the facts, and with legitimate reasons (strategically and/or financially justified).
h) **Verify their effective protection**:
   - Design and implement direct protection measures (physical, technical, operational)
   - Identify their exposure to the risk of illegal capture by third parties
   - Design and implement behavioural protection measures (awareness-raising, training of personnel according to their mission or ability to detain sensitive information)
   - Perform assessment of critical stakeholders' including suppliers' and clients' own performance in business secrecy policies (existence, robustness, history of failures, …).
i) **Specify duration of storage and then archive** together with the corresponding supports.

6.4 Make Sure Protection Lasts for a Sufficiently Long Time

It is necessary, in order to extract the most value from the business secrets, that regular monitoring takes place. First, the status may change regarding potential dual use of such information (Fig. 4). Note that a dual-use technology is a technology that can be used for both civilian and military purposes in the broader sense.

A generalized approach to business secret management will typically contain the four stages as shown in Fig. 5: audit, categorize, control, and monitor. The difference with business secrets is the level within the organization where this process operates. Unlike other forms of IP, such a process may be compartmentalized into a particular function or business unit, and hence be the responsibility of a unit head.

- **Audit:** Audit and develop an inventory of business secrets and associated documentation. This may be performed centrally as part of document management or knowledge management functions. Alternatively, the audit can be performed

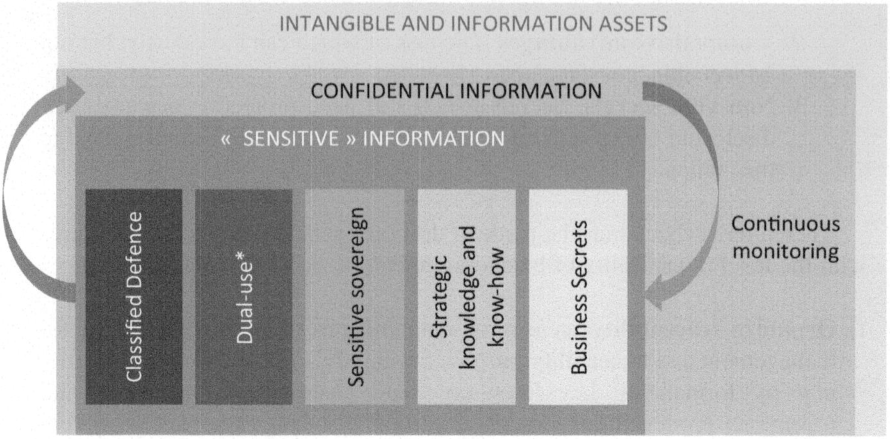

(*) a dual-use technology is a technology that can be used for civilian and military purposes in the broadest sense

Fig. 4 Monitoring from Confidential Information to Sensitive Information (credit Véronique Chapuis & Pierre Ollivier)

Fig. 5 The 4 stages of managing business secrets (credit Graham Bell, Cubicibuc)

locally where confidential information is compartmentalized in appropriate business units, functions, or project teams.

- **Categorize:** Map business secrets to appropriate business units, products, people, and partners. Understand what the business secret relates to and when it is no longer needed. Business secrets need to be maintained and actively managed in the same way as other IP. Linking or at least establishing a basic understanding of how the business secret aligns to products, processes, or systems within the business allows active management of the secrets in the next step—control.
- **Control:** Maintain copies of non-disclosure agreements and employment contracts of those with access to business secrets. Review the agreements in employment contracts, and in particular restrictive covenants. Ensure appropriate policies and systems are in place; this might include document marking, IT systems to manage and create audit trails, and physical access control to certain areas.
- **Monitor:** Report on people, companies, and agreements pertaining to specific business secrets. Allow access to be audited so that in case business secrets are exposed, a trace can be made to minimize damage. Where such systems are in place there is often value in making the systems themselves and any resultant actions visible—raising awareness of other employees when there is a breach.

At all stages of the process, it is important to think about the negative and positive impact on the people, processes, and policies of the business.

	Identify (capture, report and categorise)	Manage (Determine value, review, lapse)	Prevent loss or leakage (detect and monitor)
People			
Policies			
Processes			

Like other forms of IP management, there are compromises to be made. As discussed above, each of these stages is likely to incur associated costs, which must be balanced with the perceived benefit of protecting the business secrets. For example, implementing IT systems to secure secrets and reduce the risk of unintentional leakage will have associated costs, from the software itself, the impact of change to the business, and ongoing training costs. This should be weighed against the perceived risk and possible impact of a secret leak.

The identification stage may have a non-monetary cost, particularly if employees feel that the process is unnecessary, or may feel unincentivized to engage. It is unlikely that organizations will establish remuneration processes linked to business secrets in a similar way that patent bounties may be operated.

As discussed elsewhere locking down secrets and restricting access to secret information and data can be seen as having a negative impact on collaboration and innovation within organizations. If business secrets are managed well, they enable innovation within the organization and collaboration with external partners. However, organizations with high levels of secret information tend to act in silos which may reinforce negative behaviors, reducing collaboration both internally and externally.

Having considered general approach to managing business secrets, we turn to the other side of the coin—the loss or leakage of business secrets. The two most common forms of information and business secret loss or leakage are human-based and IT-based.

Humans can produce intentional or unintentional leakage. *Intentional leakage* is typically a result of disgruntled current or ex-employees; however, *unintentional leakage* could come from anyone within the business.

Further, *unintentional leakage* is often the result of unintended, well-intentioned actions such as speaking at conferences or to professional (technical) press media, where employees are "overenthusiastic" and share more than they should have. In some cases, this may be the result of "social engineering" where a third party is actively trying to extract the information or may just be unsolicited interest in a topic.

Unintentional leaks may also occur during discussions with potential partners and customers where employees "overshare" in an attempt to win favour. This is common where smaller companies are trying to build partnerships with larger organizations. The power asymmetry often results in the SME over-sharing to build trust or confidence from the larger entity in the early stages of relationship building.

In such circumstances, it may be difficult to rely on IT or physical barriers to deter such behaviour. As discussed, such leakage may occur in social environments, in bars, or at parties. There have been many examples of employees leaving secret documents in restaurants or in taxis—obviously careless, but with potentially damaging consequences.

Case Study

"Apple loses another unreleased iPhone", 31 August 2011.[77]

"In a bizarre repeat of a high-profile incident last year, an Apple employee once again appears to have lost an unreleased iPhone in a bar, CNET has learned.

(continued)

[77] https://www.cnet.com/tech/tech-industry/apple-loses-another-unreleased-iphone-exclusive/.

...

The errant iPhone, which went missing in San Francisco's Mission district in late July, sparked a scramble by Apple security to recover the device over the next few days, according to a source familiar with the investigation.

...

After last year's embarrassing loss, Apple reportedly has taken extraordinary steps to protect its prototype devices from leaks. Next-generation iPhones are sent to carriers for testing 'inside locked and sealed boxes so that the carriers can carry out checks on their network compatibility in their labs', according to the Guardian."

Increasingly, data is held electronically, and rather than leaving folders of data, employees may be leaving laptops, phones, or tablets in the open. IT solutions have a place here, ensuring data is encrypted, access locked down, and remote erasing of data is possible. However, as more sensitive information is stored in IT systems, these systems become attractive targets for external parties to attack—covered in the next section.

At the time of writing, we have seen a spate of news reports relating to unintentional leaking of confidential information through the use of artificial intelligence (AI) tools. Online AI tools such as ChatGPT have begun to be adopted within commercial organizations but several entities have reported users inputting sensitive information that is later extracted by external third parties. This has resulted in many large corporations banning the use of AI tools, or at least putting strict usage policies in place.

The use of online AI tools as a potential cause of secret leakage points to another, much more common aspect of IT usage which is the ad hoc use of online cloud-based tools by employees.

Case Study

Samsung employees accidentally shared confidential information while using ChatGPT, April 2023.

According to various sources, Samsung's semiconductor division had allowed engineers to use ChatGPT to check source code.

The *Economist Korea* reported[78] three separate instances of Samsung employees unintentionally leaking sensitive information to ChatGPT:

- In one instance, an employee pasted confidential source code into the chat to check for errors.

(continued)

[78] https://economist.co.kr/article/view/ecn202303300057?s=31.

- Another employee shared code with ChatGPT and "requested code optimization".
- A third shared a recording of a meeting to convert into notes for a presentation. That information is now out in the wild for ChatGPT to feed on.

ChatGPT's data policy[79] states it uses content from users to "improve" its models unless users specifically request to opt out:

> One of the most useful and promising features of AI models is that they can improve over time. We continuously improve our models through research breakthroughs as well as exposure to real-world problems and data. When you share your content with us, it helps our models become more accurate and better at solving your specific problems and it also helps improve their general capabilities and safety. We don't use your content to market our services or create advertising profiles of you—we use it to make our models more helpful. ChatGPT, for instance, improves by further training on the conversations people have with it, unless you opt out.

Following the incident, it was reported that Samsung took immediate action limiting the data that employees could upload to the ChatGPT service. Other organizations have since limited or blocked access to such online AI tools, some considering creating their own internal AI solutions in an attempt to reduce the risk of business secret leakage.

Inspired perhaps by the smartphone ecosystem, but increasingly part of the "desktop PC" experience, free-to-use applications that provide convenient single-task solutions are increasingly common and used by employees. Often these apps are free of charge, hosted as cloud solutions (meaning the actual application runs on a server at an unknown location), and do not require or offer any user authentication or security. Examples include language translation, file format conversion tools, file transfer, video conferencing, and business information directories.

While convenient, these tools represent a significant risk to organizations if users are not aware of the terms of use or security provided. Like websites, cloud apps typically collect user data which may be retained, used by the organization, and shared with unknown third parties. Likewise, data input into the applications may be stored, used, and shared. Employees using online translation tools to translate company critical or confidential information, or to convert file formats, e.g. between pdfs and Word document, are therefore risking that information effectively through unintentional sharing with an unknown party.

[79] https://help.openai.com/en/articles/5722486-how-your-data-is-used-to-improve-model-performance.

Takeaways
Pragmatic considerations
Human

- Clarify the employment contracts so that everyone has a confidential information clause.
  - Are you paying key people enough? This is a simple if not perhaps expensive way of stopping people moving elsewhere—going to competitors.
- Reinforce this at entry and exit interviews—making everyone aware that the company has confidential information that has value and takes it seriously.
  - Review where employees go when leaving and if to a competitor take additional steps to reinforce considerations around business secrets.
- Include business secret awareness, in general "quality training" for all employees.
  - If management of business secrets includes document marking, e.g. company confidential, project confidential type labelling, make sure this is communicated to all employees.
  - Where responsibility for business secrets is allocated to business units or project, identify and commission a champion responsible for the day-to-day operation. Such a role may be linked to additional responsibility credits within the organization.

Takeaways
Pragmatic considerations
IT related

- Do not let employees have phones/cameras in sensitive areas—and make examples of those that break these rules to reinforce that the company takes this seriously.
- Limit employees access to sensitive areas / access to the magic formula—this might for some forms of business secret involve locking behind IT systems that limit access and audit access attempts.
- Adopt IT systems that compartmentalize by project—make the "need-to-know" rule part of the culture of the company—although this brings its own

(continued)

set of tensions with need-to-know versus sharing info to encourage innovation:
  - Some IT solutions will provide audit reports of who and when particular files have been accessed. This may be appropriate for some business secrets.
  - Some IT solutions automatically restrict access according to project involvement, so employees don't need to think about whether they can share material—the system automatically takes care of that depending on who's involved in the project. This might become a headache if people move between projects regularly, and again become as point of tension between secrecy vs creativity.
- Put an air gap between sensitive IT systems and the Internet. Does your sensitive data need to be connected to the outside? If not, disconnect it; put it in a locked room with restricted access.
- Make sure your IT system is up to date, that phones and laptops aren't vulnerable to attack, that data is encrypted, and possibly that devices can be wiped remotely if lost or stolen.
- Consider using IT solutions that lock-down email and other communications, lock ports, limit data transfers, etc.
  - Utilize continual prompts to users to remind them / question whether they should be sharing / exporting particular information or data.

Takeaways

Pragmatic considerations

Physical

- Think about the physical environment and how it supports / encourages the management policies of the business.
  - For example, if hot-desking is the norm, does this include a clean-desk policy? How is it enforced?
  - Are project rooms locked / limited access—is access audited?
  - Are printers controlled (need the person physically present before it prints rather than leaving printer documents in the "open")?
  - Are prints audited?
- Do not let visitors near where the magic happens:
  - Segregate visitor areas from the rest of business—put an air gap in place so it's clear for visitors where they should and shouldn't go.

(continued)

  - Get all visitors to read and sign an NDA each and every time—again reinforcing that you take business secret seriously.
- Reinforce policies in the environment with signage—no camera signs, no entry signs, etc.

6.5 Issue with Data Leakage and Cyber attacks

Information leakage is becoming a major concern for companies, with an increased risk due to dematerialization, most of the time because of internal failures whether intentional or not. Indeed, according to a Verizon study,[80] 58% of information compromissions come from insider or partner errors and misbehaviour (18% by insiders and 39% by partners), and the median size (measured in number of compromised records) of an insider breach exceeds that of a third-party breach by more than ten to one. In other words, errors in information transmissions and environment configurations by employees are the top two causes of the threat.

Corruption or violation from the outside weakens innovative companies and disturbs their capacity to control and protect their business secrets; still according to Verizon, computer systems can be corrupted in only a few hours in large companies (e.g. production plants) and distributed denial of service (DDoS) attacks represent 46% of total incidents. An IBM study[81] also reports that the average cost of a data breach is nearly $4 million and is on a steady upward trend.

The protection of business secrets is organized by necessity in pain and penalizes first innovative companies. In fact, a study conducted by the European Commission in 2013[82] shows that misappropriation of trade secrets resulted in lost revenue for 56% of companies, whereas 44% incurred internal investigation costs and 35% responded by increasing their protection spending. Innovative companies are seen as the most exposed by a December 2020 memo from the French Ministry of the Interior on economic interference: this memo alerts companies, especially the most innovative ones, to the risks of undue appropriation of know-how or essential technological bricks by players from foreign countries in the context of partnerships. This risk has increased following the COVID health crisis of 2020.

In terms of economic warfare, General Thierry Burkhard, Chief of Staff of the French Armed Forces, recalls that[83] " *[…] faced with increasingly uninhibited*

[80] (Verizon) 2022 Data Breach Investigations Report—DBIR.

[81] (IBM) Cost of a data breach 2022: A million-dollar race to detect and respond.

[82] Study on Trade Secrets and Confidential Business Information for the European Commission (2013).

[83] Vision stratégique du Chef d'Etat Major des Armées (Strategic vision of the Chief of Staff of the Armed Forces), Oct 2021 (https://www.defense.gouv.fr/ema/chef-detat-major-armees/vision-strategique-du-chef-detat-major-armees-fresgb).

competitors, when the law is not an effective remedy, it is necessary to be able to impose a favourable balance of power." In addition, new practices and threats call for enlightened governance:

New practices include:

- Digitization of know-how
- AI (artificial intelligence) to capture information in servers
- Collaborative platforms to share data
- Open data and Open Science

New threats and amplification of their impacts include:

- Plundering or corruption of data following computer attacks
- Public disclosure by hackers of data from a ransomware system (e.g. APHP in France)
- Massive disorganization of a collective system (e.g. operation of a hospital, failure of an electricity distribution or transportation system).

Case Study

Examples of cyber-breaches include:

- Reported in a publication by Otto-JS on "spell-jacking"[84] (cited) "*The Otto-JS team of security researchers discovered that the Microsoft editor on Microsoft Edge and* ***the enhanced spell checker*** *built into Google Chrome send typed data, including passwords, to Google and Microsoft servers. They can also analyse all content entered into a text field.*" This breach named "Spell-jacking" by Otto-JS is transposable to any cloud infrastructure or internal company network.
- Depending on the nationality and location of the provider, **a given encryption solution** may not be sufficient to meet the security quality requirements of the user's country.
- AI opens as many opportunities as threats by facilitating the capture of data or the detection of a valuable element in a mass of unsorted data.

Cybersecurity has thus become the major concern for companies and ecosystems, surpassing other risks (Fig. 6).

[84] Google and Microsoft can get your passwords via your browser enhanced spellcheck (https://www.bleepingcomputer.com/news/security/google-microsoft-can-get-your-passwords-via-web-browsers-spellcheck/).

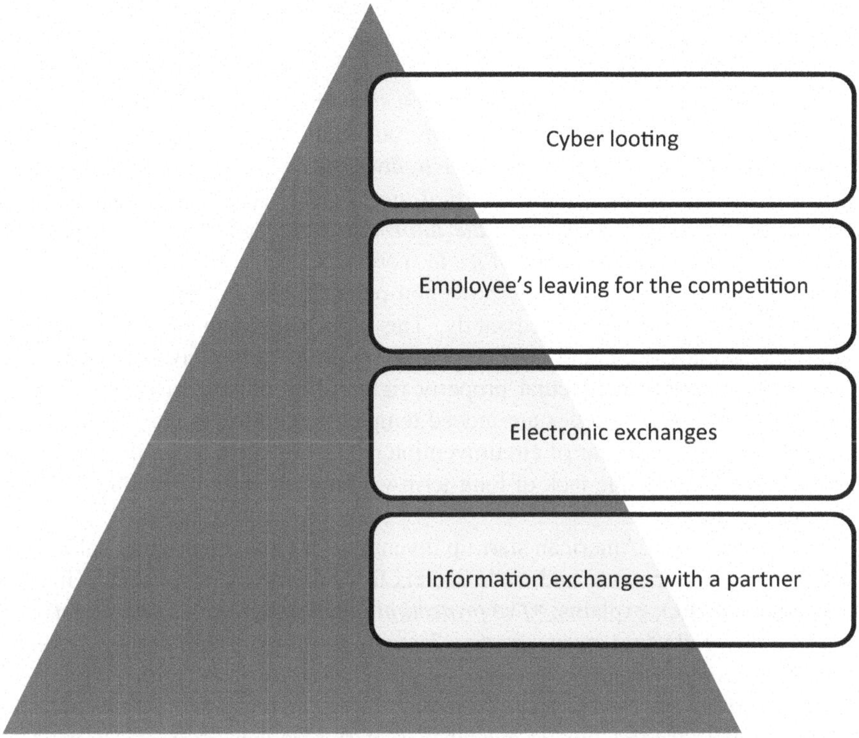

Fig. 6 Hierarchical risk structure of information exchanges (credit Véronique Chapuis & Pierre Ollivier)

The European Union, wishing that the Internet offers an environment of trust, has issued security rules in the directive on the security of networks and information systems ("SRI2" in French or "NIS 2" in English).[85]

7 Combining and Optimizing Several Protection Strategies to Increase Company Strategic Value

7.1 Issues with Business Negotiations and Commercial and Corporate Transactions

As seen above, in the competitive world of business, secrets are the lifeblood of innovation and strategic advantage. Protecting these secrets during key commercial transactions and key corporate transactions such as mergers and acquisitions (M&A)

[85] European Commission communication (https://digital-strategy.ec.europa.eu/en/policies/nis2-directive).

is paramount to maintaining a company's competitive edge and increasing its strategic value. For instance:

- Data is the new gold of the twenty-first century. Jim Pooley, former Deputy Director General of the WIPO, points out that "*Even companies that never imagined they would focus on such lightweight concepts as data, instead of cars or buildings, are discovering that their market value and sometimes their survival depends on controlling the information that gives them a competitive advantage. This is the essence of trade secrets.*"
- The range and amount of know-how, non-patentable inventions or inventions to be kept secret, augments incessantly. The French government reaffirms that a company's know-how and commercial information cannot always be protected by patent or other intellectual property rights: they must then be protected by secrecy.[86] Many companies are indeed tempted to choose secrecy as an alternative to patenting, for fear of circumvention or infringement of published patents, sometimes for a simple lack of long-term vision or for lack of funding to secure formal IP assets.
- TIATROS Inc., an American start-up inventor of a cloud computing solution for healthcare, uses patents and trade secrets to optimize its protection. Kimberlie Cerrone, its CEO, explains: "*The protection of know-how and trade secrets is an aspect of intellectual property that Tiatros, a software company, exploits to ensure its competitiveness. We have an extensive trade secret policy that applies to our employees, contractors, customers, and current and potential business partners. We take this part of our business very seriously.*"[87]

This section provides a broad view on how legal and organizational means of protecting business secrets can be employed effectively during business negotiations, execution of commercial and corporate transactions, and thereafter following execution.

Two complementary topics are explored herein: the protection of business secrets during deal-making and the contractual representations and warranties that often constitute the basis of a deal and which will legally bind parties to a deal after its execution.

Whenever relevant, we will exemplify the above with specific examples from selected industries.

---

[86] French Ministry Bercy communication (https://economie.fgov.be/fr/themes/propriete-intellectuelle/droits-de-pi/regimes-de-protection/secrets-daffaires-protection).

[87] WIPO communication (https://www.wipo.int/ipadvantage/fr/details.jsp?id=5580).

7.2 Business Secrets Protection During Deal-Making

Successful deal-making are the result of key negotiation including disclosure strategies that ensure that all relevant business secrets are shared in a controlled and secure manner. These strategies must be carefully planned and executed to protect the interests, not only of the disclosing party but also of the recipient party.

The negotiation and disclosure of business secrets play a crucial role, especially during the early phase and due diligence phases of deal-making related to business transactions such as merger and acquisition (M&A), sale and purchase of assets, joint venture agreements, collaborative development agreement, and license agreements. At all time, the disclosing party in such transaction must carefully consider the balance between *transparency* (sharing enough information to facilitate the deal) and *secrecy* (protecting their confidential information in case the deal falls through).

Disclosure Strategies

IP owners can employ various disclosure strategies to protect their business secrets during deal-making. We explore below the main such disclosure strategies: controlled disclosure, tiered or phased disclosure, and also third-party verifications, post-acquisition disclosure, and public disclosure. These strategies must be tailored to the specific circumstances of each deal and the specific nature of the business secrets involved. These strategies require careful planning and execution and should be developed with the assistance of legal and business advisors.

Controlled Disclosure

Controlled disclosure involves releasing business secrets in a controlled manner to limit the risk of unwanted leaks. This strategy is all about managing what information is disclosed, to whom, and at what point in the negotiations. The idea is to first allow the recipient party to access sufficient information to validate the attractiveness of a potential transaction and confirming an interest, before disclosing business secrets related to technologies, know-how, and process. The controlled disclosure follows the steps established by the parties in order for the acquirer, licensee, or investor to conduct its due diligence.

Data rooms technologies and services are widely used to ensure controlled and monitored access to information during the due diligence process, ensuring that only authorized individuals can have access to specific information during time-limited periods while providing data owners with evidence of access and use.

By way of example, in the pharmaceutical industry, a company might choose to disclose only confidential information such as the results of clinical trials without revealing a proprietary drug formula, mode of action or its production processes. This allows potential buyers to understand the efficiency of the drug without gaining access to information that would have allowed them to conduct retro-engineering work.

In the automotive industry, a developer of battery technology might disclose performance data, safety records, costs and pricing, and software functions, but not the manufacturing process, power management software, or source code.

In the AI field, a company might disclose the performance metrics of their AI model such as accuracy, precision, and recall, without revealing the underlying proprietary algorithms or the unique training dataset or combination of datasets. This allows potential partners or acquirers to understand the effectiveness of the AI model without exposing its enabling IP.

Tiered Disclosure

Tiered disclosure, also known as phased or staged disclosure, involves disclosing information in stages based on the progress of the negotiations, starting with the least sensitive information. This strategy allows parties to build trust gradually and ensures that sensitive information is only shared when necessary. This strategy further helps to protect sensitive information while still allowing the negotiation process to move forward. Information of a general business nature and financial information are typically disclosed in the initial phases.

For example, in the oil and gas industry, a company might initially disclose general operational data. As negotiations progress and trust is built, the company might then disclose more sensitive information, such as proprietary extraction methods.

In the software industry, a company might first disclose high-level architectural diagrams before disclosing detailed source code.

In the telecommunications industry, a company might initially disclose general information about a new communication technology they have developed, such as its capabilities and potential applications. As negotiations progress and a higher level of trust is established, they might then disclose detailed technical specifications or proprietary aspects of the technology.

In the AI field, a company might initially disclose high-level information about an AI model, such as its purpose, capabilities, and performance metrics. As trust is built, they might then disclose more sensitive information, such as the architecture of the model, the features used, or the nature of the proprietary training data. If the negotiations lead to a formal partnership or acquisition, the company might finally disclose the most sensitive information, such as the specific algorithms used or the raw training data.

Third-Party Verification

In some cases, a trusted third party can be involved to validate the existence, availability, value or authenticity of certain business secrets without disclosing such secrets to the negotiating counter-party. This strategy adds an additional layer of protection while still providing the necessary information for the deal.

For example, in the pharmaceutical industry, a third-party lab might be used to verify efficiency claims by conducting invitro tests or by reviewing statistical models, without revealing confidential process information to the potential buyer or licensee.

Public Disclosure

In some cases, what a party considers its business secrets may already be publicly available, in whole or in part, through a prior non-authorized or authorized disclosure, through independent creation, or through public disclosure by a third party. In these situations, discussions about a transaction would typically focus on operational items such as sales and brand. Typically, an acquired company that cannot rely on business secrets or IP as barriers to entry to competitors will see its value discounted. Without such protection, there may be less need for additional protection measures.

In certain specific situations, companies might opt to publicly disclose certain business secrets as part of their commercial or M&A strategy. For example, a software company might choose to open source some of its software as a way to demonstrate its value to potential buyers and to the wider market. In such case, a lower barrier to entry for a technology is compensated by the objective of a much faster market adoption, making it difficult or impossible for competitors to monetize their solutions at a profit.

Post-Acquisition Disclosure

In certain situations, it may be more appropriate to disclose certain business secrets after the completion of the deal. This strategy ensures that sensitive information is only shared with the acquiring party once the deal is finalized.

For example, in the service industry (e.g. consulting or legal services), a client list may only be disclosed upon receipt of the agreed purchase price. Contracts often include provisions to address scenarios where projected revenue or client turnover does not materialize after the acquisition. In the oil and gas industry, a company might choose to disclose proprietary extraction methods or information about its spot and long-term supply contracts only after an acquisition deal is executed.

Disclosure vs Negotiation Strategies

In deal-making situations, corporations must align their disclosure strategy with their negotiation strategies. While complete disclosure may be necessary to facilitate a deal, it is crucial to ensure that sensitive information is only shared when necessary, and only to trusted parties. Negotiation strategies, on the other hand, focus on the process of advancing discussions towards the ultimate goal of a successful transaction.

Negotiation Strategies

Using the proper negotiation strategy is also crucial to ensure a fair and beneficial outcome for all parties involved. This requires a careful balance between achieving business objectives and protecting business secrets. It is a complex process that requires careful planning, clear communication, and often, the guidance of seasoned managers with assistance from experienced external advisors.

Here is a quick rundown of well-known negotiation strategies, which can be employed individually or in combination.

Interest-based negotiation. This strategy focuses on understanding the underlying interests of both parties rather than their stated positions. Understanding this interest could lead to solutions such as stronger confidentiality agreements or phased/tiered disclosure strategies. A party reluctant to disclose a business secret may not only be concerned about protecting its IP, but may also be concerned about market positioning and pricing should the other party enter the same field, using the business secret or not. In the oil and gas industry, an acquiring company might be interested in a proprietary extraction method not just for use in a current project, but because the method aligns with a long-term strategy of securing access to a particular geological formation.

Collaborative negotiation. This strategy focuses on finding win-win solutions that benefit both parties. For example, in the electronics industry, two parties may enter into M&A discussion a cross-sale and cross-licence arrangement for intellectual property (IP) relevant to various generations of related technologies. Under such arrangement, each company gain access technologies that align with its manufacturing and distribution capabilities. Such arrangements preserve value for both entities while fostering long-term collaboration.

BATNA (Best alternative to a negotiated agreement). Understanding your BATNA is crucial in any negotiation, as it defines the course of action that will be taken if the current negotiation fails and an agreement cannot be reached, for any reason. Knowing your BATNA gives you the power to walk away from a negotiation if the terms do not meet your minimum requirements.

Value creation. This strategy involves finding ways to create additional value in the deal for all parties and focuses on understanding the value of the business secrets to each party, individually vs collectively. This could involve identifying synergies between the merging companies, exploring new market opportunities which none of the businesses can explore on its own, or leveraging combined resources for greater efficiency.

Third-party mediation. In complex negotiations, involving a neutral third party can help facilitate communication, provide an objective perspective, and help parties find common ground. This can be particularly useful when negotiating sensitive issues such as business secrets.

Other Considerations

Deal structuring. The structure of the deal can significantly impact the negotiation of business secrets and other key terms. For example, an earn-out structure, where part of the purchase price is dependent on future performance, could help align the interests of the buyer and seller and facilitate the negotiation of business secrets.

Pricing negotiation. Pricing is often a critical point in licensing or M&A negotiations. Strategies for parties to agree on the value of a corporation or on the value of a technology include future adjustment on price using ratchets, conditional on the companies meeting (or missing) milestones; valuation using the comparable market method or income method (discounted cashflow projections (DCF) and net present value (NPV)), based on assumptions that may be accepted by both parties; or reliance on independent business valuations.

Representations and warranties (discussed in Sect. 7.3 below). These are statements of fact about the company or asset being sold or licensed, on topic including ownership, governance, compliance with laws, and the accuracy of financial statements. The negotiation here will focus on the scope, accuracy, and duration of these representations and warranties. The buyer will want broad representations to have a clear understanding of what they are buying, while the seller will want to limit these to reduce potential liability.

When to Use (or Not) Non-Disclosure Agreements (NDAs)

Non-disclosure agreements (NDAs) (discussed in Sect. 3 in Chap. 6) are legal contracts that aims at managing disclosure of confidential information from one party to another party (the recipient), or between parties in the case of mutual NDA. Non-disclosure obligations are also formalized in confidential disclosure agreements (CDA) or non-competition and non-disclosure (NCND) agreements. The purpose of these agreements is essentially similar: to identify confidential information and to clarify the extent of legal obligations not to disclose such information after it has been disclosed or made available.

NDAs should be utilized when there is a genuine need to protect sensitive information and establish legal recourse in the event of a breach. Besides the legal protection it confers, executing an NDA during the early phases of discussion also enables a party to assess another party's willingness to transact and its capabilities in executing a contractual document. Consider:

- Does the NDA need to be approved by the board of directors or by a controlling entity?
- Does the other party have a legal department, or does it refer the matter to external attorneys?
- What is their reaction time?
- Does the other party require using their own contract model?
- How sophisticated or detail-oriented are they?

All of these topics are important in a deal-making process.

Discussions Without NDAs

It is essential to carefully evaluate when to use NDAs. In some cases, such as preliminary discussions, it may be more appropriate to rely on other disclosure strategies.

Generally speaking, a corporation wishing to attract investment, clients, or partners should aim at advancing discussions as much as possible before requesting its potential partner to sign an NDA. Exceptions exist, including, per example, when a corporation's decision to seek licensees constitutes itself confidential information.

Professionally managed corporations, appropriately, seek to limit as much as possible the number and extent of their legal obligations towards third parties for a number of reasons. *First*, there is the need to avoid creating legal obligations in situations where there is not a clear consideration or benefit. *Second*, the complexity of administrating these obligations must be considered. A grey zone is created whenever information disclosure under a broad NDA does not indicate and segregate confidential information from general purpose or public information.

Fundraising or licensing-out efforts offer an ideal viewpoint to the complexity and limitations of NDAs, especially for an early-stage company. In an era where ideas and technologies are considered commodities, investors, especially venture capital (VC) firms or private equity firms, often enforce a policy of not signing NDAs. These policies are supported by the need for an investor not to limit its ability to operate efficiently. Any investor active in a particular sector typically reviews a plurality of investment opportunities, with overlap in markets served, product offerings, and general technology use. Receiving confidential information under an NDA that relates to a certain market (e.g. battery cathodes) would impede the ability of this investor to assess other investment opportunities in the same market or in related markets, unless the NDA specifically allows the investor to use confidential information when assessing other opportunities. This creates a circular argument, since an NDA allowing the recipient to use confidential information in contexts other than a discussion with the disclosing party deprives the NDA of much of its usefulness for the disclosing party.

For similar reasons, large corporations receiving business opportunities including unsolicited licensing-out proposals often avoid signing NDAs or confirming confidentiality obligations, notably in email communications. Such corporations would typically only confirm receipt of information that is in the public domain, including published patents. As an example, Apple and Microsoft both enforce policies of not accepting unsolicited proposals for ideas, products, or services.

A second argument raised by professional investors relates to the very nature of their activity, based on trust, protecting their own information, and not disclosing confidential information of other parties.

Disclosures to banks and advisory firms follow the same logic. It should be noted, however, that officers and managers of financial institutions with qualifications as attorneys or accountants are bound by extensive confidentiality obligations pursuant to their professional association policies, national regulations, and statutes. Such obligation would typically extend to client and other third-party information held by their employer.

Use of a Memorandum of Understanding (MOU)

A good practice is to include confidentiality obligations in a memorandum of understanding (MOU) or agreements of a similar nature, which defines the relationship between parties and their respective objective, during discussion of a business nature. Alternatively, parties can enter an MOU after signature of the NDA.

When the parties have clarified their respective and common intent and objectives by sharing of non-confidential information, an MOU would help to define general terms and principles by which the parties will abide during negotiation and after, in either the case of a transaction or should discussion abort. The MOU would define the terms, principles, rights, and obligations set forth which shall constitute formal conditions and guidelines during the relationship between the parties, in general or with reference to a specific project.

With respect to business secrets, the MOU should include what each party considers to be its upstream or background IP (BIP)—held prior to the entry into force of this agreement, or acquired or developed independently of the project during this agreement, as opposed to the downstream, foreground or forward IP (FIP)—

comprising information created, developed, or acquired by a party during and within the frame of project covered by the MOU. FIP excludes all BIP. This construction greatly helps clarifying which information is excluded from the definition of confidentiality obligations under the exclusions discussed above.

Common Hurdles in the Use of NDAs

A frequent drawback of NDAs is that they may provide a false sense of security. An obvious case involves a corporation acting in bad faith, which will use the pretext of discussions under an NDA to obtain business secrets which it could not have otherwise accessed. The disclosing party, in such a case, may not be aware of any unauthorized uses until the recipient party launches a competing product on the market. When infringement of confidentiality obligations becomes known to the disclosing party, enforcement of the NDA can enter the legal arena. Litigation is too often a dice game for start-ups, inventors, and small corporations, and success of a disclosing party depends on its capacity to fund litigation from its free cash flow or with assistance of a lender, investor, a partner, or a law firm acting under success fee.

In any case, an IP owner, no matter how difficult its situation, should refrain from disclosing information in any situations exempt of trust. Unfortunately, this is easier said than done.

In most cases, however, difficulty to properly protect business secrets disclosed under an NDA arises from a combination of two mutually reinforcing factors:

1. A disclosure in absence of bad faith from the recipient, such as disclosure by an employee not aware of who owns the information or of existence of restrictions on its use, and
2. A difficulty to properly manage information disclosure after execution of an NDA.

Three situations are examined below.

Purpose-specific disclosure. The NDA must clearly specify which information can be used, for which purpose, and by whom. Template NDAs often lack clarity about what action a recipient of information can perform with the confidential information. The NDA must specify the purpose and the context of disclosure and be specific and limitative about the authorized uses by the recipient of information. For example, in the pharmaceutical industry, use of a business secret must be limited to specific purposes such as a research collaboration or clinical trials where some identified information can be shared with external researchers.

Difficulty in establishing proof of non-authorized use. This makes NDA less relevant in many contexts, where proof of infringement is difficult or impossible. For example, it may be impossible or very difficult to document unauthorized use of information related to source code or to formula or process in the chemical industry, since such information would be used and modified by the recipient party in the context of its own confidential processes.

Non-segregation of confidential information. Confidential information may be disclosed under a NDA but not segregated from information subject to exclusions from the definition of confidential information. In other words, confidential information is often disclosed together with non-confidential information, in the same document, page or phrase. This creates uncertainty as to the confidentiality nature of information and opens the door to far-reaching use of exclusion from confidential information definition in the NDA. The most common such exclusions include information independently developed, developed by recipient prior to disclosure, or in the public domain (in combined or separated form). For example, a vast majority of business plans include confidential information (pro forma financial statement, product and market strategy, IP strategy, list of clients, list of suppliers, etc.) combined with information of a public nature or already known by the recipient (comparative description of products, product performance metrics, data on industry size, and annual growth).

Exception to Confidential Information: Independently Developed Information

Independently developed information refers to knowledge or technology that has been developed by one party without using the confidential information of another party. It is crucial to establish clear boundaries and definitions to protect both parties' rights in an NDA and to ensure fair usage of independently developed information. It is essential to establish clear definitions and boundaries to avoid any potential disputes regarding the origin and ownership of such information.

Famously, information once disclosed cannot be undisclosed. It may be tempting then, for a recipient of information, to "fill the blanks" of its own information and claim prior knowledge.

Information subject to independently developed exception should be systematically identified (not disclosed but referred to). For example, such information may be listed in an appendix to an NDA. Ideally, such information is included in the identification of BIP, in an appendix to an MOU. In each case, such appendix could be regularly updated and bonified as a new FIP is developed, during the effective life of either the NDA or MOU.

Industry-Specific Examples of Confidential Information

While the basic structure of an NDA remains the same across industries, the specifics can vary based on the nature of the industry and the type of information being protected. The definition of confidential information in NDAs is crucial as it outlines what information is considered proprietary and protected. Here is an expanded, non-exhaustive look at what might be considered confidential in different industries:

Pharma/Biotech	Confidential information specific to the pharmaceutical industry includes proprietary formulas and processes used to create a drug; clinical trial data, patient data, efficiency data, and adverse event reports; research methodologies; regulatory strategies comprising plans and strategies for obtaining regulatory approval for drugs and terms related to compliance with specific regulations, such as the US Health Insurance Portability and Accountability Act (HIPAA)

(continued)

Pharma/Biotech	Confidential information specific to the pharmaceutical industry includes proprietary formulas and processes used to create a drug; clinical trial data, patient data, efficiency data, and adverse event reports; research methodologies; regulatory strategies comprising plans and strategies for obtaining regulatory approval for drugs and terms related to compliance with specific regulations, such as the US Health Insurance Portability and Accountability Act (HIPAA)
Oil/Gas, Energy, Chemical	Confidential information often relates to the technical and operational aspects of exploration, extraction, production, and distribution Examples include geological data; proprietary extraction methods; chemical formulas—specific formulas for chemical compounds or mixtures; geological data; environmental compliance including terms related to compliance with environmental regulations and the handling of sensitive environmental data
Electronics	In the electronics industry, confidential information often includes proprietary circuit designs, component designs, and product designs; manufacturing processes; supplier information—pricing, terms, and capabilities, FMEA results; and other reliability data
Software	In the software sector, confidential information often relates to the development and commercialization of software-based products and services: source code (code that developers write to create a software program; often the most critical asset) and compiled or executable code; algorithms—the specific computational procedures used in a software program; architectural diagrams showing the high-level structure of a software system, including the relationships between different components; personal data, including any data collected about customers, such as usage data, personal data, and payment data

Example of Restriction of Use

In the case of a product development project, use of confidential information can be restricted to disclosure of proprietary designs and manufacturing processes within a specific team, involved in the development of a new product and employed by selected contracting third parties for manufacturing, which team being subject to NDA and other organizational protection measures (see Sect. 4). The NDA would specify that this information can only be used for this purpose and not for any other activities.

In the case of an outsourced software development project, use of confidential information can be restricted to specific purposes, such as full stack development or development of specific functionalities using identified tools and languages. The use of any open-source software or part thereof by the contractor should be either prevented or automatically and systematically disclosed to the contracting entity, along with the relevant terms of licence covering such open-source code. This ensures that the use of open source does not inadvertently lead to the forced disclosure of proprietary code, sometimes publicly shared but with limitations of rights. For reference, open-source licences are categorized into two primary categories: copyleft and permissive. Copyleft licences require that any derivative works based on the original open-source code must also be made available under the same licence. This means that any software that uses or modifies the original open-source code must also be open source. Examples of copyleft licences include the GNU General Public License (GPL) and the Mozilla Public License (MPL). Other types of non-free software licences include the Creative Commons (CC) licences, where restrictions apply to at least one of the following rights (whereas proprietary and secret software prohibits all of these, and open-source software allows all of them):

1. Running the software without restrictions
2. Studying and modifying the software for one's own use
3. Redistributing the software
4. Modifying and publishing improvements

In contrast, proprietary and secret software prohibits all of these, and open-source software allows all of them.

Practically, Creative Commons software licences fall under one of the following cases (all prohibiting commercial use):

NC	Non-commercial
CC BY-NC	Attribution by name author
CC BY-NC-SA	Attribution + share alike = disclose as is
CC BY-NC-ND	Attribution—no derivatives

Disclosure Processes During Deal-Making

Use of Protection Measures

Prior to or during the earliest phases of discussing a possible business transaction with another party, corporations and other IP holders must implement effective protection measures for their business secrets. These measures can be categorized into technological and physical protection, organizational good practices, and legal protection (see details in Sect. 4):

- *Technological and physical protection measures:* involve securing digital assets, physical premises, and equipment. Examples include encrypted databases, robust cybersecurity measures, secure manufacturing facilities, access controls, and surveillance systems. These measures ensure that business secrets are protected from unauthorized access and accidental disclosure.
- *Organizational good practices*: involve the implementation of internal policies and procedures to manage and protect business secrets. These practices can include trade secret management policies, secrets inventories, regular audits, and employee training programs. By establishing clear guidelines and ensuring systematic compliance, corporations can effectively succeed at protecting their business secrets.

- *Legal protection measures*: involve the use of legal instruments such as non-disclosure agreements (NDAs), the acknowledgment of disclosure receipt by recipient parties, the insertion of non-disclosure obligations in employment agreements and service agreements, and the registration of copyrights to safeguard business secrets. Specific patent filing strategies not involving publication, may also be used.

Use of Business Secrets in License Agreements

License agreements for the use of technologies almost always involve the disclosure of confidential information, enabling the recipient party to effectively implemented the licensed rights. In the media industry, licensed intellectual property (IP) rights are often publicly known or intended for broadcast or public presentation, and confidentiality obligations of recipient party are more easily delineated. As discussed above, the disclosure of business secrets during negotiation of license agreements is a delicate process that requires a careful balance between sharing enough information for the deal to proceed and protecting the business secrets from misuse.

In terms of legal protection measure implemented in a license agreement, the owner of the industrial business secrets (in this case, know-how) would negotiate terms regarding how the business secrets can be used. By way of example, this could include:

Scope of use	The agreement might delineate some specifications as to what data, equipment or processes the licensee is permitted to use, and in what context. For example, the licensee might be permitted to use a specific manufacturing process to produce a specific product only
Training and support	The agreement might include terms on training and support, especially if the licensee needs to be trained to use the know-how and any related equipment or to carry out the manufacturing process effectively. This could involve training sessions, manuals, or ongoing technical support
Duration	The agreement must specify the duration of the licence. After this period, the licensee would no longer be permitted to use the industrial know-how, unless the agreement is renewed
Improvements	The licensing agreement might also include terms on the handling of improvements or modifications to the process or product manufactured, by recipient, its contractors, licensees and clients

Use of Business Secrets in M&A

In mergers and acquisitions transactions (M&A), a critical part of the due diligence process concerns the validation of existence of business secrets. The acquiring company would be interested in understanding the value of the business secrets, how they contribute to the company's competitive advantage, their nature, extent, use, dissemination, and how they are protected.

The due diligence would focus notably on validating that business secrets are genuinely "secret", have not been disclosed, or disclosed in a controlled manner, nor used without authorization. The acquiring company would want to know how the industrial know-how is protected. This could involve obtaining detailed information about physical security measures, access controls, and legal measures such as non-disclosure agreements.

Due diligence on business secrets is most exhaustive in the case of smaller size M&A or acquisition of a single or of a small number of business units. The idea is that due diligence of intangibles and business secrets covering reasonable validation of existence, usefulness, completeness, and accessibility of the secrets can only be performed on a finite number of technologies and IP rights, given time and resource constraints to complete a deal, whereof the acquirer relies on contractual representations and warranties of the selling parties (discussed in following Sect. 5.2).

In the case of larger mergers, scale of operations as well as complexity gets in the way, and due diligence focuses on and is often limited to financial, sales and distribution elements. The focus on obtaining regulatory anti-trust clearance, and the speed of execution, means that business secrets are rarely assessed completely prior to the execution of the M&A transaction.

In the case of industrial know-how, for example, due diligence would include assessing the efficiency of the manufacturing processes, the condition and capabilities of the assets and equipment, and the skills and expertise of the key personnel. Ideally, the acquiring company would assess the impact of acquiring the industrial know-how on the merged or acquired entity. This could involve considering how the know-how would fit into the existing operations and whether it would provide a competitive advantage.

7.3 Contractual Representations and Warranties

In addition to negotiation and disclosure strategies, contractual representations and warranties are pivotal in addressing issues related to business secrets in the context of licensing agreements and mergers and acquisitions (M&A) transactions. The provisions serve as legally binding assurances regarding the existence, completeness, accessibility, and security of business secrets, ensuring all parties to the agreement are aligned on their obligations and expectations.

General Considerations

Representations and warranties are contractual statements made by one party to another in the context of a business transaction. Representations and warranties cover notably factual elements whose existence and completeness are a pre-requisite to a licensor or buyer entering a business deal. With respect to business secrets, these statements typically include:

- *Existence*: the business secrets exist and are properly documented
- *Completeness*: the business secrets encompass all information needed and no undisclosed information is necessary for the intended purpose
- *Accessibility*: the business secrets can be effectively accessed and utilized by the appropriate parties

- *Usefulness*: the business secrets serve their intended purpose (and confer a competitive advantage).
- *Security*: appropriate measures (physical, organizational, legal) are and have been maintained at all times to protect the confidential nature of business secrets; this generally mentions that no business secrets were disclosed to third parties outside the scope of an NDA or CDA (confidential disclosure agreement) and that the list of any such disclosure is available (including the intended recipient, copy of the NDA or CDA, and detail of the date, format, and content of disclosures).

Confidentiality Representations

Confidentiality is fundamental to business secrets management. Therefore, confidentiality should be addressed in detail in the contractual documentation of any transaction, preferably in a distinct section or in the representations and warranties section of licensing and purchase agreement. Below are essential confidentiality representations with industry-specific examples and recommended documentation practices:

1. **Definition of confidential information**. At minima, the definition of "confidential information" should refer to any non-public information that is proprietary to the disclosing party. The definition can be expanded to comprise any information of a technical, business or financial nature, with illustrative items including per example, information related to intellectual property rights, business strategies, business projects, R&D projects, customers, pricing, data (financial, commercial, user-related), know-how and other trade secrets, etc. The definition can be augmented by mentioning information specific to the concerned sector of activities, for example in the AI sector, proprietary algorithms, training datasets, and machine learning models. In the cloud computing sector, the definition may include infrastructure details, specifications of customized customer software, service configuration data, and customer data.
2. **Obligation to maintain confidentiality**. Typically, the recipient party agrees to an obligation to protect confidential information, not to disclose it to unauthorized parties, maintain in secrecy, and not to use, expect for the defined intended use. Such an obligation often survives termination of the agreement, and the duration of such obligations can be set in reference to the planned useful life of the confidential information. Obligations concerning personal data would be maintained in the manner and for the duration prescribed in applicable laws.[88]

[88] Illustrative examples of laws relevant to personal data include GDPR (General Data Protection Regulation)—EU; CCPA/CPRA (California Consumer Privacy Act / California Privacy Rights Act)—USA; HIPAA (Health Insurance Portability and Accountability Act)—USA; PIPEDA (Personal Information Protection and Electronic Documents Act)—Canada; LGPD (Lei Geral de Proteção de Dados)—Brazil; APPI (Act on the Protection of Personal Information)—Japan; and Data Protection Laws in China (PIPL—Personal Information Protection Law)—PRC.

3. **Exceptions to confidentiality.** The confidentiality obligation typically includes certain exceptions, such as information that is publicly available, independently developed, or required to be disclosed by law or court order. In the life sciences sector, for instance, a company might not be required to keep a process confidential once it becomes publicly available through publication in a scientific journal or publication of a patent application.
4. **Measures to ensure confidentiality**. Parties must adopt reasonable measures to protect confidential information, such as implementing access controls, physical and digital security protocols, and employee and contractor awareness programs. For example, a biotech company or CRO (contract research organization) might implement strict access controls and encryption to protect information related to proprietary drug formulas or manufacturing processes.
5. **Breach of confidentiality**. If a confidentiality obligation is breached, the responsible party may be liable for damages, and the agreement may specify additional remedies, per example a one-time financial penalty for each event, and/or a financial penalty for each day that the recipient of information is in breach.
6. **Documentation**. Parties may be required to document compliance with confidentiality obligations during or at termination of the agreement, including records of who accessed confidential information, when, and under what security protocols. For example, a software company might maintain access logs to monitor service access, source code usage, and use of download or print functions.

Representations and Warranties Related to Business Secrets

Representations and warranties provisions are crucial elements in licensing agreements and mergers and acquisitions transactions. They provide assurances about the state of the business, the validity of the business secrets, and the rights of the parties involved.

In a licensing agreement, the licensor provides assurances about the business secrets being licensed. In an M&A deal, the seller provides assurances about the business and the business secrets being acquired. Key representations and warranties related to business secrets include:

Identification	Business secrets are often identified in contractual agreements as part of the definition of trade secrets or intellectual property. A good practice is to provide an inventory of business secrets relevant to the transaction, in a distinct appendix to the license agreement. The inventory does not disclose the secret in detail, but can include information such as referenced name, project name, function performed, list of related patents and other IPR, and reference about control or location of the business secrets, including location information (physical or digital), the department, and officer responsible for the project
Ownership	The party disclosing the business secrets (licensor or seller) typically represents and warrants that it has full ownership and the legal right to disclose the information and confer the rights stated in the agreement

(continued)

Identification	Business secrets are often identified in contractual agreements as part of the definition of trade secrets or intellectual property. A good practice is to provide an inventory of business secrets relevant to the transaction, in a distinct appendix to the license agreement. The inventory does not disclose the secret in detail, but can include information such as referenced name, project name, function performed, list of related patents and other IPR, and reference about control or location of the business secrets, including location information (physical or digital), the department, and officer responsible for the project
Ownership	The party disclosing the business secrets (licensor or seller) typically represents and warrants that it has full ownership and the legal right to disclose the information and confer the rights stated in the agreement
Validity	The disclosing party often represents that the business secrets, such as proprietary technology or process, are operational and function as described
Non-infringement	The disclosing party typically warrants that the business secrets do not infringe upon third-party intellectual property rights, ensuring that the recipient's use of the secrets will not result in IP violations
Confidentiality	A representation that the disclosing party has maintained confidentiality of the business secrets and has not disclosed them to any unauthorized third parties
Compliance with Laws	The disclosing party typically warrants that development and use of business secrets comply with applicable laws and regulations, such as IP laws, data privacy, and cybersecurity standards
Absence of liens and encumbrances	The disclosing party represents and warrants that the business secrets are free of legal claims or liens that might restrict the rights being transferred
Accuracy of information	The disclosing party warrants that all information provided about business secrets is accurate and complete. This includes any information provided during the early phase of negotiation under NDA or CDA, and during the transaction due diligence process
No breach of contract	The disclosing party often represents disclosing business secrets or granting rights over business secrets under the agreement does not violate other contractual obligations. Exceptions, if any, must be documented, generally in appendix to the agreement. Licensor or seller must validate compliance to these representations beforehand, especially in complex cases, such as when a technology originates from collaborative research, was developed with governmental aids, or includes third-party sub-systems sourced under exclusive or quasi-exclusive commercial rights

Industry-Specific Examples of Representation and Warranties

Specific representations and warranties provisions are typically drafted for commercial agreements, depending on the unique nature of business secrets and usage across sectors. Below are illustrative examples of how representations and warranties can be adapted across key industries.

Pharma industry	The pharmaceutical industry's representations and warranties are often extensive, focusing on proprietary drug formulas, clinical trial data, regulatory compliance, and intellectual property (IP) ownership. Key representations may include: • *Validity and completeness of drug formulas*: representations that the drug formulas are accurate, have been adequately documented, contain only referenced components, have a known MOA (mode of action). • *Accuracy and completeness of clinical trial data*: all clinical data obtained from the clinical investigator (submitted to regulators or not) are complete, are accurate, and were obtained in compliance with approved protocols. These representations cover preclinical safety and efficacy, clinical efficacy, adverse event reporting, and other essential data points. • *Regulatory compliance*: warranties addressing compliance with relevant health authorities (e.g. FDA, EMA) and certifying that all regulatory requirements for drug approvals, manufacturing, and marketing are met. For example, the seller may confirm that good manufacturing practices (GMP) and good clinical practices (GCP) standards are observed throughout its processes
Oil and gas, mining	In the extractive industries, representations and warranties typically focus on proprietary production methods, compliance with environmental and safety regulations, and technology rights, addressing specific challenges and risks tied to high-value resources and processes. Examples include: • *Proprietary extraction and production techniques*: extraction methods and chemical formulas are effective, documented, and compliant with environmental and safety standards. The seller may also warrant those proprietary processes for drilling, refining, or chemical synthesis that meet or exceed regulatory expectations • *Environmental compliance and safety standards*: all business activities are compliant with relevant environmental laws, health and safety regulations, and industry-specific standards (e.g. EPA standards in the USA, REACH in the EU). This also includes topics such as waste management, emissions control, and worker safety protocols • *Contractual assurances on supply and production contracts*: long term and spot supply contracts with customers, distributors, and partners are active, enforceable, and disclosed
Electronics	In the electronics industry, representations and warranties often focus on proprietary design and manufacturing processes, compliance with industry standards, and planned product updates or upgrades. Typical representations and warranties include: • *Existence and usefulness of proprietary designs*: all proprietary designs (e.g. for hardware, circuit layouts, or software integration) are fully documented, functional, and ready for manufacturing • *Compliance with industry standards and certification*: all electronic components, products, and processes comply with regulatory and industry

(continued)

	standards (e.g. CE marking, RoHS, FCC). This may include assurances on safety standards, emissions control, and electrical certifications • *Commitment to future updates and upgrades*: for products requiring ongoing development or support, the seller may warrant that it will provide updates or upgrades as per customer agreements or industry expectations • *IP ownership and supplier relationships*: representations confirming that the IP underlying product designs is owned by the seller and that critical supplier relationships are disclosed, active, and transferable
Software and AI	Software-related representations and warranties often relate to the completeness and functionality of source code, compiled code, documentation, IP rights, absence of defects, and compliance with industry standards, such as data privacy regulations. Typical assurances may include: • *Completeness and documentation of source code*: the software's source code is complete, is fully documented, and can be understood and maintained by technical staff. This may include representations about coding practices, quality assurance processes, use of open-source code, and testing documentation. • *Functionality and absence of bugs or defects*: the software functions as intended and is free from known bugs, malware, or other defects that would impede performance. This assurance often includes a description of any known issues or limitations. • *Compliance with data privacy and cybersecurity standards*: The software complies with data privacy laws (e.g. GDPR, CCPA) and cybersecurity best practices, including assurances about data encryption, access controls, and regular security audits • *AI, performance and validity of AI models*: the AI models function as described, meet performance benchmarks, and have been tested under varied conditions. The seller may provide warranties on the accuracy and reliability of the models' outputs • *AI, assurance of ethical use*: given the evolving ethical standards around AI, sellers may be required to disclose and warrant compliance with AI ethics guidelines, ensuring transparency in model design and deployment practices
Cloud computing industry	In cloud computing, representations and warranties typically include commitments regarding service reliability, data security measures, compliance with data protection laws, and IP ownership. Common examples include: • *Reliability and uptime guarantees*: warranties specifying service uptime, performance levels, and maintenance schedules and history of past issues if any. These assurances typically set minimum standards, such as 99.9% uptime, and detail remedies if standards are not met

(continued)

	• *Data security and privacy compliance*: security protocols meet or exceed industry standards (e.g. SOC 2, ISO 27001) and that customer data is handled in compliance with data protection regulations. Warranties may include assurances about encryption, intrusion detection, and data redundancy • *Compliance with cybersecurity standards*: warranties of adherence to specific cybersecurity frameworks to prevent data breaches and unauthorized access

Contractual Strategies to Protect Business Secrets

Victor De Leon and John Williamson

Abstract

In this chapter we consider the contractual protections a company can adopt to effectively protect its business secrets, which include but are not limited to trade secrets and sensitive information.

As a practical matter, in order to leverage the value of confidential business information, the information must be shared with others—employees, partners, suppliers, customers. There is no way to reap the benefits of valuable confidential information if that information is merely locked away in a vault for no one to see or learn or use.

Protecting confidential business information through contract is a ubiquitous practice. Those who share or receive confidential information in their day-to-day responsibilities are no doubt familiar with non-disclosure agreements. Sometimes the use of such agreements becomes so commonplace that little thought may be given to the strategic implications of the agreements. But recent developments in law and policy suggest that owners of confidential business information should carefully evaluate their contractual protection strategies. Specifically, the fundamentals regarding contractual protections in the context of disclosures to employees, other entities, and even end consumers can be evaluated and considered as part of an overall strategy to protect business information through the use of contracts.

In this chapter we consider the contractual protections in three contexts, when sharing (1) with employees, (2) with external entities, and (3) with end customers.

V. De Leon
Manila, Philippines
e-mail: vnlllb@gmail.com

J. Williamson (✉)
Washington, DC, USA
e-mail: john.williamson@finnegan.com

P. Ollivier et al. (eds.), *Business Secrets Management*, Management for Professionals, https://doi.org/10.1007/978-3-031-82512-5_6

1 Introduction

Without strong contractual protections, a company will be unable to effectively protect its business secrets, a subset of confidential business information further addressed here. As a practical matter, in order to leverage the value of confidential business information, the information must be shared with others—employees, partners, suppliers, customers. There is no way to reap the benefits of valuable confidential information if that information is merely locked away in a vault for no one to see or learn or use. If a company develops a new manufacturing process, for example, it must be shared with employees on the manufacturing line or with manufacturing partners so that the efficiencies can actually be practiced and realised. But once the confidential information is shared with others, what prevents them from accessing the information and disclosing it the information publicly, or using the information for their own benefit? Contracts serve as the primary vehicle to protect confidential information in such circumstances.

A duty of confidence is the foundation of all legal protections for confidential information that is deliberately shared with others. That duty can be implied in certain circumstances. For instance, a duty of confidence might arise between two parties that owe fiduciary duties to one another. Or such a duty might arise between an employer and employee. But more often than not, owners of confidential business information prefer to use contracts to clearly and unequivocally create a duty of confidence and define the contours of that duty.

The use of contracts to protect confidential business information brings countless benefits over reliance on only implied legal duties of confidence. For one, some courts that have evaluated the issue refuse to recognise information as confidential and refuse to recognise information as a trade secret under the law, if it is shared without the protections afforded by contracts. Moreover, when contracts are used, parties can exercise control, clearly delineating their understandings, rights, and obligations concerning the specific information at issue. Finally, traditional legal doctrines and implied duties may not be well suited to address ownership, control, and responsibility for information in the context of new and emerging technologies, AI in particular. In uncharted and developing areas, contractual protections give parties more comfort and certainty than leaving the matter to traditional legal doctrines.

For these and other reasons, protecting confidential business information through contract is a ubiquitous practice. Those who share or receive confidential information in their day-to-day responsibilities are no doubt familiar with non-disclosure agreements. Sometimes the use of such agreements becomes so commonplace that little thought may be given to the strategic implications of the agreements. But recent developments in law and policy suggest that owners of confidential business information should carefully evaluate their contractual protection strategies. Specifically, the fundamentals regarding contractual protections in the context of disclosures to employees, other entities, and even end consumers can be evaluated and considered as part of an overall strategy to protect business information through the use of contracts.

In this chapter's next sections, we consider these three contexts:

1. Sharing with employees.
2. Sharing with entities.
3. Sharing with end consumers.

2 Contracts with Employees

2.1 Dealing with Employees and Confidential Information

As discussed in this book's previous chapters, company confidential information is likely to cross the desks of employees in nearly every function of the business. Whether in administration, finance, accounting, business development, marketing, management, research and development, human resources, legal, information technology, or any other job, employees will be trusted to handle company confidential information of all types. And many employees will develop and generate new company confidential information as part of their job responsibilities.

While employee exposure to company confidential information has always created a risk of leakage or misuse of information, those risks are heightened in an era of remote work, increased employee mobility, decreased employee loyalty, and the proliferation of technologies that make copying and transferring information seamless.

Theft of company confidential information by departing employees is on the rise, and many companies are revisiting their employee training, culture building, and physical and virtual security systems in light of such trends. But while practical security tools and training are important, it is the employment agreement that forms the core of any strategy to protect company confidential information in the hands of employees, both during and after employment.

Contracts between the employer and employee may contain a number of provisions designed to protect company confidential information, including:

1. Non-disclosure and use restrictions during and after employment,
2. Training requirements and policies regarding handling of confidential information,
3. Ownership of new confidential information developed during the course of employment,
4. Non-solicitation after separation of employment, and
5. Non-competition after separation of employment.

2.2 The General Employee NDA and Associated Confidentiality Policies

The most important and effective of these provisions is the non-disclosure and non-use obligation. Here the employment contract explicitly defines what constitutes the company's "confidential information" and explicitly sets forth the employee's obligations to protect such information. As a general matter, those obligations preclude the employee from disclosing "confidential information" outside of the company, or to anyone who is not under a duty to protect the confidentiality of the information. To the extent that an employee's role involves outside disclosures (e.g., M&A, joint research and development, etc.) protocols are identified for making such disclosures or obtaining management approvals. Similarly, the obligations typically require that employees may only use company "confidential information" for purposes of performing their job responsibilities. Because many courts recognise that such restrictions are necessary to protect legitimate business interests, the provisions tend to be broad in scope. Often the obligations will have no geographic limitations and will not expire unless and until the information at issue becomes publicly known. While courts are hostile to provisions that would restrict an employee from using general skills and knowledge in future endeavours, with that caveat most courts will enforce broad non-disclosure and non-use provisions. While relatively straightforward in concept, these basic obligations can be hotly disputed when employees depart for their next job, often with a competitor.

Disputes tend to centre on the scope of the defined "confidential information" as well as on the practices and policies of the company. For example, if in practice a company marks certain documents with a "CONFIDENTIAL" legend, or otherwise segregates or restricts access to certain information, employees may incorrectly believe that any information not so marked or segregated—even if it might fall within the contractual definition of "confidential information"—would be free for the taking. Regular training programs and policies therefore become important to correct such misunderstandings. Companies may adopt specific information handling policies or tiered structures that require marking certain information "CONFIDENTIAL" or segregating certain information for specific sensitive projects or personnel, all while preserving the confidentiality of other company information that does not fall, for example, in the highest tier of confidentiality. Policies with tiered structures that provide examples of information that falls within each tier (e.g., highly confidential, confidential, sensitive, and public) and outline specific obligations that apply to each tier are becoming common (see also Chap. 5 "Protecting Business Secrets to Improve Value Creation" of this book for more details). But employees need to know and understand the practices and policies. Absent training programs or policy manuals that explain how and why the company handles different types of confidential information in different ways, misunderstandings may become commonplace. If that happens, employees may be more likely to walk out the door with confidential information (and courts may be more likely to interpret the contractual "confidential information" definition in the NDA narrowly in light of customs, practices, and course of performance).

The scope of the definition of "confidential information" is also sometimes the source of confusion and disputes. Companies have every incentive to define "confidential information" as broadly as possible so that the non-use and non-disclosure restrictions will protect all company information in the case of a departing employee. But casting the net too wide comes with risk. This is because employees are entitled to use their general knowledge, skill, or facility in future employment. Accordingly, to the extent that the definition of "confidential information" extends to cover public information or general knowledge, the provision might be invalidated in a legal action. Similarly, statutes in certain jurisdictions dictate that employees may disclose trade secrets and confidential information for specific reasons and in specific contexts (for instance, to report a violation of law). These statutes are colloquially known as "whistleblower" protection provisions, and failure to account for such statutes can also result in the loss of rights for the employer. Because the law generally seeks to strike a balance between protecting legitimate business interests in the confidentiality of information on the one hand, and an employee's right to use general skills and knowledge on the other hand, many companies are carefully revisiting the scope of their definitions of "confidential information"—explicitly including carve outs that recognise employee rights and statutory provisions—so as to avoid invalidation of the NDA agreements or loss of other legal rights.

2.3 Contracts Addressing Ownership in the Employment Context

A thorough contractual strategy for protecting a company's confidential information requires consideration of ownership of confidential information that is developed by employees of the company. Typically, employers require employees to assign all right, title, and interest in any inventions and other work product that is related to the employer's business and is derived by the employee while working and while using the employer's resources. Without such a provision, it is possible that ownership of newly developed confidential intellectual property and inventions might vest with the employee, not the employer. Similar to the situation with employee NDAs, assignment and ownership provisions are highly jurisdiction specific. In many jurisdictions, for example, additional compensation may be due to the employee in exchange for the assignment. Similarly, certain jurisdictions may have statutes that preclude assignment of certain types of information or require specific notices to be provided to employees as part of the execution of any assignment provisions. So just as with NDAs, assignment and ownership provisions must be carefully crafted to conform to the laws of the local jurisdiction where the employment contract will be implemented.

2.4 Restrictive Covenants That Protect Confidential Information

Although the primary contractual strategies in the employment context centre on non-disclosure, non-use, and ownership as discussed above, companies may also implement restrictive covenants—restricting an employee's behaviour post-employment—that might, as a practical matter, further bolster protections for company confidential information. Generally speaking, restrictive covenants are heavily scrutinised by courts, disfavoured in some respects, and outright banned in certain jurisdictions. To the extent that they are enforceable, restrictive covenants must be directed to protect only legitimate business interests, must be narrowly tailored so they do not unduly burden employees, and must not harm the public. Three often used restrictive covenants are:

1. No-hire provision,
2. Non-solicitation provision,
3. Non-compete provision.

The no-hire provision generally prevents former employees from seeking to recruit or hire away their former colleagues on behalf of their new employer. Such provisions may help to prevent departing employees from targeting others in the company who have access to trade secrets, confidential information, or unique client relationships. These are all recognised as legitimate business interests that may be protected by a properly tailored no-hire provision. As a practical matter, no-hire provisions may also help prevent the type of *en masse* departure where many key employees resign and join a competitor all within a short time frame. While protecting against massive departures might not, by itself, stand as a legitimate business interest, it is worth noting that many disputes concerning misappropriation of company trade secrets and confidential information involve *en masse* departures. Measures designed to discourage such departures, therefore, will also limit risk of misuse or misappropriation of company confidential information. In order to achieve such benefits, however, even in jurisdictions that will consider enforcing no-hire provisions, it would be prudent to include narrowly tailored limitations in geographic scope, limitations in time, and limitations as to the type of employees subject to the provision to help in demonstrating the reasonableness of the provision.

Non-solicitation and non-compete provisions are typically more disfavoured by courts than no-hire provisions. These provisions prohibit departing employees from soliciting the company's customers for business or from joining a competing firm. Because such provisions sharply limit an employee's ability to use general knowledge, skills, and facilities in a subsequent job (or event to hold a subsequent job altogether), many jurisdictions refuse to enforce these types of restrictive covenants. In the United States, for example, the 50 states are split as to whether, and under what conditions, non-compete agreements may be enforced. The U.S. Federal Trade Commission is now weighing in on this split, proposing rules that would invalidate all non-compete agreements in the U.S., even in states that have long recognised and enforced such agreements. Accordingly, while non-solicitation and non-compete agreements have served as a powerful and effective contractual strategy to protect company confidential information in the employment context, companies should not rely on such agreements alone given the uncertainty and widespread disfavour in the current climate.

Takeaways

General Employee NDAs

While the nuances of the scope of the non-disclosure and non-use provisions in the employment contract will be subject to local law and interpretations, the bottom line remains that this provision is the foundation of the protection of the company's confidential information in the context of the employment relationship. Without an express non-disclosure and non-use provision covering the company's confidential information, in many jurisdictions a company will have little recourse in the event that employees depart with sensitive company information. Even trade secret rights might not be available to the company in such situations because many courts consider the use and enforcement of non-disclosure and non-use contracts to be something of a pre-requisite (a necessary "reasonable measure" to preserve confidentiality) when evaluating whether information should qualify as a trade secret under statutory or common law. For these reasons, implementation and management of a well-balanced non-disclosure and non-use provision is paramount to managing the company's "confidential information" in the employment context.

Ownership

Similar to the situation with employee NDAs, assignment and ownership provisions are highly jurisdiction specific, and compensation may be due to the employee in exchange for the assignment. Ownership by the company is a necessary step, but must be performed with care.

Restrictive Covenants

No-hire, non-solicitation, and non-compete provisions maybe available, but should always be used in combination with NDAs and ownership provisions and not as a substitute, given the risk that courts many find such clauses unenforceable.

For all of the above, the vital first stage must be a clear delineation and identification of confidential material. A regular review and refresh of such material is also likely to be a necessary part of "reasonable measures" to demonstrate that the employee was made aware of these policies and materials and was likewise "encouraged" by the organisation to act within the bounds defined in those policies.

3 Contracts with Entities

Just as is the case with disclosures of confidential information to employees, any deliberate disclosure of confidential information to another entity—for example a corporation, university, partnership, or government—places the continued confidentiality of the information at risk. Such disclosures should be made only where a duty of confidence is established, as in the employment context. Likewise, any disclosures should account for expectations regarding the permitted uses and ownership of the information and any new innovations or information derived through use of the disclosed confidential information.

3.1 Non-Disclosure Agreements

Non-disclosure agreements with other entities are commonplace in many commercial contexts. Joint R&D projects, grant applications, due diligence for potential acquisition, co-marketing arrangements, regulatory submissions, supply arrangements, and consulting projects are just a few examples where contractual clauses addressing non-disclosure and restricted use of information are routinely implemented. As a general matter, such contracts are regularly enforced by their terms given that such agreements are typically executed between commercial entities at arm's length and do not involve policy considerations regarding the ability of employees to maintain gainful employment in the future, as in the employment context. While such agreements can be highly complex, and often stand as one part of much larger and more significant commercial agreements and relationships, certain terms and issues arise frequently and warrant careful consideration.

The definition of "confidential information" in such agreements is critical. The benefits and burdens associated with the non-disclosure and restricted use provisions will turn on this definition. In commercial contexts, receiving parties typically demand a far more concrete and specific definition than that which may be found in other contexts. For instance, for a receiving party to agree that it will maintain certain information as confidential and will not use the information in its business, it may demand that such information be expressly marked with a particular legend when initially disclosed so that there can be no confusion as to whether any particular disclosure in the course of a commercial relationship triggers the non-disclosure and non-use burdens. Anything not marked with the agreed upon legend, therefore, will not restrict the receiving party in any way. The disclosing party, on the other hand, may attempt to achieve a more flexible definition of "confidential information" (e.g., information that is marked or should be understood to be confidential given the circumstances).

Just as important as the definition of "confidential information", parties to NDAs between entities should give due consideration to the required limitations and standard of care that must be exhibited for information that meets the definition. Typically, a disclosing party will articulate express restrictions on access, disclosure, and use of the information at issue. For instance, if information is disclosed during a due diligence the information may be provided in a restricted access "data room", where only specified individuals may access the information and where the use of the information is limited to a narrow evaluation of the technology or business under consideration. Or where information is disclosed as part of a consulting relationship, it may be limited to use in a specific laboratory or other physical location. A disclosing party will often articulate such technical and practical limitations in the

NDA so as to create an enforceable contractual obligation to support the technical and practical limitations. More generally, parties typically agree that any information disclosed in the course of the relationship may only be used for furthering the commercial purpose stated in the contract. Similarly, parties often require that a receiving party must generally exercise the same standard of care with the disclosing party's confidential information as the receiving party exercises with it is own information. While such general terms are useful, narrow and specific obligations (e.g., limitations to specific individuals or locations) tend to be more effective in maintaining confidence.

Temporal limitations regarding the burdens associated with protecting confidential information are particularly important when negotiating an NDA between entities. Many entities will sharply resist unlimited perpetual confidentiality obligations, instead insisting that the confidentiality obligations should have an expiration. For instance, a receiving party might prefer a rolling expiration (e.g., 3 years after any specific confidential information was first disclosed to it) or a triggering expiration event (e.g., 1 year after termination of the underlying commercial arrangement). As a practical matter, many NDAs between entities include an expiration on the confidentiality obligations as perpetual obligations can be difficult to manage and may derail an important commercial opportunity if the parties cannot reach a compromise on the temporal limitation. But with respect to trade secrets, a disclosing party should carefully consider the costs and benefits when agreeing upon an expiring confidentiality obligation. Once the obligation expires, a court is likely to determine that the disclosing party forfeits any protections under trade secret law as of the date of the expiration. Once the information is in the possession of another entity with no confidentiality obligations attached, the disclosing party will likely be deemed to have forgone the "reasonable measures" necessary to protect the information in confidence as of that date. Parties may try to navigate this tension by allowing confidentiality obligations to expire for most of the information disclosed in the course of a commercial relationship, but preserving the obligation as a perpetual one for specific information (e.g., a particularly valuable formula), to allow trade secret protection to continue for a subset of the information disclosed between the entities.

Whether, and to what extent, parties agree on temporal limitations for confidentiality obligations, in most situations a receiving party will desire to protect itself against having to bear the burdens associated with "confidential information" disclosed under the NDA once that information has become public through no fault of the receiving party. Similarly, a receiving party may want to be relieved of any non-disclosure or restricted use obligations in the event that the receiving party is able to independently develop the confidential information without reference to or use of any confidential information provided by the disclosing party. While details vary, such terms are often found in NDAs between entities.

Choice of law and choice of venue clauses are also often found in NDAs between entities. In some circumstances, such clauses might be simply imported from an entity's other standard commercial agreements. Parties should carefully consider the implications of the choice of law and choice of venue provisions in NDAs. While parties may be familiar with the particular contract interpretation and application principles in a certain jurisdiction, it is likely that if a dispute arises a court may elect to apply the selected law not only to the contractual aspects of the dispute but also any attendant trade secret disputes. Trade secret law can vary between jurisdictions in ways that may not be fully appreciated unless advance consideration is given to the choice of law. For instance, jurisdictions may vary significantly as to what types of remedies are available to a trade secret owner.

While there may be many other provisions and details in NDAs between entities, the particular provisions covered here tend to be addressed in typical NDAs. Given that legal actions for misappropriation and misuse of confidential information can result in a company being enjoined from even participating in the market, and can result in significant economic damages awards, the tension and negotiation over matters such as the definition of "confidential information", the specific limitations and standards of care, temporal restrictions, relieving conditions, and choice of law and venue should not be taken lightly, as the outcome of significant future disputes may turn on these terms.

3.2 Licence Agreements for Trade Secrets and Confidential Information

Like NDAs, licensing agreements are also commonplace in modern commercialised industries. In essence, a licensing agreement grants one entity (the licensee) the right to use, make, or sell the property of another entity (the licensor). Due to the number of intellectual property rights a licensing agreement can cover, it is important for the licensor to properly ascertain the specific subject matter of the licence agreement. Specifically in the context of trade secrets, licensing agreements see the licensor grant the licensee access to valuable confidential commercial information, with the licensee having the obligation to keep said information from public disclosure and, in some instances, pay a fee for the use or access to said information, commonly referred to as a "royalty".

Since licensing agreements are, in essence, contracts, they are subject to the rules of contract interpretation and enforcement, and must thus contain clear definitions, terms and conditions, and accurately delineate the boundaries between the licensor and the licensee. Some common clauses found in licensing agreements include the following:

1. The ever-important non-disclosure agreements and/or confidentiality clauses,
2. Warranties and representations regarding the ownership of the secrets and the licensee's recognition of such on the part of the licensor,
3. The licensor's explicit grant of permission to the licensee to use or assess said information,
4. Clauses governing quality control and the extent to which the licensee can access the trade secrets and confidential information given by the licensor,
5. Clauses stipulating the payment of royalties, if applicable,

6. Clauses governing export and distribution,
7. Termination and term limit clauses, and in cases of breach,
8. Indemnification and penalty clauses, and,
9. Conflict and alternative dispute resolution clauses.[1]

Furthermore, in the context of trade secrets, the manner in which the information is to be shared to the licensee should be embodied in the agreement.[2]

Provisions that are improper or are contrary to the law should be avoided in licence agreements. For example, some jurisdictions impose restrictions that could result in the decimation of a trade secret, such as restrictions regarding the amount of control the licensor has over the prices of goods under a licence.[3] Terms in a licence agreement that violate such restrictions could render "[...]the destruction of the trade secrets or a declaration that the licence is null and void".[4] It is important to note as well that a licence agreement should be carefully structured so as to limit the disclosure of any trade secret to a subcontractor.[5] Hence, to protect trade secrets, licence agreement provisions should be written with great caution regarding confidential information and should be compliant with existing laws.

When licensing agreements are maximised to their fullest potential, they present a mutually beneficial arrangement.

For the licensor, licensing agreements take advantage of the modern Specialisation of organisations and economies of scale by outsourcing processes like production and manufacturing to more capable, cost-efficient entities. The licensor is also able to generate licence-related revenue and can commercialise products and realise income from their trade secrets much faster.[6] For instance, a licensor that is not in a position to fully exploit the potential of its trade secrets due to budgetary or technological constraints may seek additional revenue and aid in exploiting said trade secret via a licensing agreement.[7] In some instances, licensing agreements may also have an indirect effect of reducing competition by turning possible competitors into licensees that are contractually bound not to disclose the information they gain access to.

For the licensee, the benefit lies in being given access to proven trade secrets and information without needing to conduct R&D to replicate the same.[8] The licensee is

[1] Joel W. Mohrman, "Capitalizing on Intellectual Property: An Introduction to Licensing," Brief 38, no. 2 (Winter 2009): 36–48.

[2] Arthur H. Seidel. What the General Practitioner Should Know about Trade Secrets and Employment Agreements (2).

[3] *Id.*

[4] *Id.*

[5] *Id.*

[6] Robert A. Schroeder, "Licensing of Rights to Intellectual Property," Albany Law Review 50, no. 3 (Spring 1986): 455–474. https://heinonline.org/HOL/P?h=hein.journals/albany50&i=476.

[7] *Id.*

[8] Richard P. Rozek, "Protection of Intellectual Property through Licensing: Efficiency Considerations," Journal of World Trade 22, no. 5 (1988): 27–34. https://heinonline.org/HOL/P?h=hein.kluwer/jwt0022&i=505.

also provided with a valuable asset to profit from and reduced uncertainty when it comes to production and testing.

Notwithstanding all the positives of licensing agreements, they do carry a certain amount of risk, depending on the situation. Necessarily, the execution of a licensing agreement carries with it the disclosure of trade secrets and confidential information to the licensee, and it is possible that the licensee, whether intentionally or not, discloses the same to the public or to a third party. While it is common for licensees to have the duty to safeguard confidential information granted to them even after the expiry of the period of the licensing agreement, other problems may arise, such as a possibility that the licensor loses control over the details of the exploitation of its trade secret, with possible problems in quality control and manufacturing.[9] In specific instances, it may also be possible that a licensee is constrained to continue paying royalties and fees for a trade secret even after the same has been disclosed to the public.[10] Though these problems are inherent in the concept, they could be solved, or at the very least, minimised, with a combination of airtight terminology and clause-writing in the licensing agreement and a consistent and effective quality control mechanism.

In some jurisdictions, such as the Philippines, private and public research and development institutes ("RDIs") that engage with a Government Funding Agency ("GFA") may seek protection of undisclosed information in their work by way of three guidelines:

1. Mechanisms for the protection of undisclosed information should be developed by RDIs and such protection will be at the institutional level;
2. The GFA should be informed in writing if the RDI believes that the IP should be protected solely as undisclosed information, where after review by the GFA, the RDI may not be obligated to file an application for protection; and,
3. Regular reports on IP that is protected as undisclosed information are to be submitted by the RDI to the GFA.[11]

In fact, protecting undisclosed information should be seen as a priority to the owner of such intellectual property as the law mandates "all disclosures of potential IPRs shall be covered by confidentiality agreements".[12] Confidential information will be kept from public disclosure until the RDI can file a national or international IPR application or when the RDI notifies the GFA allowing public disclosure. The purpose of this provision is to "ensure that any information pertaining to a potential IPR does not become part of prior art or prejudice the novelty of the national IPR

[9] Thomas M. Apke, "Acquisition and Licensing of Intellectual Property," Managerial Law 40, no. 6 (1998): 1–16.

[10] Robert A. Schroeder, *Licensing of Rights to Intellectual Property*, 50 ALB. L. REV. 455 (1986).

[11] Joint DOST-IPO Administrative Order No. 02-2010 The Implementing Rules and Regulations of Republic Act No. 10055, Rule 12.

[12] *Id.*

application [...] or the international application for IPR that the RDI may file in a foreign country or in such other IP authority".[13]

Takeaways
Several jurisdictions have recognised that the protection of business and trade secrets in licensing agreements is important in order to ensure the owner of such secrets may maintain their intellectual property rights and reserve the privilege to file national or international applications with IP authorities.

While greater public access to technology and innovation is necessary to further economic growth, there must be a balance between this policy and protecting the owner's intellectual property rights.

Hence, it is highly recommended to ensure that one's intellectual property rights are exercised even in light of an existing licensing agreement, in order to ensure the protection of commercial trade secrets. Awareness of laws that shield business secrets and confidential and/or undisclosed information, and implementing said laws in the business entity, is the key to avoiding breaches in protection of valuable business secrets.

4 Contracts with End User Customers

As a general matter once a product is launched in the market, any trade secrets that can be understood by inspection or study of the product are essentially extinguished. Trade secret law will not protect information that is publicly known or easily ascertainable from public sources. Reverse engineering of products that are available in the market is typically understood to be a proper means of discovering information from the public domain. That is not to say that all trade secrets associated with a product are necessarily extinguished once the product is publicly available. For instance, while the general design and components of a product might be ascertainable from inspection, manufacturing techniques or tolerances might not. Likewise, some products may be so complex that their characteristics cannot be understood by inspecting the product. But generally speaking, when a product is placed into the market some protection over the information about the product that was confidential before launch is necessarily forfeited.

In certain situations, however, a trade secret owner may try to use agreements with customers and end-users to protect trade secrets in information about a publicly launched product, even information that would be ascertainable by inspection of the product. Software is the primary example of such conduct. Software owners often licence their product to end-users, rather than sell it in the traditional sense (where title would pass to the customer). As part of these end-user software licence

[13] *Id.*

agreements, the software owner often contractually prohibits any decompiling or reverse engineering of the source code for the licensed software. Because the end-user would therefore have to violate a contract in order to perform the reverse engineering, such activity is not deemed proper for purposes of obtaining information about the product. Software owners employing this strategy can successfully maintain trade secret protection over their source code, despite that the code is contained in a launched product that likely could, as a technical matter, be reverse engineered.

Specialised equipment that is leased rather than sold may also contain similar provisions restricting the lessee from reverse engineering the product. Essentially, if the owner of the technology and product organises its business such that title to the product does not pass to the end-user, then arguably the end-user does not necessarily have the right to disassemble and study the product at issue. As long as the owner of the product includes appropriate restrictions on use, it is possible for an owner to preserve trade secret protections over aspects of the product that are otherwise discoverable through reverse engineering as a technical matter.

Similarly, in some industries the supply chain simply does not allow for a meaningful reverse engineering opportunity. For instance, medical devices that are designed to be implanted in a patient might be manufactured by the owner of the information, then provided to specialised distributors (who are contractually precluded from opening or inspecting the devices), then provided to physicians who surgically implant the devices. In such situations, there is no practical opportunity for inspection and reverse engineering, enabling the designer to maintain trade secret protections over the information about the devices, despite that the devices have been launched in the market.

Accordingly, in unique scenarios contractual provisions with end-users or distributors might enable an information owner to continue trade secret protections for products launched in the market.

Takeaways

Trade secret law will not protect information that is publicly known or easily ascertainable from public sources and hence as a general matter any trade secrets that can be understood by inspection or study of the product are essentially extinguished.

Routes to limit "reverse engineering" may be available to certain types of products and services, typically software-based where end-user licence agreements. This implies a change to traditional commercial model where an end-user is the owner to one where they become licensee or subscriber.

Dispute Strategies to Protect Business Secrets

Antonio Di Bernardo and Mattia Dalla Costa

Abstract

This chapter is about practical guidance on what to do in case you suspect that your business secret has been stolen, which can sometimes be a trade secret or a sensitive information; this guidance is on how to develop the pre-litigation strategy (i.e. what to do before starting any litigation) and the possible protection given by civil and criminal law.

No matter which protection measures you take, business secrets still can be stolen, e.g., by a hacker breaching your electronic protection measures or by an unfaithful/disgruntled employee having full access to manage these trade secrets. In either case you need to know what to do and which steps should be taken.

For both civil and criminal law this chapter evaluates the potential pros and cons of each of these legal remedies implementing protection measures to secure your business secrets. Protection measures are not only useful to safeguard your company's value but are also a pre-condition to obtain legal protection.

Many countries protect trade secrets through civil and criminal laws; this allows different strategies to be implemented by the IP manager.

A. Di Bernardo
THINX S.r.l., Milano, Italy
e-mail: a.dibernardo@thinx.expert

M. Dalla Costa (✉)
CBA Studio Legale, Padova - Milano, Italy
e-mail: mattia.dallacosta@cbalex.com

P. Ollivier et al. (eds.), *Business Secrets Management*, Management for Professionals, https://doi.org/10.1007/978-3-031-82512-5_7

1 Introduction

Implementing protection measures to secure your business secrets, as disclosed in Chap. 5, is not only useful to safeguard your company's value, but is also a pre-condition to obtain legal protection.

No matter which protection measures you take, business secrets still can be stolen, e.g., by a hacker breaching your electronic protection measures or by an unfaithful/disgruntled employee having full access to manage these trade secrets. In this case you need to know what to do and which steps should be taken.

Many countries protect trade secrets through civil and criminal laws; this allows different strategies to be implemented by the IP manager.

This chapter provides some hints on what to do in case you suspect that your trade secrets have been stolen:

1. Section 2 considers pre-litigation strategy, i.e., what to do before starting any litigation.
2. Section 3 considers the possible protection given by civil law, while
3. Section 4 considers criminal law.

For both civil and criminal law this chapter evaluates the potential pros and cons of each of these legal remedies.

In this comment, reference has sometimes been made to the Italian judicial system: Italy is in fact the EU country with the highest number of court cases relating to the misappropriation and infringement of trade secrets, because Italy, since Legislative Decree No. 198 of 19 March 1996 (thus 20 years before DIRECTIVE (EU) 2016/943 on trade secrets), has specific legislation to protect trade secrets and considers trade secrets as intellectual property rights with the same status and protection as, e.g., a patent or a registered trademark. Moreover, the vast majority of Italian proceedings concerning trade secrets are brought before a specialised IP court (92%).

According to the study made by the European Union Intellectual Property Office (EUIPO) in 2023 (TRADE SECRETS LITIGATION TRENDS IN THE EU for 2017–2022) after implementation of Directive (EU) 2016/943 on trade secrets, Italy is by far the country with the most litigation involving trade secrets (151 cases). The other European countries have less cases: for example, France (52 cases), Germany (39 cases), Spain (50 cases), the Netherlands (32 cases).

Moreover, Italy has provided since 1939 (R.D. 29 June 1939, n. 1127, *Testo delle disposizioni legislative in materia di brevetti per invenzioni industriali*) for the investigation procedure of the *Descrizion*e (see below) as an enforcement that can be used by the owner of an intellectual property right in case of infringement of an IP right and therefore has an experience of almost 80 years in the management of description procedures and judicial inspections of competitors' establishments.

2 Pre-Litigation Strategy

The misappropriation of trade secrets is not always obvious; sometimes a given business entity only has a suspicion that its former employees or third parties have misappropriated a trade secret.

Such suspicion may arise when an employee moves to work for a competitor and the competitor, suddenly and in a very short time, manages to successfully close an industrial gap or produce products similar to the ones of the employee's former employer that the competitor was previously unable to produce.

Case Study
In a case brought before the Court of Milan a few years ago, a company producing industrial fans realised that a few months after one of its former employees transferred to a competitor, the latter had marketed three models of fans aesthetically identical to those produced by the company concerned. Since the production of industrial fans requires considerable research and development and very demanding and expensive wind tunnel tests to determine the performance characteristics of the fan, the company therefore suspected that the employee had stolen sensitive company information.

When such a suspicion arises, the manager responsible for protecting the company's business secrets should:

1. Verify whether there has been an actual misappropriation of the company's secrets,
2. Define the best strategy for the company, and
3. Prepare the necessary documentation to implement the chosen strategy.

2.1 Verifying the Removal of Secrets

If it is suspected that an employee has stolen business secrets, some checks may be carried out on the company server and the employee's computer/lap top.

Computers
The worst thing to do in this situation is logging into the former employee's computer to check whether he/she has downloaded, duplicated, or misappropriated relevant documents or information, and whether he/she has transferred them to the competitor. The company's accessing and operating of the computer could, in fact, alter the evidence of the misappropriation and make the evidence unusable in proceedings such as criminal proceedings, where there must be a very strong certainty that the evidence has not been altered.

The best thing to do is to make a forensic copy of the employee's computer and data in order not to alter its content and to be able to provide it in the event of a trial as evidence. The search for evidence of misappropriation should then be carried out by the company on a second working copy of the computer that will be used for internal verification and will not be produced in court.

Confidential information, usually stored in electronic documents, can be transferred in a number of ways, e.g.:

- By e-mail via an e-mail client installed on a PC,
- Via e-mail by uploading to a mail site, e.g. Gmail,
- Via transfer to USB devices,
- Via sites such as WeTransfer that offer the possibility of transferring large amounts of data.

There are commercially available programmes such as Agent HX or DeviceView® that enable organisations to check which USB devices have been connected to the PC. This check will make it possible to verify whether the employee has used unauthorised USB devices. This alone does not prove the theft of confidential information, but it is a first clue. The presence of files transferred, perhaps in bulk, at the connection windows of these USB devices may reinforce this further suspicion.

A simpler check of the employee's e-mail box makes it possible to verify whether the employee has sent confidential files to his/her personal e-mail address or, even worse, to unauthorised third parties.

Browser history analysis, on the other hand, allows access to file transfer sites or web mailboxes to be verified.

By analysing the computer, one can therefore find evidence that proves with certainty the theft of business secrets (e.g. the sending of e-mails with attached files) or other indications of possible illegal behaviour. Understanding what elements it was possible to collect is important to define the strategy to be pursued.

Server

Some companies store their data in remote servers or virtual machines that are accessed by employees' computers. These systems usually keep track of access to the various work areas, so, by analysing the logs, it is possible to check whether an employee accessed work folders other than those of his/her normal company role or exceeding limits of competence and access, especially if there is an internal company regulation setting different levels of access and authorisations. For example, a salesperson accessing work folders containing specific technical drawings of company products, or administration folders, could be suspicious.

Such logs may also allow access to individual files to be audited. In this way, it is possible to check whether an employee has made a copy of documents on his or her computer when leaving the company. A mass copy is easy to identify: you have a large number of documents that are accessed one after the other seconds apart.

2.2 Deciding on Strategy

The misappropriation of business secrets may be punishable under both civil and criminal law. The choice of which strategy to implement depends on several factors, including but not limited to: the role of the employee in the new company, compensation for damages, the costs of action, the need to gather further evidence of the misappropriation, and the amount of available time.

The choice of proceedings through civil or criminal court depends on the result one wishes to pursue.

The main purpose of a civil action is to compensate the person who has suffered damage. A criminal action is more aimed at prosecuting those who commit offences; the compensatory aspect, in criminal action, is secondary.

If the goal to be achieved is to negatively impact the competitor who took advantage of and used the stolen trade secrets through the unfaithful employee, then a civil action against both the competitor and the employee is the one to be preferred.

If, however, the unfaithful employee has set up his/her own business and exploits the stolen business secrets to take advantage of the start-up of the new company, then criminal action could be preferable. In fact, an action against the start-up will not recover much in damages, whereas a criminal action, by striking the unfaithful employee, will be more efficient in convincing him/her to stop the illegal action.

In addition to a criminal action, it may be advisable to file a civil preliminary injunction in order to obtain an injunction to stop the abusive activity. Such a preliminary injunction does not then compel the automatic duty to start a civil suit on the merits, being limited to obtaining an injunction against the unfaithful former employee.

Another factor to consider is the costs of the action, which are higher in civil than in criminal cases. In a civil trial, in fact, each party bears the costs of the case and often the plaintiff is also called upon to bear, at least in the initial phase, the costs of any technical consultancy that may be ordered by the judge. In criminal proceedings, on the other hand, investigations are conducted by the prosecutor and the judicial police, with costs that are borne by the public authorities (and ultimately by the State itself), not by the person making the criminal complaint.

In choosing the proper strategy to be implemented, another important factor to consider is the evidence gathered during the analysis phase of the company's computers and servers. If there is only general circumstantial evidence of misappropriation, it is sometimes better to proceed in civil court in order to acquire new evidence, and then possibly file a criminal complaint on the basis of more concrete facts and evidence.

Finally, the timing of procedures must be considered when choosing a strategy. Civil interim procedures, like the request of a preliminary injunction and/or the seizure of the infringing goods, may be obtained within a short timeframe (i.e. some days or weeks) depending on the jurisdiction. On the contrary, criminal procedures are slower.

2.3 Prepare the Necessary Documentation

Regardless of whether civil or criminal proceedings are started, the manager must prepare all necessary documentation to give evidence of the infringement.

It will therefore be the manager's task to gather the necessary documentation to prove whether the business secrets qualify for recognition by law as trade secrets and thus enjoy the protection provided by law.

For example, in Italy and the EU Member States the conditions to be satisfied for business secrets to be accorded protection by law are found in Article 2 of the DIRECTIVE (EU) 2016/943 *on the protection of undisclosed know-how and business information (trade secrets) against their unlawful acquisition, use, and disclosure.* These conditions are (similarly in the USA) that the information:

1. Is not easily accessible to the public,
2. Has economic value, and
3. Has been subject to adequate measures to keep it confidential

(so-called 'test of protection').

The manager will therefore need to gather all the necessary documentation to prove that the stolen information meets said three requirements.

In addition, it will also be the manager's task to gather evidence of the misappropriation and to provide the lawyers/prosecutors (if one chooses the criminal route) with all evidence of the misappropriation and of any damage suffered because of the misappropriation.

It is therefore extremely important that the action is well prepared from its initial stages.

The foregoing notwithstanding, it may also be possible in some jurisdictions that business secrets are entitled to protection even without satisfying the above mentioned test of protection: under some general rules or law, it may be possible to protect business secrets as 'know-how'.

3 Civil Law

The civil process system offers various opportunities to protect business secrets, differing from country to country and with interim procedures that allow decisions to be obtained more quickly than in an ordinary trial on the merits, which often follows the interim procedure for the determination and quantification of damages.

In the following sections, we will provide a brief picture of the most common and useful procedures to be used in the fight against the violation of business secrets.

3.1 Interim Procedures

When the owner of an industrial property right or of a trade secret cannot wait for the normal timeframe of an ordinary procedure on the merits, in many European countries (such as Italy) he/she has access to interim procedures that allow decisions to be obtained more quickly, so-called under urgency.

To be eligible for interim measures, however, proof is required of the following conditions precedents:

(i) The *fumus boni iure*, i.e. the reasonable certainty that one's right has been violated, and
(ii) The *periculum in mora*, i.e. the reasons why it is important to obtain a decision as a matter of urgency without waiting for the normal time of justice of an ordinary procedure on the merit.

Since it is the manager's job to decide how to act in defence of the business secrets, it is appropriate for the manager to have a smattering of what elements considering in the evaluation.

With reference to *fumus boni jure*, the owner of a business secret will have to prove:

a) The existence and validity of the right,
b) Reasonable suspicion that his/her right has been violated.

The right-holder shall therefore prove that the confidential information has the status of a trade secret, i.e. that the information that, according to article 2 of DIRECTIVE (EU) 2016/943, is not easily accessible to the public in its form or precise constitution, that has economic value, and that has been placed and protected under security measures by the company or the business entity. Furthermore, the right-holder will have to provide evidence of the misappropriation or suspected misappropriation by conducting a good preparatory phase as explained in the previous section.

Regarding the requirement of *periculum*, it is necessary to know that this is assessed differently in different countries. For example, in Germany established case law provides that a request of an interim measure must be filed within 1 month from the moment the holder becomes aware of the infringement. In Italy, on the other hand, jurisprudence is more flexible, allowing the request an interim measure of seizure and injunction even after 6/8 months from the knowledge of the infringement. All that considered, the enforcement strategy in different countries should be prepared accordingly.

In some countries, such as Italy, the owner of a trade secret is entitled to request the Court the following measures: injunction and/or '*Descrizione*' (a form of search and investigation procedure) and/or the seizure of the machines producing the infringing products and/or the infringing products, i.e. of the goods manufactured by a third party by infringing his/her business secrets. The request of a *Descrizione* proceeding and/or the seizure is usually accompanied with the request of an injunction. However, the injunction can be requested alone and is stand-alone: it keeps its validity without the applicant being forced to request, in addition, the *Descrizione* and/or the seizure.

In other countries, such as the United States, it is possible to bring out the full picture of wrongdoing through other means, such as disclosure.

Case Study

Descrizione in Italy

The *Descrizione* proceeding in Italy has a long tradition (dozens and dozens of years of application and use in Italian courts) and is a very useful tool in cases of misappropriation of trade secrets, because it allows the right-holder to ascertain the extent of the misappropriation. As explained above, sometimes checking the employee's computer may reveal evidence of a file transferred by e-mail or raise awareness that an unauthorised USB device has been connected to the *laptop*. Very often, the evidence found at the preparatory stage is only the tip of the iceberg and the *Descrizione* brings to light what could not be ascertained by analysing company computers alone. Precisely because of this characteristic, *Descrizione* is also advisable when it has been verified with a given certainty that confidential information has been stolen by the unfaithful employee and it is desired to verify whether and in what quantity such secrets are used by the competitor in its industrial or commercial activity.

The *Descrizione* proceeding may be requested *inaudita altera parte* (*ex parte*), i.e. without the other party being pre-alerted by the Court, so that the alleged infringer cannot prepare and conceal evidence. By gaining access to the premises of the alleged infringer, the right-holder can thus search for said evidence, such as (i) files and documents proving the misappropriation of trade secrets, (ii) commercial documents (for example, invoices of clients and suppliers) relating to profits and revenues deriving from the infringement, (iii) documents allowing reconstruction of the commercial chain in which the products produced by means of the trade secrets are involved.

In order not to cause harm to the alleged infringer and to prevent the procedure from becoming an abusive means of investigation and taking in bad faith other business secrets away from competitors, by law all precautionary measures necessary to preserve the secrets or confidential information of the subject undergoing the *Descrizione* may be granted by the judge. Often, the judge also appoints an external attorney at law (obliged not to alert the alleged infringer) to take part to the *Descrizione* at the plant of the alleged infringer to verify that the alleged infringer's rights are not violated during the enforcement of the measure. The Court may also decide that the information acquired during the *Descrizione* shall be made accessible only to the attorneys and outside consultants of the holder of the trade secrets who acted in

(continued)

requesting the *Descrizione*, obliging the attorneys and consultants not to disclose to their client the technical information acquired at the competitor's plant/offices.

The *Descrizione* is normally carried out by a bailiff (i.e. a judicial officer) with the assistance of the right-holder's attorneys at law and his/her technical consultants. Usually, when it is necessary to access computers, the judge appoints and entrusts the task to an IT consultant in order to assist the bailiff and acquire a forensic copy of the possible means used for the infringement: computers, e-mails, mobile phones, USB sticks, etc. The forensic copy is then analysed at a later stage in the presence of both parties' technical consultants who, as mentioned above, may also be obliged to maintain confidentiality towards their clients and not to disclose other business information not relevant for the dispute.

Typically, these operations allow for the acquisition of large amounts of data, and searching for stolen information can be a difficult task. To facilitate this, it is important that with the request for a *Descrizione*, the owner attaches a list of the files that constitute his/her secret. The list can be kept secret and be used to compare the data acquired to identify potentially stolen data by means of a simple hash code comparison. This comparison makes it possible to find identical files, i.e. the original misappropriated files, but not to locate changes made to the files, such as changing a logo or a minor modification; this will require a more thorough search of the files.

Another feature of the *Descrizione* that must be considered by the manager is related to the fact that its enforcement, once started, can be carried out in multiple venues also at other parties involved in the offence (even unknowingly) or in the office of the accountant of the person who violated trade secrets in order to collect data, invoices, and evidence of the sale of the counterfeit products and the list of suppliers (whose identity is often also stolen by the former employee to enable his new employer to manufacture a specific product requiring special raw materials or components).

Seizure and Injunction

Further interim procedures that can be requested in civil proceedings are the seizure and injunction.

Seizure makes it possible to deprive the person subjected to it of the availability of the business secrets, all products and goods incorporating them or manufactured according to the stolen trade secrets and machines used to manufacture the abusive products. This request is therefore very important when secrets are incorporated into consumer products because it could lead to the potential seizure of thousands of products.

Consider, for example, the case where a trade secret consists of software to optimise the consumption of an electronic product, such as a television set-top box or a smart phone. These small products are produced in large batches kept in stock. To seize the products incorporating the misappropriated trade secret means to prevent the competitor from marketing the goods in stock and to profit from the sales of illicitly produced products.

Sometimes seizure may be indispensable to 'crystallise' the counterfeiting scenario at the time of search. Consider the case of a business secret used on a high-value product, such as a yacht or sports car. The interim phase, having a tight time frame, may not allow all the analyses to be fully carried out and sometimes would be too costly buying such a product later on, before starting the procedure on the merit, in order to verify the counterfeit. As a matter of fact, seizure is aimed to collect and provide evidence that can be analysed in more detail in the subsequent ordinary proceedings on the merits.

The request of granting a seizure is usually accompanied by a request for an **injunction**, but the latter may be made by the trade secret's owner independently without being forced to request also the seizure. The injunction issued by the judge, usually accompanied by a penalty for non-compliance with the judge's order, allows the use of trade secrets by the infringer to be blocked. In trade secret matters, the court usually orders an injunction prohibiting the use of files containing trade secrets and the sale of products incorporating the secret.

Under Italian law, if an interim procedure for *Descrizione* and/or seizure (in addition or not to a preliminary injunction) is sought, then an ordinary proceeding on the merit must be commenced; otherwise, the previous order granting the interim procedures lapses and is no longer valid and enforceable. There is also a subsequent risk that the person requesting the interim procedures (which were not followed by the ordinary proceedings on the merit) could be condemned by the Court to pay damages to the person who had to suffer the interim procedure that lapsed because the action on the merits did not start.

On the contrary, in the case of requesting and obtaining a preliminary injunction without requesting also a *Descrizione* and/or seizure, it will not be necessary to commence an ordinary proceeding on the merits. One says that the order of preliminary injunction stands alone. Similar to the German rules of procedures, also under Italian law the party suffering the preliminary injunction can then decide to start an ordinary proceeding on the merits against the order of preliminary injunction enacted by the Court in order to try to revoke it.

3.2 Ordinary Proceedings on the Merit

In countries where interim measures exist, ordinary proceedings on the merit are usually a continuation of the interim measures. Different countries also have very different procedures, which we cannot summarise here in one chapter, but it is good to remember that the civil procedure is the solution that allows one to recover the damage suffered; therefore, it is important for the business manager to know that in order to obtain compensation for the damage, it is necessary to initiate proceedings on the merits and to know what elements contribute to determining the damage.

Different jurisdictions provide for different procedures for calculating damages, the following are the main items that make up the damages in the case of trade secret misappropriation.

Actual damage	Actual damage consists of the costs incurred to repair the damage. In the case of misappropriation of trade secrets, actual damages may consist of 1. The loss of value of the trade secret, which, if, for example, it is made public, can no longer be qualified as a trade secret and can cause enormous damage to its owner (think, for instance, of if everyone knew the secret to making the soft drink Coca-Cola) or 2. The decrease of the turnover and the closure of production facilities because the misappropriation of that trade secret no longer allows the owner to be the only manufacturer of that trade secret product and to sell significant quantities, but also, 3. The costs incurred for computer consultants and legal fees incurred in taking legal action against the infringer. If the trade secret was not only stolen, but also deleted from the server/computer, the costs of restoring the server/computer to recover the stolen data also constitute actual damages.
Loss of profit	Loss of profit, on the other hand, is the loss of profit resulting from the infringement. In the case of trade secret misappropriation, the lost profit may be the turnover from the sales made by the competitor using the trade secret. Proving lost profits is never easy and requires proof that the lost sales are closely related to those realised by the competitor with the infringed trade secrets.
Retroversion of profits	Some laws, such as those in Italy, provide for the possibility of requesting the retroversion of profits, i.e. to request that the profits earned by the infringer through the infringement be returned to the trade secret owner.
Punitive damages	In some countries, like USA, it is possible to request a punitive decision, i.e. that damages be increased by an amount that in some cases can be up to three or more times the actual damages.

4 Criminal Law

Criminal proceedings aim to impact the criminal and punish him/her for the crime committed. Criminal proceedings are thus brought against all the physical persons who knowingly committed a crime and against the company where the physical person is operating usually if the company got economic advantages from the infringement. Some countries, such as Italy or Germany, provide that the managing director and/or CEO of the company who contributes to the crime may also be indicted as being responsible for the company. For example, a managing director could be indicted if the company where he/she is working hires an employee of a competitor in the knowledge that this employee is able to and will bring in and disclose the competitor's secrets for the benefit of the new employer.

As with civil law, criminal law also varies from country to country, but it is important for the manager to be able to identify those behaviours that, in general, are considered criminal offences, to then be able to ascertain with the criminal lawyers whether offences have been committed and to check whether to file a complaint. By implementing the DIRECTIVE (EU) 2016/943, European Members States also provide for specific criminal rules in the case of misappropriation of trade secrets.

4.1 Strategic Considerations

Criminal proceedings have two advantages:

1) It is a very effective tool in forcing the infringer to the negotiating table. However, the prosecutor may still decide to continue the criminal proceedings against the offender, even if the owner of the misappropriated trade secret is willing to settle the dispute with the payment of a given amount of money as compensation for damages.
2) It allows the expertise and broad powers of investigators to be used by the prosecutors to detect the misappropriation.

The first advantage listed above is that the criminal proceedings affect the natural person, typically the unfaithful employee and/or the managing director of the competing company that exploited the business secrets stolen by the unfaithful employee, and in some jurisdictions also the company itself that hired the employee (as a legal person's liability). In civil proceedings, a company director/manager may be concerned about the damage to be compensated, but the money belongs to the company and, barring objective liability, his/her assets and his/her person are not usually endangered by the lawsuit. In criminal proceedings, on the other hand, the director/manager is personally liable, risking not only his assets but also his/her freedom—facing potential jail time. For this reason, criminal proceedings make the offender much more susceptible to litigation and, therefore, more inclined to reach an agreement with the owner of the right to withdraw the criminal complaint-suit and convince the prosecutor not to continue the criminal prosecution, even if—as already mentioned—the prosecutor is not always inclined to dismiss the complaint.

The other advantage of criminal law is that investigations are conducted by the prosecutor and the police, thus using the means and personnel at their disposal. This can be particularly useful when the company has been subject to a hacker attack and it is necessary to carry out intensive and costly investigations to trace the hacker. By filing a criminal complaint, the prosecutor often has broad powers to carry out the investigation and is more able to find the hacker.

While the independence of the authorities in carrying out investigations can be an advantage, the same independence can sometimes turn out to be a disadvantage, as the person who initiated the criminal complaint-suit does not have control over the conduct of the investigation. It can sometimes happen that the prosecutor, in the absence of urgent and striking situations (such as the transfer of secret information to companies in countries subject to technology export restrictions), decides to devote few resources to the case, proceeds slowly or decides not to prosecute. It is therefore important to clarify with an experienced criminal lawyer which courts are more active and quicker in prosecuting certain crimes, and it is often a good idea to speak with the prosecutor beforehand to explain the seriousness of the case and to understand his/her availability in terms of time and resources.

Moreover, as mentioned above, criminal proceedings do not allow full compensation for damages. Although some jurisdictions allow the offended party to also join as a civil party in the proceedings and obtain compensation, the amounts awarded are usually lower than what can be obtained in civil proceedings.

In some jurisdictions it is not possible to initiate civil proceedings for damages if compensation has already been claimed in criminal proceedings. It is therefore important to carefully consider whether to initiate criminal proceedings in parallel with civil proceedings; this is possible, but care must be taken with the claims in both fora.

4.2 The Complaint-Suit

For criminal proceedings to begin, the prosecutor and police must become aware of the facts that could constitute a criminal offence.

Unlike crimes such as murder, where the police act independently once they are informed of the offence, when we talk about crimes related to trade secret theft these are often punishable on complaint by the offended person.

It is important to know that different national laws impose different timeframes within which a complaint must be filed.

The complaint-suit must contain an indication of the infringer (who may be unknown) and the criminally relevant facts. Thus, if during the analysis of an employee's computer, traces or evidence of a crime are found, then from this moment onwards the time limits for filing a complaint start and it will be necessary to indicate to the police what crimes have been committed and by whom. If, on the other hand, the company understands that it has been attacked by a hacker who has stolen business secrets, according to Italian law it shall file a lawsuit against unknown persons within 3 months of becoming aware of the theft of information and documents.

4.3 Sanctionable Behaviour

To illustrate, below are some behaviours that are generally are considered offences under Italian law.

Theft	Theft is the theft of an asset that one did not previously have possession of. When a hacker breaches corporate computer systems and steals

(continued)

Theft	Theft is the theft of an asset that one did not previously have possession of. When a hacker breaches corporate computer systems and steals information, he/she commits theft. Similarly, a supplier who, while visiting the company, appropriates confidential material he/she finds in the company is committing theft.
Misappropriation	Misappropriation differs from theft in that the person misappropriating the property was previously in possession of it. This is the scenario of a disloyal employee who, having access to business secrets for work, on leaving the company takes with him/her documentation that should have remained in the company.
Unauthorised access to computer systems	In some countries, such as Italy, unauthorised access to a computer system is an offence punishable by imprisonment. In Italy, the Court of Criminal Cassation, in its judgement 565 of 2019, ruled that the offence of abusive access to a computer system is committed not only when there is a violation of the computer system, but also when the employee's behaviour is in conflict with the duties of loyalty and fidelity of the employee.
Removal and disclosure of scientific, industrial and commercial secrets	In general, an offence is committed if a person learns trade secrets or information intended to remain secret about scientific discoveries or inventions and discloses or uses them for profit. For this offence to take place, it is therefore necessary that a profit be made from the disclosure or use of business secrets. This offence is therefore not committed if an employee leaves the company and takes secret documents with him without using them.

Takeaways (from Chapter 7)

The misappropriation of business secrets may be punishable under both civil and criminal law. The choice of which strategy to implement depends on several factors, including but not limited to:

- The role of the employee (in the new company and in the previous company),
- Compensation for damages,
- Cost of action,
- Availability of evidence and ability to gather more,
- Available time.

(continued)

The choice of proceedings through civil or criminal court depends on the result one wishes to pursue.

A civil action is to compensate the person who has suffered damage.

A criminal action is more aimed at prosecuting those who commit offences.

In choosing which strategy to be implemented, an important factor to consider is the evidence gathered during the analysis phase: general circumstantial evidence of misappropriation may be more appropriate to proceed in civil court to acquire new evidence, and then possibly file a criminal complaint on the basis of more concrete facts and evidence.

Civil interim procedures, like the request of a preliminary injunction and/or the seizure of the infringing goods, may be obtained within a short timeframe depending on the jurisdiction.

The *Descrizione* procedure is then one of the most effective tools for understanding whether a competitor is misusing a third party's business secrets and in what manner; it also allows one to take copies of all sales invoices to customers as well as invoices issued by suppliers, to then easily determine the damages that can be claimed against the infringer.

As mentioned in the introduction, Italy is the EU country with the highest number of court cases related to the misappropriation and infringement of trade secrets, because Italy, since 1996 (thus 20 years before DIRECTIVE (EU) 2016/943), has specific legislation to protect trade secrets and almost 80 years of experience in handling description procedures and judicial inspections of competitors' factories.

Correction to: Protecting Business Secrets to Improve Value Creation

Pierre Ollivier, Véronique Chapuis-Thuault, Ferzana Haq,
Katarína Račková, Victor De Leon, Graham Bell, and Sylvain Roy

Correction to:
Chapter 5 in: P. Ollivier et al. (eds.),
***Business Secrets Management*, Management for Professionals,**
https://doi.org/10.1007/978-3-031-82512-5_5

The author's name was misspelled in the original version of the manuscript as Ferzana Hacq. This has now been corrected to Ferzana Haq.

The updated version of this chapter can be found at
https://doi.org/10.1007/978-3-031-82512-5_5

P. Ollivier et al. (eds.), *Business Secrets Management*, Management for Professionals, https://doi.org/10.1007/978-3-031-82512-5_8

Correction to: Business Secrets Increase Asset Value

Graham Bell, Véronique Chapuis-Thuault, André Gorius, Aldona Kapacinskaite, Pierre Ollivier, Katarína Račková, and Philippe Simon

Correction to:
Chapter 4 in: P. Ollivier et al. (eds.),
***Business Secrets Management*, Management for Professionals,**
https://doi.org/10.1007/978-3-031-82512-5_4

The original version of the chapter was inadvertently published with the incorrect figure legend for Fig. 1, which has been updated as below.

Fig. 1: Profit split of licensable intangibles in percent of enterprise value (credit: les Nouvelles, 2015, Uniloc, C. Binder and A. Nestler). Source: markables.net

The updated version of this chapter can be found at https://doi.org/10.1007/978-3-031-82512-5_4

P. Ollivier et al. (eds.), *Business Secrets Management*, Management for Professionals, https://doi.org/10.1007/978-3-031-82512-5_9

The manufacturer's authorised representative in the EU is Springer Nature Customer Service Centre GmbH, Europaplatz 3, 69115 Heidelberg, Germany. If you have any concerns regarding our products, please contact ProductSafety@springernature.com

Printed and bound by CPI Group (UK) Ltd, Croydon, CR0 4YY
01/10/2026
02225925-0005